Praise

Gatecrashing Paradise

'Revealing aspects of a surprising little tropical nation wholly unknown to holidaymakers, Gatecrashing Paradise *compares honourably with Arthur Grimble's* A Pattern of Islands.'

—Alexander Frater, former chief travel correspondent of the *Observer*, author of *The Balloon Factory*, *Tales from the Torrid Zone*, *Chasing the Monsoon* and *Beyond the Blue Horizon*

'Tom Chesshyre bravely and entertainingly exposes the dimensions of the Maldives that the tourist board is strangely shy of illuminating.'

—Simon Calder, Travel Editor of the *Independent on Sunday*

To Dexter and Florence

Gatecrashing Paradise

Misadventures in the Real Maldives

Tom Chesshyre

NICHOLAS BREALEY
PUBLISHING

London • Boston

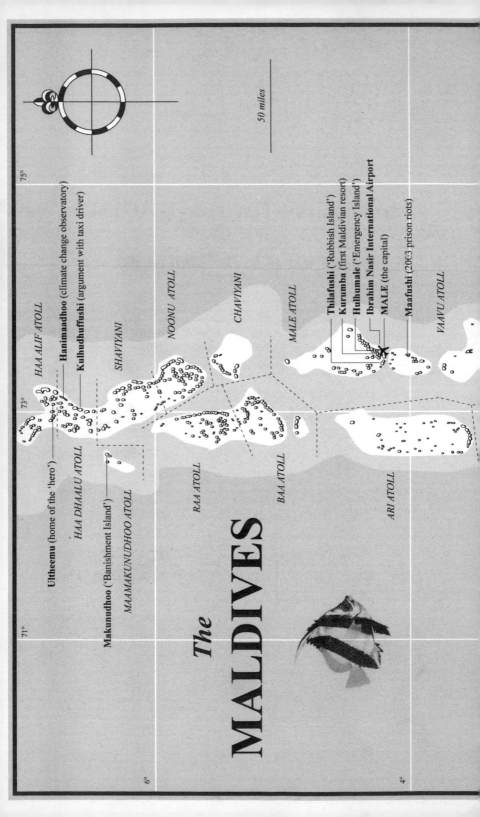

The
MALDIVES

HAA ALIF ATOLL

Ultheemu (home of the 'hero')

HAA DHAALU ATOLL

Hanimaadhoo (climate change observatory)

Kulhudhuffushi (argument with taxi driver)

Makunudhoo ('Banishment Island')

MAAMAKUNUDHOO ATOLL

SHAVIYANI

NOONU ATOLL

RAA ATOLL

CHAVIYANI

BAA ATOLL

MALE ATOLL

Thilafushi ('Rubbish Island')
Kurumba (first Maldivian resort)
Hulhumale ('Emergency Island')
Ibrahim Nasir International Airport
MALE (the capital)
Maafushi (2003 prison riots)

ARI ATOLL

VAAVU ATOLL

50 miles

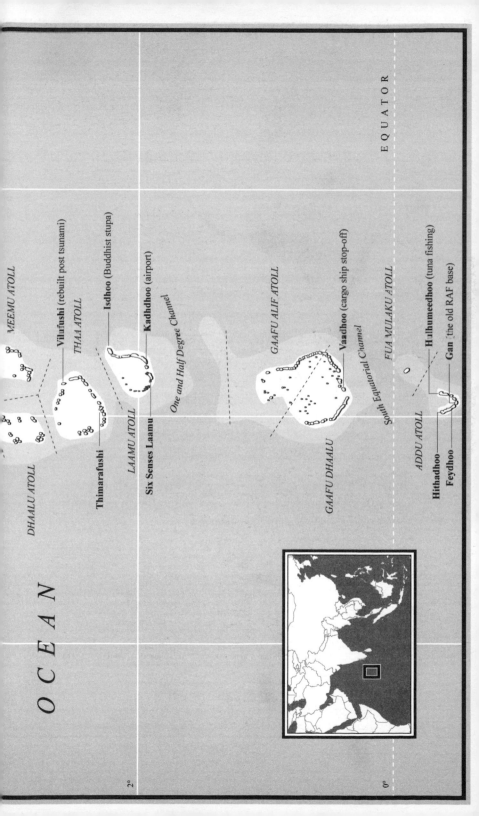

First published by
Nicholas Brealey Publishing in 2015

3–5 Spafield Street
Clerkenwell, London
EC1R 4QB, UK
Tel: +44 (0)20 7239 0360
Fax: +44 (0)20 7239 0370
www.nicholasbrealey.com
www.tomchesshyre.co.uk
@tchesshyre

20 Park Plaza
Boston
MA 02116, USA
Tel: (888) BREALEY
Fax: (617) 523 3708

ISBN: 978-1-85788-627-6
eISBN: 978-1-85788-937-6

British Library Cataloguing in Publication Data
A catalogue record for this book is available from the
British Library.

Maps by Matthew Swift

Printed in the UK by Clays Ltd, St Ives plc

Contents

Preface

Our whole mindset regarding going abroad has altered beyond recognition in the last few years. I began as a journalist on the travel desk of the *The Times*, hoping to see the world, inspired by writers such as Paul Theroux, P. J. O'Rourke, Jonathan Raban, Eric Newby, Bruce Chatwin, Jan Morris, Dervla Murphy, Norman Lewis and Bill Bryson. Heading out with a notebook to explore backwaters, meet unusual characters, experience the sights, sounds and smells of distant climes – travel journalism was a romantic notion. Apart from travel literature, guidebooks, radio broadcasts, newspapers, films and television documentaries (presented by the likes of Alan Whicker and Michael Palin), there was no other way to learn about distant shores. Travel was expensive and knowledge was unreliable; guidebooks soon became out of date.

In the years between the late 1990s, when I was starting out, and now, I continued with travel writing despite a growing feeling that the internet, as it developed and boomed, could tell you almost anything you needed to know before you took off from Heathrow or caught a train through the Channel Tunnel. Reporters were increasingly becoming tied to their desks. 'Newshounds' found themselves attached to screens that flashed wire stories and, more recently, tweets. But as a travel writer, by definition, you had to get out and about, see things with your own eyes.

After taking several journeys to unpronounceable places on low-cost airlines' 1p flights, I wrote a travel book entitled *To Hull and Back*, describing some of the least likely places to spend time off in the UK. This was a reaction to taking so many easyJet flights; I wanted to stay on the ground. It was also in the spirit of Alain de Botton's engaging book *The Art of Travel*, in which the Swiss-British philosopher ruminates on finding the extraordinary in the ordinary.

With the internet so pervasive and travel becoming almost ludicrously easy, I liked the idea of slowing down and taking a closer look at places that were less trodden. I stayed on the ground once more to see Europe by high-speed train (*Tales from the Fast Trains*) before visiting Tunisia, Libya and Egypt a year after the Arab Spring (*A Tourist in the Arab Spring*). News of the uprisings, which some were comparing to the fall of the Berlin Wall, was coming thick and fast on television and over the internet. But I wanted to see it for myself, rather than relying on information that flashes up on a screen.

Some people suggest that the (apparent) omniscience of the World Wide Web makes travel writing redundant. It is a dying genre, the doom merchants say, as everything is out there already: every corner of the earth covered and accessible at the click of a computer mouse. There can be no Wilfred Thesiger-style journeys through the Empty Quarter of Arabia, no quixotic rambles through the Hindu Kush à la Newby, no Bruce Chatwinesque immersions in African nomadic tribal life. And perhaps that's true. The surprise element no longer exists when you can read about most places on your smartphone.

Most places, but not all. And in the Maldives, I wanted to take a different approach. Before I went, I had little idea what islands I would visit and what I would come across. I had no grand plans mapped out on the internet, no instant information to show me the way, no World Wide Web at my fingertips. Escaping a Google world by ditching my smartphone and laptop, I had little alternative to following my nose and letting instinct lead the way.

I had some rare time off work, annual leave that had somehow stacked up: a honeymoon period of sorts, an unexpected break from daily life. And there was a certain irony to this. I was heading to one of the globe's most renowned honeymoon hotspots – the Maldives – on my own: my girlfriend and I had split in the weeks before I decided to go. We had been together a while and it felt like a turning point, a 'spring clean' moment of anything being possible. I was stepping off the treadmill of the ordinary. Goodbye commuting. Goodbye deadlines. Goodbye to everything connected to worries. Hello sunshine. Hello sea. Hello to discovering a distant country from the ground up, without monitors bleeping messages I really did not want to read.

That's why I bought a ticket to the Indian Ocean.

'We heard the boom of breakers from miles offshore as they crashed upon the reef. It was a sound new to our ears, a note of majesty once heard, forever remembered.'
Arthur Grimble, *A Pattern of Islands*

'The first guests at the Brisas del Mar arrived in some style in a chauffeur-driven Isotta-Frashini at the end of May, providing instant and final confirmation of the villagers' belief that all outsiders were basically irrational, when not actually mad.'
Norman Lewis, *Voices of the Old Sea*

'Later I realized how foolish it had been to have any scruples, for big hotels are quite merciless towards their employees.'
George Orwell, *Down and Out in Paris and London*

'When the rate of return on capitalism exceeds the rate of growth of output and income, as it did in the nineteenth century and seems likely to do again in the twenty-first, capitalism automatically generates arbitrary and unsustainable inequalities that radically undermine the meritocratic values on which democratic societies are based.'
Thomas Piketty, *Capital in the Twenty-First Century*

PART ONE
Into the Indian Ocean

Arrival in Male, the capital – and a journey by cargo ship, sleeping next to sacks of onions on a deck floor, to the southernmost point in the country: Addu Atoll, south of the Equator, where there is a visit to the old RAF base and a night spent tuna fishing in what was once the United Suvadive Islands

'There are a lot of mysterious things about boats, such as why anyone would get on one voluntarily.'
P. J. O'Rourke

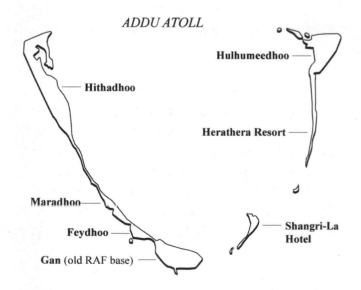

ADDU ATOLL

The Sunny Side of Life

Down below there was water – lots of water. The screen on the maroon seat on my plane from Colombo in Sri Lanka to Male, capital of the Maldives, showed that we were crossing the 'Indischer Ozean'. Thin white streaks of waves broke on a peninsula bristling with jade-topped palm trees: our last glimpse of the mainland. Then there was blue – an enormity of blue. The Indischer stretched to the horizon, gargantuan, all-encompassing, seeming to roll onwards for ever.

It was a mesmerising sight. On the surface of the sea I could make out the faintest of movements, an almost imperceptible sway. The tiniest of undulations, the briefest stir, visible for a split second... then gone. The motion returned and went away once more. From 30,000 feet, far from the peaks and troughs of the swell, the ocean was a lumbering creature, somehow alive, quietly breathing in and out.

Rust-red cargo ships stood sentinel on the gently pulsing sea. They appeared hopelessly lost, miniscule man-made outposts in the infinite seascape. And as we rose through ribbons of cloud, the surface of the aqueous world began to alter. Glimmers of silver emerged, spreading outwards and blooming into a metallic sheen. The blue, after a tantalising spell of indigo, morphed into a mercurial swirl. As I looked through the oval window I began to readjust my place on the planet. From now on it was water, not land, that mattered.

The Indian Ocean nation of the Maldives is the flattest country on earth (the highest 'hill' is 7ft 10in) and stretches about 515 miles from north to south, bulging to just 80 miles at its widest point. Among the 1,192 islands, 100 are

'resort islands', for tourists only, while 198 are categorised as 'inhabited'. All the islands and reefs and lagoons
together amount to 35,300 square miles, about the size of
North Island in New Zealand, but the territory is 99.9 per
cent water, and most of the 0.1 per cent of land is about 3
feet above the sea.

There was water, water everywhere – and some
beyond-luxurious hotels on perfect white-sand beaches. If
you wanted to escape for a while, what better place than the
ultimate vision of paradise? The honeymoon dream of holiday brochures: criss-crossing palm trees, tropical flowers,
colourful coral, long sunny days crowned by blazing sunsets. Not to mention the glass-bottomed bathtubs, private
terraces or 37" flatscreen televisions in palm-roofed villas
perched over the Indian Ocean.

It sounds great, but I have to admit I'd always imagined
the Maldives to be dull. Too boring, too obvious.

I did, however, have a plan. I had heard of a change in
Maldivian law that allowed visitors to travel off the beaten
track to islands that were not official tourist islands. From
the 1980s until 2009, foreigners had been banned from visiting places populated by locals, other than on stopovers in
the capital. Government officials had been concerned that
Western influences might rub off and spoil the Islamic way
of life. These were worries dating from the hippy trail, the
ban on outsiders 'going local' designed to prevent a cavalry
charge of folk with long hair smoking funny cigarettes and
behaving in other odd ways.

With hippies long gone, the policy had been eased and the
idea was to allow poorer parts of the archipelago the opportunity to enjoy the spoils of tourism. It was early days, with
the first guesthouses opening around the time of my visit. Few
people seemed to have heard about this new way of seeing

the country. It was a bit like Greek island-hopping when that travel phenomenon began, except that the weather would be hotter, the scenery even more beautiful – and you could get a tuna curry just about anywhere you went.

A whole new country had effectively opened up, hundreds of islands seldom seen by outsiders. It's not all that often something like this happens in the twenty-first century. Yes, I was looking forward to making the most of paradise, but I was intending to take a voyage around the edges of perfection, travelling on cargo ships and ferries to these newly accessible islands. By skirting this periphery I hoped to get an insight into Maldivian life away from the shiny, glitzy presentation of the tourist board and public relations officials. Journalists are only too familiar with PR gloss. I wanted to capture the bigger picture.

With these thoughts in mind, my first sight of Maldivian terra firma came in the form of a beetle-shaped island with curving leg-like jetties studded with hotel villas. Thick green palm groves at the centre of the island acted as the beetle's back. The land was almost perfectly circular and surrounded by a flawless rim of white sand. Beyond, the ocean disappeared in a swirl of clouds in the direction of Africa.

This beetle was followed by another bug-shaped creation, and another, and then a series of islands that appeared uninhabited. These were thin and stretched out in irregular ovals. They were unlike anything I'd seen before. There was something almost Daliesque about their wobbly shapes, the way they undulated in long curves adorned by foaming waves.

Many of the circles barely rose above the ocean. I already knew that what I was seeing was the tip of coral reefs that ringed ancient underwater volcanic peaks. These now-extinct volcanoes were the result of the meeting of tectonic plates. They had once towered above the water, but over the millennia had subsided, leaving both lagoons and the higher ground on which Maldivians lived.

Charles Darwin, no less, had first recognised coral reefs – known as atolls when the reefs encircled a lagoon – and explained their formation when pottering about the world's oceans in the 1830s on HMS *Beagle*. The peaks were part of an enormous ridge that ran from Madagascar to India, the submerged mountain range to which I was headed.

The plane's wheels hit the runway on Airport Island with a screech. I followed couples down steps onto the baking concourse. We shambled bleary-eyed and blinking through fierce heat to a humid hall with a low ceiling.

So much so normal – an airport like any other. We might have been in Malaga. Then we shuffled through the exit… and things were very different.

Outside, men in crisp white uniforms held signs with the labels of luxury tour operators, including Cox & Kings, Island Voyage, Coco Collection (this was much more upmarket than the Costa del Sol). They were not there for me, though. I strolled past and a few paces further came to the sea. A sign told me I was entering 'THE SUNNY SIDE OF LIFE'.

And so I was. I crossed a traffic-free street to a small jetty with a concrete walkway covered by an awning. In the shade at the far end of this sun cover was a rickety kiosk.

This was not upmarket at all. This, I soon gathered, was where you caught the ferry to Male. I may have only been in the country for a few moments, but already I was taking to the ocean. I waited in a queue with a Maldivian man wearing a Union Jack sleeveless top with a hood and matching shorts. He was accompanied by a woman in a burqa. They made a very odd couple. I handed over 10 rufiyaa (about 40 pence) and hauled my luggage across the bow of a short, covered wooden boat. A wiry ferryman neatly stacked my bag by a heap of cardboard boxes filled with chocolate-milk powder.

We settled in and waited for the seats to fill. The boat bobbed and gurgled at its mooring, smelling of diesel. Water trickled against the quay. I had squeezed onto a bench next to a passenger in pinstripe trousers and an untucked pink shirt. If you ignored his flip-flops, he might have been returning from a day at a city stock exchange. Others were less formally dressed; mainly airport staff, it appeared, going home after shifts. I was the sole Westerner (those on the plane had peeled away after the customs check to meet their holiday reps). Most but not all women wore headscarves, with only the single burqa.

Our ferry must have been 30 feet long. The floor consisted of old wooden boards with peeling battleship-grey paint. A faint breeze stirred through the windowless stern. When all the benches were occupied, the engine growled into life. We backed out of the mooring, swaying in the churning waves, heading into choppy sea beyond a breakwater.

Then I saw Male for the first time. The capital was an extraordinary sight, a mini-Manhattan of tower blocks painted pink and aquamarine, jammed onto a small island across half a mile of ocean. It seemed totally out of place, as though the buildings had been transferred from a city in the USA, dropped one by one by helicopters in the middle of the sea and painted pastel colours.

We rocked and rolled in the direction of this candy-coloured mirage and as we did so I was struck again by the feeling of entering some kind of water world. Little black fish darted close to the surface, looking like leaves blown in an under-water wind. Speed boats from tourist resorts raced by, causing us to bob in their wake. We chugged forwards towards a tower with HITACHI written in red on its roof. The sky was turning purple, streaks of pink feathering the surface of the surging sea.

We entered a small secondary harbour and moored, bow first, by the quayside. A man wearing a T-shirt emblazoned with the message 'SMILE MORE: WHY NOT?' swung my bag over the harbour wall. I grinned and stepped onto Male. I had arrived in paradise, amid skyscrapers, bustling crowds, honking mopeds, bright pink election banners announcing 'YOUTH! ECONOMY! HOPE!', yellow bunting tied to lampposts in honour of the Maldivian Democratic Party, and tiny warren-like alleys.

I entered one of these and was almost flattened by a moped. A stream of traffic flew past as I came to a corner with a mosque and muezzin beginning a call to prayer. I walked cautiously across another busy, narrow road lined with tall loping trees whose emerald branches formed a canopy of shade. Locals walked past, their posture erect, arms swinging casually at their sides, paying little attention to the foreigner in their midst. I passed a shop selling brightly coloured headscarves, turned left at a whitewashed Islamic college, hopped to one side to avoid a taxi, and came to the pistachio-green walls of Skai Lodge. By some stroke of luck after all the labyrinthine lanes I'd made it to my guesthouse – where 'comfort and affordability are synonymous... the price is worth value for money', or so said the website blurb.

The entrance was in a cramped courtyard with a high wall lined with tropical plants. I edged down a dimly lit passageway into my first abode in the Maldives. Tinny Bollywood music played on a television. A fan whirred. Pictures of beaches lined with palm trees adorned the walls. Well-thumbed magazines advertising diving breaks were stacked on a coffee table by a squashy sofa. A man in a tangerine shirt hunched on the sofa quietly tapping on a smartphone, a cigarette resting on an ashtray. A tired-eyed receptionist wearing a headscarf looked up, startled, from behind a counter.

Her expression was owlish. She was little more than 5 feet tall and seemed to have been engrossed in the Bollywood video. She raised an eyebrow and gave me a look that suggested: 'What on earth are you doing in a suburb of Male near the ferry port?' I was, I admit, thinking something the same myself.

I confirmed my identity. Where were the welcome drinks? The cool towels? The charming staff in crisp uniforms with Nelson Mandela collars? But I didn't mind. The receptionist handed me a key and I heaved my bag upstairs.

I had made it to a 'destination [that] reigns supreme over all others', according to the tourist brochure I had read on the plane: the 'magical Maldives'. I had '1,200 idyllic islands' to investigate and I was about to take a good look at paradise – warts and all.

The Money Islands: A Little Bit of History

What is known of the people of the Maldives goes back more than 3,500 years. What is not known is who exactly lived on the islands at around that time. Some archaeologists believe that a sun-worshipping people called the Redin existed on the archipelago, although the sun motif found on slabs of stone as 'evidence' of this was commonly used by Buddhists. Whoever they were, it is established that settlers later came from southern India and Sri Lanka at around 500 BC, bringing with them Buddhism and Hinduism. It is likely that many of the first Maldivians did not arrive willingly; some were almost certainly the victims of shipwrecks in these famously treacherous waters.

Arab traders visited the islands for several hundred years, from around 200 AD onwards. The Maldives were then nicknamed the Money Islands, as they were a rich source of cowry shells, used at the time as a form of currency across the globe. Various dynasties ruled the nation before Arab influence left a lasting mark. In 1153 a Moroccan traveller named Abul Barakaath Yoosuf Al-Babari dropped by and converted the islanders to Islam. He knew the Koran by heart and his preaching impressed the then sultan. A copper plate from the period describes the subsequent execution of Buddhist monks in the southern islands.

The first record of a 'tourist' comes from the fourteenth century. Ibn Battuta, the great Moroccan explorer, spent about eight months in the Maldives in 1344. During this time the famous wanderer is believed to have taken a total of six wives, divorcing as necessary so that he did not exceed the accepted limit of four under Islamic law. He was temporarily made *qadi* (judge) in the court in Male, during which he attempted to enforce the need for women to cover the top part of their body in public; before this Maldivian women apparently went about bare chested. Yet he found the local female population in general to be 'delightful' and commented: 'It is easy to marry in these islands because of the smallness of the dowries and the pleasures of society which the women offer ... When the ships put in, the crew marry; when they intend to leave they divorce their wives. This is a kind of temporary marriage. The women of these islands never leave their country.'

The next moment of note came in the late fifteenth century. The Portuguese, led by Vasco da Gama, rounded the Cape of Good Hope and opened up the spice route by sea in 1498. They landed in Calicut and it was not long before Portuguese mercenaries were attacking the Maldives. In 1558 they invaded and for 15 years the Portuguese flag hung in Male until a group of rebels, against the odds, defeated the occupiers, a famous moment that is marked by the Maldives' National Day (the first day of the third month of the lunar year).

This was the only time the Maldives was to be occupied. The country was fiercely independent and when European ships washed up on the reefs the crews were often taken hostage. Loose agreements were signed with the Dutch, the French and then the British, who took over Ceylon from the Dutch in 1796 and chartered the Maldivian waters in the 1830s. These deals were required to defend the islands from Portuguese, Bengali and Malabar attacks. The relationship with the British was formalised in 1887 when a treaty recognised the nationhood of the islands under a 'protected status' – which fell short of being a full protectorate.

This set-up left internal affairs to the islanders and it held firm until Mohammed Amin Didi proclaimed himself president of the first Maldivian republic in 1953. The republic lasted less than a year before he fell due to an internal revolt. There followed a shaky period during which parts of the south attempted to break free, even declaring a new nation: the United Suvadive Islands, which existed from 1959 to 1963. Mohammed Amin Didi's brief rule as president of a republic eventually paved the way for full independence under another republic in 1968, when the president elected was Ibrahim Nasir, after whom the international airport is named.

It was during this period that the British were granted the right to develop an airbase in the most southerly atoll in the Maldives: Addu Atoll. This was important, as it gave Britain a foothold in the region in the wake of India's independence in 1947 and Sri Lanka's the following year, providing a crucial refuelling station for planes flying between Singapore and Europe. The Royal Air Force base existed until 1976 when it was closed for financial reasons under Prime Minister Harold Wilson; the parts that remain were the first 'target' of my visit.

Politics since independence had a rollercoaster quality. Nasir ruled until 1978, when Maumoon Abdul Gayoom took over for 30 years, enjoying a series of elections with suspiciously large majorities, usually attracting well above 90 per cent support. Political parties were not allowed in elections, either for the president or parliament. However, this changed after a 19-year-old prison inmate named Hassan Evan Naseem was beaten to death by guards on the island of Maafushi in 2003, prompting a jail uprising in which three further prisoners were shot dead. Protests were held in Male about the brutality, and government heavy-handedness in general, and a state of emergency was proclaimed. Then came the 2004 tsunami, during which more than 100 people died. Repairing the destruction caused by the surging sea cost more than half of the country's gross domestic product of US$6,566 per capita.

International pressure was applied to the Indian Ocean nation to get its politics in order. The country was in a dire financial state and the desperately needed aid potentially depended on its achieving reform. This was how democracy and the presidential election of Mohamed Nasheed of the Maldivian Democratic Party came about in 2008. Everything went swimmingly for four years, before Nasheed was forced to step down at gunpoint in a coup claimed to be orchestrated by figures connected to the former regime of President Gayoom.

Matters are a little murky after this point. It was claimed by many that the taxes Nasheed had introduced were unpopular among wealthy resort owners, so the coup had been organised to protect their profits. There was also a belief that the Gayoom family hoped to gain power once more by having Abdulla Yameen Abdul Gayoom, half-brother of the ex-president, put in charge following elections that would be 'finessed' in his favour. These elections were to be held not long after my trip and in the meantime the country was being run by an interim leader, Dr Mohammed Waheed Hassan, who was regarded as pro Gayoom.

All in all, affairs in paradise seemed surprisingly turbulent. Yet this country of 1,192 islands has a proud past and a multi-party democracy, a pretty rare scenario for an Islamic country.

As for tourism, the first holidaymakers arrived in the early 1970s, when the inaugural resorts were opened. The recently lifted ban on outsiders visiting 'inhabited' islands dated from 1984, and tourism as a whole accounted for about a third of GDP. It was the country's biggest industry ahead of fishing and agriculture. About 1.3 million tourists go to the Maldives each year, roughly three times the population total, which was 393,500 at last count (up from 82,068 in 1946).

Tourism and religion had a cagey relationship. Officially it was against the law to practise any religion other than Islam and holidaymakers are warned on immigration arrival cards not to bring in 'materials contrary to Islam, idols for worship, pork and pork products, alcohol or dogs'. In theory bibles were forbidden, as was wearing jewellery with a cross. In practice officials turned a blind eye, although it would not be a good idea to wear a large cross or bring in more than one bible. Alcohol is confiscated at the airport, with all bags put through an X-ray machine; not having properly realised the rules, I had foregone a bottle of Bombay Sapphire gin purchased at Colombo airport. Booze is prohibited throughout the 'inhabited' islands, although it was permitted on 'tourist' islands, where it was highly priced and an important source of income. On most of the islands I was visiting I would not be able to get a drink – at least, that was how it would appear.

The Maldives incorporates 26 atolls in what is described by geographers as a 'double chain' and the long, thin outline of the islands resembles a garland – *malodheep* in Sanskrit – which is where the name of the country is believed to have originated. From 'Money Islands' to 'Tempest Haunted Islands' (as some ancient mariners knew them) via garlands and the 'necklace islands' (*Maala Divaina* in Sinhalese)… I was about to explore a place that had, over the centuries, been anointed with many a name.

'You never know where you'll be in the Maldives'

I crashed out on the hard single bed in my sparse room at Skai Lodge, accompanied by an albino gecko on one of the walls. Mopeds puttered past and voices rose from the street. From my balcony I could see a ramshackle apartment block that looked as though it might topple over at any moment. Great bundles of bright washing were tied on lines, giving the effect of a tall ship with all its flags on display. To the right of this was a large white building with 'COLLEGE OF ISLAMIC STUDIES' written above a double door. Through open windows I could see rows of children bent over paperwork at their desks, with green books (presumably Korans) by their side. At night footsteps echoed in the hall and a fridge hummed in a corner.

In the morning, cockerels cried out from backyards as I was served slices of papaya with lime, an omelette laced with chilli, a thin, inedible hotdog, and a cup of instant coffee. I was the only diner. In the dimly lit room by reception the Bollywood soap opera was promptly switched off in honour of the English-speaking guest. Instead BBC World was on, with an item on Margaret Thatcher's death.

'Who is she?' asked Mimal, the Sri Lankan waiter and cook.

It was difficult, I was already finding, to escape the outside world. He was staring at the screen, seemingly fascinated by the former Conservative Party leader. It was interesting to meet someone who had no idea who she was. Mimal had kind grey eyes that matched the colour of his hair, and a lingering manner, as though he enjoyed letting time slip by, gently musing on matters in the company of others. When he talked, he had a habit of shaking his head softly from side to side, as though weighing up his thoughts.

'A former prime minister of the United Kingdom. She's died,' I said.

'When?' he asked.

'A few days ago,' I said.

His visage shifted from side to side for a few moments. 'What happened?'

'A heart attack.'

Mimal looked at the screen, his eyes glazing over. Then his head began to oscillate as though a big thought was arriving; first, though, it had to be properly shuffled into order. 'Air,' he said, apropos of nothing.

'Sorry?' I replied, my own head beginning to move about. The trait seemed to be catching.

'Air?' He pointed to a fan in the corner. His interest in the former prime minister was abruptly over. Did I want the fan on?

I did. It was already a scorching day, the temperature easily above 30 °C. Mosquitoes buzzed in the breakfast room, entering through an open door leading to an alley and the kitchen. I had been bitten a couple of times on my arms, but the fan kept the insects away.

Mimal told me he had come to the Maldives for work because of financial problems back in Kandy, Sri Lanka. We talked about cricket. He considered India's Sachin Tendulkar to be 'selfish', England's Kevin Pietersen to be 'very good, yeah, yeah, yeah' (lots of headshakes) and Pakistan's Saeed Anwar to be the best: 'Respect, respect! Oh yes!'

Skai Lodge may not have been as plush as Traders Hotel, part of the prestigious Shangri-La group and Male's chief residence for international visitors (mainly those on overnight stays before or after flights), but it had a down-to-earth, relaxed feel that no five-star hotel could hope to emulate. Mossies and all.

Sometimes it's wise to throw yourself into a journey: leap in and hope for the best (even if you don't quite know where to start). This was my approach in the Maldives. I wanted to get on the move, out to the high seas on the way to little-visited islands I imagined sweltering under the sun, waves lapping on palm-fringed shores. To head out on the water and try to find out about this sandy sea-world so far from home. Never mind about getting lost every now and then, just take to the waves and see what happens.

My only problem was: how?

As far as I could discover, no website listed ferries between the islands; I was not entirely sure whether services even existed. Yes, local boats clearly sailed between 'Airport Island' and Male. You simply had to turn up at the right jetty and off you would eventually go. For longer trips, however, for those who were not staying at resorts and jetting about on sea-planes, moving around seemed a little trickier.

My circular route was to start in Male and move to the south of the archipelago, before sailing to the far north, then down again to the capital – in fact, the journey would be more like a giant figure of eight. Male is roughly in the centre of the long chain of islands that stretches to Addu Atoll in the south. Addu is shaped like a heart and is divided from the rest of the country by the formidable expanse of the South Equatorial Channel. Its population is about 20,000 on seven islands, with 9,500 on the island of Hithadhoo, which had the biggest town outside of Male. The atoll seemed like a sensible first port of call: an exotic, distant place, removed and isolated even in a country that was pretty well cut off from the rest of the world.

The voyage from Male to Addu is approximately 330 miles. Before leaving the UK I had established there were no ferries on this particular route, and instead I would need to take a cargo ship. Many apparently travelled this way and they offered berths to passengers in an informal arrangement. So I had phoned the mobile number of a ship I found online and spoken to Captain Naseem of the Best Line cargo company. Over crackles and hisses, via satellites circling near the Equator, he had said: 'Maybe we go Friday. You come to docks.'

So, it being Thursday, I was about to make my way towards what I thought were the docks. I followed a narrow road festooned with yellow and pink bunting: further evidence of the imminent election. The pavements were crowded with upright locals swinging their arms in the manner I had noticed the evening before. On average people are shorter in the Maldives than in the West, and it was almost as though they were straining to make the most of the inches they had. I was wearing jeans, as I had seen that most men in Male covered their legs; perhaps this was a Muslim sensitivity. However, while they wore flip-flops or sandals, I was in trainers and socks. I felt hot as I passed the 'Tip Top' grocery shop and a youngster in a T-shirt with the slogan 'WISH I AM THERE.'

Maldivians clearly love clothing with a quirky message. I was quickly to come across 'IRONY: THE OPPOSITE OF WRINKLY' (my favourite), 'GAME OVER', written as though it was from a computer game and with an accompanying picture of a newly wed couple, and 'LICENCE TO BITCH', worn by a sweet-looking teenager who seemed to want to add a little attitude.

Aside from these fabric thoughts, there was a liberal scattering of graffiti. While people appeared generally carefree and chilled out, inscriptions on walls brought out the under-current of bother. 'FREE ANNI!' was written on the corner of a road leading to parliament and the presidential palace. This was the nickname of Mohamed Nasheed; since being deposed he had been arrested twice on charges of having broken constitutional laws during his rule. The graffiti must have referred to one of his spells inside.

Further on, someone had scrawled on a wall by a café the enigmatic 'NO JUSTICE, NO PEACE.' Meanwhile, a message by the seafront declared: 'COPS = PROSTITUTES. MALDIVES SOLD FOR $$$.' The latter was written near a monument in honour of the tetrapods that covered the shoreline. These star-shaped concrete blocks were stacked at key points to dissipate large waves. They could handle most sea surges, with the ocean at its current level, and had helped protect the capital from the full effect of the tsunami. On the northwest-ern tip of the island was a tall memorial to 2004's victims, at the base of which a group of men sat smoking, looking vaguely conspiratorial, staring across the waves. Were these seething insurgents plotting yet another uprising? Or were they just good old boys passing the time of day?

Beyond an avenue of lime-green trees was the colourful façade of the 'Official Residence of the President'. This was quite a sight: playfully bright, with a mosaic of pastel tiles as though it were the home of a character in a children's book rather than the epicentre of so much controversy. Solar panels glistened on the roof and black crows flickered in branches in the garden. The president's home was next to Sultan's Park, where I rested on a bench, taking in my new surroundings. There was something extremely peace-ful about this enclave of ancient trees, its pools of shadows tucked away from the bustle of the main streets. The soft, warm air had a soporific effect, and for a short while I closed my eyes, soaking up the heat. Had I lain down, I would have fallen fast asleep.

After a while, as I refocused, I found I was being observed by a skeletal man with a yellow-toothed grin. He had joined me on the bench.

'Mister, shopping?' he murmured.

'No, thanks,' I said, as I got up and walked on.

The man trailed me round the park, sidling close as though he were an old friend. He did not seem likely to cause much harm, so I didn't hurry. We strolled in step with one another. Trees loomed upwards with Spanish moss hanging from their branches, beneath which figures lazed on the other benches, some lying flat on their backs. A lizard fell from above, dropping by my feet. For a moment it appeared stunned, shaken by the fall, then scuttled away.

'Shopping?' Yellow Teeth persisted, seeming to want to take my arm and march me somewhere else.

'No, thanks.'

'OK, afterwards: shopping,' he relented, mysteriously pointing to a lane where there was a mosque with a golden dome.

Sticky pavements led to a tourist bazaar offering shark jaws and knick-knacks made of turtle shell, both sold illegally. There were no tourists. At the end of this parade was Republic Square, where more men stretched out on benches and lawns. It seemed to be siesta time.

I passed through the square, crossed a busy road, and arrived at a muddle of fishing boats. I had found the docks.

It was a cacophonous place. Fishermen in flip-flops were dragging buckets piled with red snapper towards a market with white-tiled floors slimy with tuna and swordfish. While much of Male appeared to be napping, here it was all action. Folk scurried about in the direction of another building, which I took to be a fruit and vegetable market. Great heaps of coconuts marked the doorway to a warren of tumbledown stalls.

I asked a fisherman clasping a tuna if he knew the whereabouts of Captain Naseem of the Best Line cargo company. He shrugged and hurried onwards. It was like *Alice in Wonderland* – nobody seemed to hold still for a moment. My chances of bumping into the captain seemed slim.

In the shadow of a spice stall I called him on the local mobile I had bought cheaply. He answered and told me that he was not in Male after all. He would not be there for a week.

'It is just the way,' he said in a drawl. 'You never know where you'll be in the Maldives.'

Those words sinking in, I glanced around, wondering what to do. For a while, I admit, I had a sense of utter hopelessness. I was in a fruit and veg market in the depths of the Indian Ocean, with no ticket to go anywhere whatsoever. I had arrived, but what was I to do? Maybe I should just head for the nearest (least expensive) holiday island and spend a couple of weeks reading novels and drinking sundowners by the pool.

It was tempting.

I found a stall selling thin, crisp slices of areca nut. These had a brain-like pattern, with swirling red marks around a white centre. Their circumference was about the same as a ten pence piece. Men were buying the nuts and sprinkling on them a cinnamon-tinted, curry-like powder, before wrapping this concoction in small green leaves and chewing. As I watched and considered giving this delicacy a try, a middle-aged man with glasses and a beard stepped out of the gloom.

Meeting Mr Malik

Mr Malik, Deputy Director General of Fisheries and Agriculture in the Maldives, was having a day off and doing a bit of shopping. He told me, by way of introducing himself, that he was reading for a Master's in food technology quality assurance and had attended Hull University, where he had been an undergraduate in fish processing and marketing. His positions, I quickly learnt, also included working for an NGO entitled Green Future Maldives (responsible for searching for renewable energy sources), the Environmental Protection Agency and the parents' association of his children's school. He was a man with many responsibilities, and he wanted me to know.

'Come with me, I take you to the *Aagalaa Queen*,' he said.

Before I knew it I was on the back of his metallic-blue Honda Wave moped. As we darted along the back streets, Mr Malik shouted over his shoulder: 'Don't worry, I am not crazy driver!' Then he added, somewhat randomly: 'Fishing stocks! We are very worried about fishing stocks!' The Sri Lankans had been fishing for tuna in Maldivian waters, he yelled backwards as we narrowly avoided a scaffolding crew. This was putting pressure on native fishermen who were struggling to make a living. It was clearly a deplorable situation.

The *Aagalaa Queen* was a white cargo ship, about 100 feet long, with a blue sign and a chief cashier named Hussein, who was petting a small scarlet bird. He was sitting at a table next to a tower of boxes of instant noodles. Hussein had tan skin and carefully maintained his triangular minigoatee beard halfway down towards his chin, like a floating comma.

'We are waiting for two containers. Maybe we go next week,' he said, sounding both Zen-like and Captain Naseem-like, too.

'I want to go earlier than that,' I said, realising I was coming across as a typical pushy Westerner.

I was, whether I liked it or not, quite a TPW. I could already tell that Maldivians were several degrees more laid back than me. This seemed to be an 'island thing'. Local pride in this super-relaxed attitude to just about everything – so long as politics and fish market negotiations were not involved – was frankly annoying, at least at first. But I would simply have to get used to the unspoken rules in the Indian Ocean, which appeared to be: take it easy, my friend, or else you'll never understand us.

So I tried to sound patient as I asked about heading south. Hussein shrugged and stroked the bird's feathers. He pondered matters for a moment. Then he shrugged once more and suggested we try the *Naza Express*, a smaller cargo ship with a green sign, just a couple of berths away. He thought it might be leaving sooner, he said. Smiling whimsically, he scratched his goatee.

Mr Malik and I walked through a dust cloud rising from bags of concrete to the ship, where we met Ahmed, the captain.

'We depart tomorrow!' he pronounced. The *Naza Express* was going in the right direction, or so it seemed, all the way to the Addu Atoll. They could squeeze me in, sleeping on a lino floor in the hold.

Ahmed was another relaxed fellow. He was wearing a royal-blue T-shirt that bulged at the waist and he had content, steady eyes, neat hair with a central tuft, and a chubby complexion. His facial expression was enigmatic but upbeat: a male Maldivian Mona Lisa. He was not a person given to fluster; a good quality in a captain, I immediately felt. The journey would take 35 hours and cost 500 rufiyaa (about £20). I was to turn up the next day at noon, and pay on arrival. At 57p an hour or 6p a mile, it all seemed quite a bargain.

The Deputy Director General of Fisheries and Agriculture and I went for a drink to celebrate. Not an alcoholic one, naturally. We had a Lavazza coffee, an Italian brand for which Maldivians have a penchant, and discussed Hull.

'My first flat was burgled,' Mr Malik said, a far-off gaze in his eyes. 'Downstairs: they broke in with screwdrivers. I was scared. I coughed and they ran away. I informed the police, then I moved to another flat.'

He had more trouble at his next lodgings. 'The other students didn't pay the electricity bill,' he said. He grimaced at the recollection of their power being cut off.

We talked politics. Mr Malik said that he was neutral. 'I am a civil servant. No matter what the president: I work. They cannot fire me.'

He paused, looking pleased for a moment or two. Then he frowned and continued matter-of-factly: 'Everyone is so politicised in the Maldives. So they don't work together. Multi-party democracy is not a good thing. It segregates people: the social cost is huge.'

He did not seem especially enamoured by the introduction of a fair voting system. 'Democracy is expensive,' he declared with a flourish. 'It costs a lot of money.'

He let that thought linger, before adding: 'We are so geographically spread out. When there were island chiefs, it worked well. Now there are five or six elected councillors. I don't like it at all.'

We sipped our coffee. It was good and strong, and Mr Malik was a talker. After his denunciation of democracy, communicated sincerely as though letting me into a secret, he turned to the subject of higher sea levels. Some scientists predicted that the Indian Ocean would lift by as much as 80 centimetres by the end of the century, and many locals were concerned that rising waters could lead to the islands being flooded. With 80 per cent of the Maldives at about one metre above sea level, this could, in theory at least, mean mass evacuations in the future.

'I am not much worried,' Mr Malik said. 'There was a time when the world temperature was higher.'

He shrugged and smiled.

'So you're a climate change sceptic?' I asked.

'Well, yes,' he replied, beaming broadly.

We finished our drinks and Mr Malik rushed off: there was a fisheries meeting and then a parents' association event to attend. I watched his Honda Wave hurtling in the direction of the pastel pink presidential palace.

Hitting the High Seas

The Albino gecko was still occupying a corner of my room at Skai Lodge. I ate a fiery tuna curry in the breakfast room, which doubled as the dining room when required, and got an early night listening to a fellow guest snoring loudly through a wall. In the morning, reports on Thatcher's funeral on BBC World showed horse-drawn carriages and vast crowds. 'The bells of Big Ben were silenced as a sign of respect ... not since Churchill has London seen such pageantry for a prime minister,' intoned the reporter. The former Conservative Party MP Michael Portillo looked as though he was about to cry.

I ate my papaya with lime and a chilli omelette, and had a chat with Mimal about the weather. 'Very hot' was the forecast. Then I went out to search for a camping mat, or something like it, plus a cushion perhaps, and a supply of groceries for the long journey on the ship.

That was when I realised that all the shops were shut. It was Friday, the Islamic day of rest. The streets were quiet, apart from the plaintive echo of prayers. I was about to spend 35 hours on a cargo ship and I would have to sleep on the hard deck floor. Would there be food or water? I had no idea.

In the hope that somewhere might be open, I went for a walk. I soon became lost, which was easily done on Male. The island has the fourth highest concentration of population of any in the world with an overall total of 105,000 – that's 53,000 people per square kilometre, greater than Manhattan where the figure is a mere 26,900. The result is that everything in the capital is crammed between teetering apartment blocks. The streets are both extremely confusing to navigate and usually packed with people. The alleys I walked down led to dusty football pitches, a cracked wall with 'SAY NO TO GANJA: THINK HEALTH' daubed in black paint, a café with men sitting outside playing checkers (seemingly OK on a Friday), numerous mosques, and many shops, all of them closed.

Nearby was a small man-made beach. It was a striking sight. The water was almost full of women bathing in burqa swimsuits. They splashed about, occasionally shrieking, while hairy-chested men in swimming trunks idled in the shallows. The beach was built behind a curve of tetrapod blocks with a gap in the middle to allow in fresh seawater. At one end, a brightly coloured Juice Lounge sold coffees and fruit cocktails. One of these was advertised as the 'Hangover Cure' and consisted of pineapple and banana: 'Highly recommended even if you don't have a hangover: replaces lost five vitamins and rehydrates instantly!' Meanwhile, the cafe's 'Liver Booster' smoothie of apple, lemon and beetroot promised to 'detox the liver and protect it from excessive alcohol consumption, it is our liver's best friend'.

All rather strange in a country with a booze ban.

When I got to the *Naza Express*, sacks of onions were being lifted into the stern. Despite this action, it did not seem as though we were likely to go anywhere in a hurry. A group of fellow passengers huddled in the shade of a warehouse.

Noticing I was at a loose end, a short man in a garish Hawaiian shirt waved me over. This was Figo, an off-duty tour guide who was soon to become my chief companion on board. He was jockey-sized and had a quizzical, deeply lined face with several teeth missing. I took him to be in his 60s. He was with Mohamed Rasheed, a hotel administrator with a brush moustache, stripy purple polo shirt and a reserved manner. He was to become my second-best cargo ship pal. Sitting on a wall was Didi, who worked at a souvenir shop. He was bulky, with protuberant brown eyes. I asked him about the shark jaws and turtle shells on sale and he quickly told me that they came from Indonesia, so they were technically legal.

Figo, Mohamed Rasheed and Didi were on their way to Vaadhoo, an island with a population of 1,700 on the Gaafu Dhaalu Atoll. This was the final atoll before the South Equatorial Channel. I had not realised we were stopping along the way.

The forthcoming elections were on their minds and Figo began to talk about former President Gayoom.

'He was very crazy. Very problem,' he said. 'Not like Nasheed. Very good man.'

'For 30 years, we didn't want him,' said Didi, who was returning to Vaadhoo to visit his parents, one of whom was ill.

They nattered for a while, bandying names of politicians about, their voices becoming heated. I had no idea what they were discussing. Then, as quickly as matters had flared, they cooled down.

'This ship take cements, potatoes,' said Mohamed Rasheed to me, seeming to want to include the outsider once again. 'The *Aagalaa Queen* is meant for passengers.'

He pointed at the sleeker vessel, still moored nearby.

'This is not.' He pointed at the *Naza Express*.

Figo helpfully added, by way of explanation and looking over at the *Aagalaa Queen*: 'This is big.'

'This is small,' he went on, eyeing the *Naza Express*.

This was interesting information to me.

Their English was not great, but then again, neither was my Dhivehi. I was not exactly fluent in the ancient Sri Lankan language spoken in the Maldives, which came with Arabic mixed in. In fact, just about all I knew amounted to *shukuria* (thank you), *haalu kihine* (how are you?), *barabah* (great), *a-salem alekum* (hello), *salam* (peace) and *boodu raalhu*. The latter meant 'big waves' and was how some Maldivians referred to the threat of the rising sea. Our little group could just about communicate, though, thanks to the English the others had picked up talking to tourists.

We chewed the fat for a while. I was ready for a lengthy wait, but to my surprise, Figo soon urged me to board the ship. We were about to depart. I jumped onto the stern after edging through a handful of women in burqas and head-scarves who were saying goodbye to loved ones. They waved and chuckled, peering into the gloom of the lower deck.

It was 1.30pm. The dozen or so other passengers and the crew had already bagged spaces on the lino floor. This meant I had the worst spot, next to a pile of doors and sacks of onions. My head, I later discovered, was to be a few inches from the feet of the ship's cook. The *QE2* this was not. Others had laid out mini-mattresses, blow-up mats and pillows. I marked my berth with a towel and a few clothes to rest my head on.

There was a splash as a member of the crew wearing a snorkel leapt overboard. It was his job to untangle the ropes holding the *Naza Express* in place. I ascended a ladder to watch, climbing through a hatch and entering a covered section full of bagged noodles and toilet rolls that led to the upper deck by the wheelhouse. The water was oily and the web of ropes of tightly packed ships appeared impossible to untangle. Eventually it was, though, and the engine rattled into life.

The man with the snorkel rejoined us. We were moving, inching out of the harbour into the watery 99.9 per cent of the Maldives, slipping past a mountain of cargo ship containers and a long wall of tetrapod blocks. Light glistened on the golden dome of a mosque. A child waved at us from the harbour.

The sea was indigo and the swell was low. In the wheelhouse, Captain Ahmed was looking calm and Maldivian style cool in a 'G-STAR RAW' T-shirt and shades. With his eye on the horizon, he told me there were eighteen passengers and eight crew, four Maldivians from Addu and four Bangladeshis. The 80-foot, 20-tonne ship had a top speed of 7.5 knots. It had been in Male for six days 'to get the items'. They did not take livestock, but he had once captained another ship transporting '30 to 40 goats'.

'Was that a fun journey?' I asked.

'No,' he said quickly. 'We had to keep them separate. Bad smelling. Keep pissing and shitting.' He pulled a face.

Near the ship's wheel were various electronic monitors and a Toshiba computer. Next to this laptop was a copy of the Koran and a box containing areca nuts and accompanying spices. Captain Ahmed sat on a leather swivel chair.

Was he worried about anything on the trip?

'The weather mostly.'

How frequent were foreign passengers?

'About three times a year. Mainly Bangladeshi.' The previous year he had taken an Australian expat who had time off from working at a resort. He liked to have foreigners on board, as it broke the monotony of the journey. No 'holidaymaker', it seemed, unless the Australian counted, had been on the ship.

Figo's head poked out of the hatch. He gestured urgently for me to follow him. Something very important was happening below deck and I had to come quick. It was almost as though we were about to sink. As it turned out, it was lunchtime. Maldivians, particularly those on cargo ships, are keen eaters. I climbed down the ladder to a shadowy space by the stern.

There, amid sacks of onions and potatoes, the cook had laid out two pans. One contained chicken curry, the other white rice. I was handed a plastic plate on which there was a drumstick, some sauce and rice, along with four slices of roshi bread (a flatbread similar to chapati) and a poppadom. Figo directed me to an upturned blue plastic bucket on which I sat, leaning against a sack of onions, gazing across the churning wake. As an afterthought, the cook provided me with a fork. The others ate with their hands.

Abdulla, the cook, was elderly and bald with a head shaped like a squashed rugby ball, narrow eyes and enormous ears. He watched to see that I was pleased. I was: it was a very good curry. Abdulla had a space the size of a couple of telephone boxes in which to produce this feast using a small gas stove. Everyone ate in silence, sitting wherever they could amid boxes of ginger, cabbages, calculators, Tiger energy drinks and carrots. The ship was stuffed full of anything and everything.

Then we did what we always did after eating on the *Naza Express*: we fell asleep on our spots on the lino. The heat and the effort of digestion induced almost immediate lassitude. Nobody fought it; barring those on the bridge, of course. Figo kindly lent me a pillow. Snores echoed across the peculiar chamber of humans, onions and energy drinks. And nobody seemed to pay me much attention. Even the three elderly women passengers seemed to have accepted the Westerner in their midst.

I could have slept for hours, drifting southwards to the Equator. The ship shimmied and shifted, a breeze stirring through its open sides. I could see the tips of gentle grey waves. Horizon haze rose in the misty-blue sky. Nothing much happened. No passing ships. Not even a seagull. Just the slosh of seawater; a faint smell of diesel; the judder of the engine. I had a patch of cargo ship on which to lay my head in a distant ocean. I felt as though I had stepped off the edge of the planet. I was already glad I'd come.

'The sun won't break'

Hours slipped by. Half asleep, I noticed a tap on my shoulder. It was Figo, looking out for me as it was teatime. We were soon back on our buckets drinking milky tea and eating biscuits served on plates that bore the words 'FASHION AND LIFE'. Nobody said much. We were still sleepy and anyway, the engine was noisy, so it was hard to communicate other than in nods.

I climbed upstairs to see what was happening. The captain was in the wheelhouse praying on a mat unfurled on the floor. A shirtless figure was steering the ship. I sat on the narrow deck with my back against the wheelhouse and my feet on the railing. The sky had turned solid blue and bright light danced on the surface of the metallic sea.

Tinny music emanated from the bridge. Prayers had ended and Captain Ahmed was on his swivel chair. He was 46 years old, he told me, and had once worked at a holiday resort as a receptionist alongside Australian staff. This was where he had picked up English. When a member of his family had fallen ill, he had left the job and returned to Addu to help. He had been a tuna fisherman for 12 years, and then taken a government navigation course to learn to become a captain. He had been on the *Naza Express* for half a year after three on another ship.

He showed me various electronic panels, which gave information on water depth, high tides and moonrise times.

'What would happen if the computers failed?' I asked.

'We'd manage,' he said. 'The sun will be there and the sun won't break.'

We looked southwards, where caterpillar-like islands emerged from time to time. For long periods silence

descended as the captain chewed on areca nuts. The cama-
raderie that came from being out at sea seemed not to
necessitate talk, though every now and then Captain Ahmed
would pipe up with another nugget of information.

He had a dim view of politics. Of the former President
Gayoom, he said: 'Good for ten years, but not after that. He
developed Male, but places like Vaadhoo are 30 years behind.'

He paused. 'Here everybody talks politics, but nobody
knows politics. We are new to the party political system.
Maldivians have too many opinions.'

'What about the rising sea?' I asked, wondering if he
might have a different view to Mr Malik.

Captain Ahmed chewed on another nut as he considered
this. 'Of course it is rising. Dig one foot or two feet down
on any island and you will find water. Any island. It was not
always like that.'

A silvery flash appeared before us. A dolphin leapt ahead
of the bow, sailing high into the Equatorial sky. This acro-
batic stunt signalled the start of a show. It was as though the
local champion had been called forth to catch our attention.
A family of underwater creatures flipped, flopped, careened
and spun. The setting sun began to bloom in pink and
orange, the waves turning cinnamon.

Figo lit a Camel cigarette as he watched. He enjoyed his
journeys on cargo ships, he said. His nickname, he told me,
came from the Portuguese footballer of the same name.

I dangled my legs over the rail as darkness descended.
The stars shone brightly and a crescent moon hung low on
the horizon.

There was a tap on the window. It was Abdulla, the cook,
gesturing to enter the wheelhouse. He was serving crispy
pieces of fried breadfruit, a crisp-like snack. The crew never
seemed to stop eating for long.

Captain Ahmed told me that his father had been an engineer at a power station on Addu Atoll, when the islands were home to the Royal Air Force base. 'He could speak English better than me,' he said. 'The British would come to our house every Eid day. We would have a party for them.'

We passed an island with a holiday resort attached. The lights of a golf buggy moved along a jetty with villas on stilts, perhaps collecting honeymooners to go to dinner. I imagined four-posters billowing with mosquito nets, plunge pools, glasses of chilled wine.

Abdulla called us down for another chicken curry. We sat on our buckets and ate. 'Ah, spicy, spicy food!' said Figo, who wolfed down his portion and promptly smoked another Camel.

Then we clambered up to the lino decking, found our spaces and lay down. Figo unfurled a 'Haji Special Mat With Inflatable Pillow'. The metal studs on my jeans dug into my side as I tried to drift off. The ship gently swayed. The Equator was not so far away; we'd reach the famous landmark in the morning. A cockroach scuttled harmlessly across the galley floor. Someone muttered. The engine rumbled. Water gurgled. The air smelt of salt and onions.

We were closing in on Vaadhoo, where Figo and the others would disembark, travelling across the One and Half Degree Channel. We had already passed Vaavu, Meemu, Thaa and Laamu atolls, and beyond were the mysterious islands of Addu.

In the dead of night, my subconscious noticed that we had stopped moving. There was a stirring around me. I opened my eyes and sat up. The cook was yawning and stretching, his feet poking into my shoulder. Figo was rolling up his mat. We had arrived in Vaadhoo.

Within moments, the other passengers disembarked and scattered homewards or to stay with friends. Figo and Mohamed Rasheed waved goodbye. 'Tomorrow morning, show you island,' the latter said.

Captain Ahmed stepped through the hatch and explained we would be staying overnight. Originally he had planned to arrive before nightfall, but we had run late. We would unload the cargo for Vaadhoo in the morning before proceeding to Addu. Would I like to join him at the café?

Beyond a dusty yard I could make out the shape of a small rectangular building with a sloping roof. A single light bulb illuminated a sign that said 'CAFE DE MILZIANO'. A few plastic chairs were arranged around a couple of tables at which a handful of men sat. There was no other sign of life on Vaadhoo, just shadows in the palm groves and stars up above.

I was soon being introduced to Shiyaz Ahmed from the island's council. He was young and enthusiastic, with a beard and wearing a pale-blue T-shirt and flip-flops. I was tired, blinking to keep my eyes open, but Shiyaz Ahmed was wide awake; the people of Vaadhoo seemed to do without sleep.

He pulled a chair close and began to tell me about his life. 'I have been in hospitality for nine years,' he said. 'My first position was at the Four Seasons. I was a steward, so I started at the bottom. Then I was storekeeper. Then cost controller. Then front office assistant. Then executive housekeeper.'

He paused to make sure I was following him. I nodded and blinked a bit to assure him I was getting the gist.

'Then I left the Four Seasons,' he continued. 'I went to Vilu Reef on Dhaalu Atoll. I was reservations chief. Then transport manager. Then I joined a private company as general manager. Then utilities manager.'

Shiyaz Ahmed had had a lot of jobs. We sat in silence for a while. The fellows on the other table were lounging back in their seats. They had been listening and appeared to approve of this shooting the breeze, although they had not expected a visitor from a northern European country to arrive in their midst that night.

From Shiyaz Ahmed I learnt that the local population was 1,421, of which 400 lived on the island at any one time, the rest working on Male or at tourist resorts. The island consisted of 178 hectares and was mainly agricultural, relying on '15 types of produce'. These included cabbages, cucumbers, watermelons, chillis, pumpkins ('baby and normal'), tomatoes, papaya and honeydew melons. Farming accounted for 60 per cent of Vaadhoo's income, while 10 per cent came from fishing and 15 per cent of people worked for the government. One in three young men was unemployed.

'We need development. We want to build a cooking gas plant here, but the government has blocked the plans,' Shiyaz Ahmed said. He looked glum about this and shook his head, seeming a bit hopeless.

The light bulb buzzed. Captain Ahmed chewed on an areca nut. The *Naza Express* bobbed at its mooring. The island was as flat as a pancake and so removed from the rest of the world that it seemed as though Vaadhoo had to fend for itself, no matter which politicians ran the metropolis in Male.

I asked Shiyaz Ahmed what it was like living on such an isolated island. Did he ever think about the possibility of rising sea levels?

'Actually we are very scared. In 20–25 years maybe it looks like sinking. We are really very worried. Very danger, here,' he said.

That night I slept on the empty lower deck of the *Naza Express*, awaking to a blaze of golden light. Wanting to explore, I hopped off the deck and walked down a dirt lane lined with rudimentary dwellings, incongruous satellite dishes dominating their front gardens. A tattered yellow flag bearing the scales-of-justice motif of the Maldivian Democratic Party hung from a pole. Cockerels called and small birds danced amid banana plants.

I continued down Jamaaluddin Magu Street, saying hello to a series of surprised elderly women fastidiously brushing leaves from the lane outside their properties. Some of the houses were constructed of coral, others of concrete. At the end of the road I came to a mosque with a rocket-like minaret, topped with a golden cupola. Palm trees shot upwards, their trunks criss-crossing.

I sat on a funny little chair made of scaffolding-style poles with a string seat – these are known as *jolies*, public benches found throughout the islands – and put my hands behind my head. I was in the shade of a mango tree, its pale-green fruit hanging from branches thick with star-shaped leaves. It is hard to convey the serenity of the setting.

Then I heard a voice. It was Mohamed Rasheed, who had changed into a blue shirt with 'OFFICIAL' on the back and was wearing sunshades with a Prada logo. He signalled for me to follow him, and we retraced my steps to a coral house next to a red-and-white telecommunications tower. Mohamed Rasheed's wife Aminath was summoned to make coffee. Figo joined us and we were soon drinking sugary Nescafé.

Mohamed Rasheed began talking about work on the tourist islands. 'The English are the best tippers. The French are the worst,' he said definitively. 'The Russians and the English drink the most. The Russians drink wine and the English drink beer.'

Figo cut in. 'Sometimes in the morning, whisky and Bacardi. The Russians. Big size glasses.'

Had they ever been tempted to taste alcohol?

'No, because we are Muslim,' replied Mohamed Rasheed.

'Younger people, maybe,' said Figo. 'And brown sugar. A lot of people.' He wasn't talking about booze – he was referring to a form of heroin known as brown sugar that had become a problem on Male.

For a while we were silent, feeling the heat of the day increase, the sunlight turning yellow and burning down on the bougainvillea in Mohamed Rasheed's garden. I was bitten on the ankle by a mosquito; I had already gone native and bought flip-flops on Male. An elderly man wearing a pale-blue sarong shuffled down the street and wordlessly joined us, raising his eyebrows momentarily as a 'good morning'. There was an uncomplicated sense of community on Vaadhoo.

A Bangladeshi's Tale

The *Naza Express* puttered onwards into the South Equatorial Channel, swaying into a bigger swell. Almost everyone, including Captain Ahmed, fell asleep. A Bangladeshi crew member took the wheel. As we crossed the Equator I had a picture taken on the bow. There was nothing but water as far as the eye could see, though occasionally we would spot a *dhoni* on the horizon, a traditional wooden fishing boat with ostentatiously curved bows.

The captain began to snore, but after a while he awoke and sat up. He had been resting on a mat on the floor of the wheelhouse, using an arm as a pillow. He rubbed his eyes and I asked him about his Bangladeshi crew. Did they enjoy being in the Maldives? I could not communicate with them, so he asked a few questions on my behalf.

The Bangladeshi steering the ship was named Moonim. He was shirtless and had a blue string tied around his right forearm, apparently for good luck. He was in his mid-20s, with buck teeth and carefully coiffed, spiky hair, as though he were a member of a boy band.

'They are not happy here. I can give you the answer without asking him,' said Captain Ahmed, but then he relented and questioned Moonim directly.

'He says that it is OK in the Maldives, but he is not happy as some fraud things have happened. In Bangladesh he paid people to come to work in the Maldives: an agent. He paid 240,000 rufiyaa.' That's over US$15,000. 'The agent told him that he could earn 20,000 to 50,000 rufiyaa a month. So he came and he got a job on a construction site, but the pay was just 10,000 rufiyaa a month, about $650. Most Bangladeshis earn much less than this, just $120–150. That is the range. It is not enough. They become trapped. There are about 120,000 foreigners working in the Maldives. They come from India and Sri Lanka as well, but more than half are from Bangladesh.'

Moonim muttered his responses to Captain Ahmed's enquiries in a soft voice, keeping his eyes on the waves ahead.

'He speaks broken Dhivehi,' said the captain. 'Many Bangladeshis don't know a single word. They are cut off from the rest of us.'

I asked him to find out what Moonim's plans were for the future. What were his dreams?

'The people who come to the Maldives to work are actually very poor. They have nothing much. They come to make money, but nothing goes to plan. If he went back home he would have to do agriculture, rice and vegetables. He says he has no dreams. Once the plan fails: no dreams.'

Back in Bangladesh, Moonim had sold his house for US$3,400 in order to help raise funds to come to the Maldives. 'He says that he still has not recovered that amount and he has been here two years. Maybe one year more and he will have got it back. He says that if he could get his hands on the agent in Bangladesh, he would kill him. Their own people have cheated them. That's the problem. Everyone has the same story. His "owner" in the Maldives, the man running the construction site, did not pay him for six months. So eventually he left. He now has no visa or passport, as the owner has his passport. Once they come over here and this happens, what can they do? They can do nothing. Human trafficking, that's what it's called, right?'

Abdulla appeared through the hatch, balancing plates of *garudia*. This Maldivian speciality consists of smoked tuna with lime, chilli and onion in a thin, spicy soup. It is served with plain white rice and is delicious.

Captain Ahmed explained that Abdulla was aged 72 but continued to work, because 'mostly Maldivians are hard working: they keep working late in life'. He was from the Fuvahmulah Atoll, which we could see far away to the southeast. He had left home to work on ships when he was 20. 'Our life is best on boats: travelling, fishing,' murmured the captain.

We were steaming on to Addu Atoll now. Captain Ahmed changed back into his 'G-STAR RAW' T-shirt, styled his hair so his signature central tuft was angled perfectly, and put on a cool pair of shades. His house was on Addu and he was looking forward to returning. He told me about the United Suvadive Islands, explaining how the southern atolls had formed the breakaway nation in 1959 as a reaction against the rulers in Male, who they thought had given up caring about their welfare. For a while the British at the RAF base had worked with the new 'country', and when it collapsed in 1963, its leader, Abdullah Afeef, fled thanks to a lift on HMS *Loch Lomond*.

'The British took his whole family to the Seychelles,' said the captain. 'The man who would have been president. Every person in Addu respects him. That's why I say that the British supported us.'

The captain believed that the RAF base had been good for the people of Addu, as it provided jobs and meant that locals learnt English. 'The southern people are more intelligent. You will notice this when you visit the north,' he said.

We talked about giving up smoking. Captain Ahmed had high cholesterol and had been forced to quit, he told me. He was also trying to cut back on his coffee intake, currently about 12 cups a day.

And then we saw Addu, a thin strip of land beneath the pale-blue sky. Towers of clouds billowed beyond it. As we entered the atoll, the water became flat and smooth with a dark, almost oily sheen. Captain Ahmed began to sing a gentle melody. We passed through a section of sea where currents met, the surface rippling and bubbling as though it were boiling. A large grey ship was moored near an uninhabited island. 'The fish collectors,' said the captain. 'Government owned. They take the fish to Kooddoo.'

The journey from Male had taken 52 hours. My eyes stung from sun cream and sunshine. My hips were sore from the lino floor. I had two-day stubble, and had bashed my head on the ceiling of the sleeping deck more times than I could remember. My polo shirt was covered in watermelon sack dust. My jeans were grimy. Captain Ahmed, on the other hand, looked as fresh as a daisy, smelling of aftershave and humming as we pulled up to the dock on the island of Feydhoo.

'Money, money, yes sir'

Feydhoo was connected to Hithadhoo by a road that led across a causeway. This road was said to be the longest in the whole of the Maldives, stretching nine miles and dating from the time of the British. The captain had called ahead to a friend who ran the Ocean Shore Guest House on Hithadhoo; considerately, he had also phoned to book a taxi.

The sun was about to set and huge clouds had gathered above Addu looking like nuclear explosions. The air was humid. The road was empty. My taxi was parked by the water's edge. After saying goodbye to Captain Ahmed and the crew, I sat in the front seat. The driver, wearing ludicrously bulbous shades, had a pronounced lower jaw and did not say much. We drove at a sedate pace past a picture of former president Mohamed Nasheed and the slogan 'A LEADER WITH VISION', followed by low-level houses painted lime-green and graffiti on a wall that said 'MONEY, MONEY, YES SIR'.

After crossing a causeway onto the island of Maradhoo, we traversed another onto Hithadhoo. I had picked up three new islands in the space of a few moments, bringing my total to six, including Airport Island, Male and Vaadhoo. On Hithadhoo we had to slow, as a group of women were walking straight down the middle of the road. It was the job of the taxi to move to one side, edging onto a dusty verge. 'They do this,' commented the driver, noticing my surprise. Turning down a potholed track, we pulled up at the Ocean Shore Guest House.

My lodgings seemed to be in a residential area, behind a crimson gate next to a mosque. The captain had told me that the guesthouse was run by Ibrahim Hamed. I entered a lounge with black leather sofas and Indian Premier League cricket playing on a television. A twenty-something man was sitting on one of the sofas, beneath a picture that would light up and show a waterfall if plugged in. The electrical cable hung from the frame.

The man was glumly watching the game and he turned to look at me.

'Are you Ibrahim Hamed?' I asked.

'Yes,' he replied. His gaze returned to the screen. He seemed to be extremely laid-back to the point of horizontal. Perhaps he hadn't heard me right. I asked again if he was Ibrahim Hamed.

'Me?' he answered.

'Yes, you,' I said.

'No,' he responded.

We weren't getting anywhere particularly fast.

Eventually I discovered that he was looking after the guesthouse. He showed me to Room 101, next to the lounge and lit by a red bulb. After the lino deck on the *Naza Express*, this was a palace. There was air-conditioning and an en suite shower room. The nightly rate was £21.50, breakfast and a chicken curry dinner included.

The caretaker returned to the cricket. I could hear the Australian commentators from the room ('that was top-drawer stuff … the brute force … the finesse'). But I didn't care. I had a fantastic shower, lay in the cool air for a while and ventured out to see about dinner.

The caretaker was still on the sofa.

'Curry coming. Chicken curry,' he said. As if to empha-sise the food's imminent arrival, he switched to a Bollywood soap opera. The Ocean Shore Guest House had its own way of doing things.

Ibrahim Ahmed arrived with the curry. He had a clipped, business-like air about him and was full of bustle. 'We've got seven rooms. No foreign tourists come. Not yet. Only locals,' he told me. He talked about the new government policy of allowing foreigners to travel around the islands independently. 'It is good for the country. Not everyone has 20 million rufiyaa to invest in a big hotel. But if you've got 2 million rufiyaa it's enough to build a place like this.' That was about £80,000.

With that, he left. He was in a rush to get to the mosque. A muezzin had begun a loud call to prayer next door.

I ate the top-notch curry and rice in the company of the caretaker, whose name I learnt was Aktar. He was 24 and from Bangladesh.

'I don't like it here,' he said sullenly, in reference to the Maldives. 'In four to five months I go home.'

Like Moonim on the ship, he seemed to have had a bad time. He had also recently been mugged: 'No good people. Twice they take pocket money, and phone.'

I sympathised with him. He shrugged as if to say, 'That's just the way life is.'

I retired to my luxurious room, soon to discover that another quirk of the Ocean Shore Guest House was its morning wake-up call. At 4.50am I was almost shaken out of bed.

'Woooo-dooo! Der doooooo! Der doooooo!' an imam began. At least that's how it sounded to me. 'Woooo! Wanna-woooo! Der doooooo!'

I looked at my watch in disbelief. I was all for getting a taste of the real Maldives, but I hadn't expected this. The imam stopped after a minute or so. I closed my eyes and tried to sleep once more. He started up again, sounding as though he were suffering from some terrible, grief-stricken woe. Other imams began in a similar vein, almost as if they were competing with one another. Wails and moans echoed across the palm trees.

After a while I got used to them and fell asleep, waking again in time for breakfast. Aktar had told me that this would be served at 8am, but there was no sign of the caretaker and the front door of the guesthouse was locked. I waited in the lounge until another guest passed by. Assessing the situation, he knocked on a bedroom door down the hall. Aktar emerged, rubbing his eyes. He smiled sheepishly and disappeared to the kitchen.

The Ocean Shore Guest House had a *Fawlty Towers* quality that was much more memorable than your average upmarket hotel. With places like this and Skai Lodge I was seeing the other side of this watery nation – and I was enjoying every minute.

The Old RAF Base

One of the highlights of Addu Atoll was the former RAF base on the island of Gan, where the servicemen's quarters had been converted into a small hotel named Equator Village, a very simple 'tourist island'. The pictures I had seen showed a bar with a snooker table dating from RAF days, a pool, and neat rows of low-level houses that still looked a bit like a military camp. Most resort islands were only accessible by boat, but because of the nine-mile road anyone could pop by to this one, so I did.

I hopped in a taxi whose driver asked 'You Muslim?' and was disappointed when I said I wasn't. Seawater rushed in a torrent through channels below the causeway. Once on Gan, the taxi passed along a lane leading through a metal gate and beyond a security hut. Bougainvillea, mango trees and well-trimmed hedges filled a pretty garden between the old quarters.

I entered the reception. There was no one on the front desk, so I wandered through a lounge scattered with wicker furniture. To one side was the bar, with a sign behind a shelf of drinks that read 'ALL-INCLUSIVE'. A sign behind another shelf of drinks said 'NON ALL-INCLUSIVE'. A shirtless man with a pot belly was ordering four Carlsberg beers and a whisky and Coke. It was 9.35am. Apart from him and his companions, the place was deserted.

'*Spaceba*,' he said, taking the drinks to the pool.

Eventually Abdullah Zuhair arrived, the reservations office manager. He wore a pink striped shirt, jeans and gold-framed glasses. He was good-natured, curious about my journey on the cargo ship, and had a precise, particular manner.

He spelt out his name. 'Abdullah with an "h". I do like it with an "h". Abdullah means "slave of God". When we spell Allah it is with an "h", so I like it with an "h".'

He joined me for a can of soda. The hotel had 78 rooms, he told me. 'Basically these are exactly the same buildings that the RAF had. There's the same mess hall. The steel on the bar and the plywood, the same. We have changed the partitions between the rooms because they were not concrete. The snooker table is there,' he pointed to a corner. 'Same room.'

We were sitting by the former sergeant's mess. 'My father worked here,' Abdullah told me. 'He was a nurse at the hospital. He worked for a long time for the RAF. Three weeks ago, 16 of them came: RAF. They called it RAF reunion. Some of them told me that they had bought their houses in London with money they earned here.'

Abdullah turned dreamy-eyed. 'We'd like them to come back. When they left in 1976, a lot of things changed. We had to wait long time to fix stuff. Everything shut down.' This included a generator made by the British. 'But the government didn't want anything to do with it. So people had to migrate. A lot of equipment was shipped to Male: things like X-ray machines from the hospital. From 1976 to 1989 we had no electricity. It was really dark. We had to carry torch lights. We used kerosene to light up oil lamps. The influential, educated people went to Male.' The British had established schools and taught pupils to pass their O-Levels. 'That was before Male even had O-Level exams.'

He looked thoughtful, almost sad. We stared out at the Russians by the pool. They were reading books without talking, drinks by their sides. Waves crashed into a concrete breakwater by the shore. Up above a dark, heavy-looking bird flapped out from the fronds of a palm tree, winging laboriously in the direction of the causeway. It looked as though it was having trouble staying airborne.

'Fruit bat,' said Abdullah, correcting my thoughts. 'Not bird. Plenty of fruit bats on Gan.'

Equator Village was so quiet. Did Abdullah enjoy living and working in Addu Atoll? He chuckled and sipped his soda.

'I like to work here,' he replied carefully. 'But the income is not so good.'

He sighed, then smiled. I got the impression he felt cut off from the world, a long way from the machinations of Male, and quite content to be that way.

Abdullah showed me a dog-eared album with black-and-white pictures from the RAF days. The photos captured 'monthly mosquito killings' (blue smoke wafting from a building that looked like the sergeant's mess), RAF Lightnings, Victors, Shackletons and VC10s parked by the runway, figures gripping pewter tankards in the bar, *dhoni* races, a visit by the Duke of Edinburgh (dressed in a shirt, tie and long trousers despite the heat, whereas the officers wore khaki shorts), another visit by Sir Alec Douglas-Home (when he was foreign secretary, before briefly becoming prime minister in 1963). He, unbelievably, was wearing a full suit. The shots were fascinating glimpses of another existence: 'eastern bloc spy ships' taken from plane windows, an art deco-style 'Astra' cinema (which still stands near the entrance to Equator Village), a cricket team in crumpled whites, a disc jockey spinning tracks for the island's own radio station.

A few words about those days were included in the old album, written by Ian Morrison, a technician who had served at the base for a year in 1959–60. In his mini-memoir, now sheathed in plastic in a folder in a bar in a faraway land, he explained how the events of 1956 led to Britain seeking an airbase in the Indian Ocean. The Suez Crisis, which saw President Nasser of Egypt renationalise the Suez Canal, forcing Britain to withdraw, had a knock-on effect: the prime minister of what was then Ceylon feared that RAF bases could be used for military action in the Middle East. The Sri Lankans did not want to be drawn into a conflict, so Britain had hastily to find an alternative staging post. Representatives were sent to Male, where a deal was signed to lease the island for £2,000 a year.

Morrison's recollections are of rough quarters and high jinks. At first the servicemen slept in simple dwellings and high tide sometimes flooded the floors. They often suffered dysentery brought on by infestations of rats. Many were so badly affected by prickly heat they would lie down in monsoon ditches to let water rush over their bodies.

When not in a bad way, they enjoyed themselves greatly, living it up almost nightly at the NAAFI bar, where they would regularly induce yet more hardship in the form of shocking hangovers. These were tolerated by the authorities 'due to the nature of life' on an isolated island, and victims would be given a day off in the sickroom, where they were served a potion that 'worked splendidly' to cure sore heads.

There were fire extinguisher fights, attempted attacks on visiting Royal Navy ships (RAF men once tried to paint silly faces on the ships' hulls and were pelted with potatoes when discovered by those on board), nights so drunken that people slept wherever they happened to pass out. Alcohol seemed to be integral to keeping boredom at bay. Most of the men were badly homesick and they kept 'chuff charts' marking the days they had left on the island – when all the days were crossed off, they were 'chuffed' to be able to return to Britain. For a bit of fun, crude address labels were stuck to coconuts, which would be posted home to surprise

friends and family: 'No doubt to be cursed by the poor post-
man delivering it in the UK,' Morrison wrote.

While in the control tower one day, he watched as a
Hastings plane coming into land hit the runway much too
hard, lost its undercarriage and careered off to one side in
a dusty heap. All the passengers and crew ran safely from
the wreckage, but the accident made the RAF aware of the
mirage of heat haze that came off the white surface of the
runway, confusing pilots over the altitude. Black lines were
drawn on the surface to create a better perspective and prevent further mishaps.

At the time of Morrison's visit the islands had broken free
of control from Male, during the temporary period of the
United Suvadive Islands. In one incident, two *dhonis* from
Male were intercepted and 60 invaders captured. They were
'armed' with great bundles of limes. Puzzled, the RAF men
asked what they were doing with all the limes and were told
they 'were to be cut open and sprayed in the eyes of sleeping Adduans as a sort of terror campaign'. If only terrorists
would take citrus fruit into battle these days.

Abdullah took me to the television room by reception,
where he left me to watch *The Lonely Men of Coral Command*,
an Anglia television documentary about life on the RAF base.
The programme was shot in 1970, narrated in a crystal-clear,
old-fashioned BBC voice by a presenter named Michael
Robson. For a while I lost myself in another era.

During the time of the documentary, a decade after
Morrison left, a bar existed on the island named the 'Not
Having Inn'. This was a reference to the lack of female com-
panionship, 'save one British woman', who was a coun-
sellor. The RAF men found the island a difficult place to be
stationed: 'It can produce in the most level-headed men, a
profound claustrophobia … at the beginning of the stay on

Gan it is not unheard of for men to weep at the sheer geo-
graphical isolation.'

On leave, married men would return to the UK, while the
unmarried would visit Singapore with its 'thieves, pickpock-
ets and hermaphrodites ... but it also has girls'.

Robson commented how unusual it was for outsiders to
visit the country. 'The Maldivian Republic discourages contact with the outside world, so this concession is an enormous one,' he said, referring to the RAF station, before
going on to describe Gan as 'not much larger than Wembley
Stadium'. He was struck by its 'harrowing tranquillity'.
Hence the need for the island shrink.

Tuna Fishing

It was battle stations on the South Equatorial Channel. The sun had lifted off the horizon in a blast of orange, the light catching shelves of thin grey clouds rising from the undulating water. The colours of the sky seemed to mutate and shift each moment: tinges of hazy peach, layers of brown, hints of emerald, streaks of jade. Shafts of purple merged into violent pinks followed by delicate blues interrupted by a bloom of exquisite egg-yolk yellow, soon infused with plumes of scarlet. At the risk of rattling on about sunsets – which I suppose I just have – I cannot recall seeing such a good one.

We were steaming ahead on a 99-foot tuna fishing boat with 25 crew, hurtling at a rate of knots towards three boats circling in the distance. The reason they were turning circles was because they had found tuna. 'We' consisted of myself and the crew. The captains, Saeed and Hamad Dideed, had been peering through binoculars on the top deck desperate to see some indication of the fish, but they'd had no luck. Fortunately, the other boats had done the work for us and located a shoal of tuna.

'Oi Oi!' exclaimed Saeed. 'Oi Oi!'

Tranquillity was over. The hunt was on.

At the sound of his cries there was movement on the deck below. The fishermen had been sprawled out, sleeping where they could, resting before the action. They were in a ragbag of polo shirts, football jerseys (one was wearing the Roma top of Francesco Totti), crumpled cricket-umpire hats, hard hats (preferred by some for protection against errant hooks), baseball caps, sunshades, surfer shorts, cut-off jeans and tracksuit bottoms. Their physiques were a mixture of rugby player and Homer Simpson, though they were all strong. They had to be. Each had picked up a rod shaped like a medieval jousting lance, about 15 feet long, and had made his way to the stern.

We pulled up close to the other boats, near enough to see the faces of the crews. Then the bait-man reached into the hold at the centre of the bottom deck, from which he scooped out little fish that we had been collecting through the night. These were tossed into the water at the rear of the boat, where a spray was being fired into the sea. The purpose of the spray was to make the water appear as though it was alive with many more bait fish than were actually there.

We moved slowly forwards. The tuna were fooled into drawing near. This was when the men trailed their lines with hooks that looked like little fish. Suddenly the most remarkable spectacle began, the great jousting rods flipping backwards over the fishermen with tuna attached to the hooks. As the rods passed the fishermen's heads, the tuna flew off the hooks, which were not barbed, and arced through the air before hitting the long blue deck with a thud and sliding into a wall with another thud. The deck was soon hopping with bloody dying fish, which were swiftly moved by a deck-man into another hold. This is how we get 'line caught tuna' (as it says on the tins in the supermarket).

The flitter-flop of fish rose from the deck. The engine rumbled. The thuds came in bursts, depending on whether we had located a patch of tuna. The 16 fishermen kept at it, hooks and fish flying manically. Earlier, I'd asked Saeed if I could have a go, but for reasons of safety and because the fishing was business and he didn't want an amateur messing up during a good patch, he had sensibly declined. Seeing the amount of skill required I was glad I had left it to the pros.

During a good moment there were as many as eight skipjack tuna soaring through the air. Often, though, the rods would go still. The captains would confer. And soon we would charge off in another direction, usually in pursuit of the other fishing boats. This was a game of cat-and-mouse, the rules appearing to be that there were no rules. If you found a good patch, you had it to yourself until the others turned up, as they inevitably would. The binoculars were constantly trained on the horizon, checking out the movements of the four main tuna vessels operating in Addu Atoll.

During a lull in the action, the ship's cook began singing happily: 'Dirty bay ah! Dirty bay ah!' At least, that was how it sounded. He repeated the words over and over. It was tuneful and seemed potentially saucy. I asked Hasan what the words meant.

'It is not a song!' he replied with a twinkle in his eye and steadfastly refused to translate the lyrics, though another member of the crew said the tune was known as Amintha, a Maldivian woman's name, and the words meant something along the lines of: 'Oh you're so good, so very kind.'

The cook was chopping onions, preparing lunch. Suitably, we had already breakfasted on tuna curry, with freshly fried *roshi*. The curry was delivered in tin bowls and was alive with spices; the tuna was, of course, straight out of the sea. The fishermen of the Maldives, like its cargo ship workers, ate very well.

Their routine was gruelling nevertheless, involving fishing six days a week, with Friday off. 'It is good money,' said Ahmed Nashid, who wore the Totti top. He was in his 30s, a hulking figure and constantly cheerful. 'We get about 10,000 to 14,000 rufiyaa a week.' That's about £400-500. 'In a resort, you would get less.'

A particularly good morning's haul of fish would come to between 10 and 20 tonnes, he said, though 4 tonnes was common. 'Now it is more difficult as boats are taking fish with nets from Sri Lanka and India. They're breaking the law.'

Each day the tuna were weighed and sold to the government boat I had seen when the *Naza Express* was coming into Feydhoo. This would take the catch to the big canneries in the north. The good news was that the price per kilogram paid by the government had gone up significantly in recent years, from 3.5 rufiyaa per kilo to more than 20 rufiyaa.

Ahmed Nashid told me that the oldest member of the crew was in his 60s and the youngest was 15.

'You have to be fit, it is hard work; there is no need to go to the gym,' he said.

'Are there many injuries?'

'Oh yes, I've been cut many times,' he replied.

Each night at 11pm, the fishermen met on the island of Hulhumeedhoo, the combined name given to two neighbouring villages, Hulhudhoo and Meedhoo. This was where I had joined the boat the evening before, after catching a ferry from a harbour close to Equator Village. We were about a mile northeast of the sleepy hotel. Between 11pm and midnight the fishing vessels would leave the docks and drop anchor in the vast lagoon in the centre of Addu Atoll. Two floodlights were then shone into the water to attract bait fish.

I had spent the night sleeping on a narrow bench with a tattered foam cushion in a hall adjacent to the captains' wheelhouse, waking at 4.30am to watch the bait fish come in, to be dropped into the tank at the centre of the lower deck. At 6am the anchor was raised and by 7am the aim was to have located shoals of tuna and begun fishing.

The biggest skipjack tuna would be about 8 kilograms, while a typical size would be around 1–5 kilograms; it simply depended on your luck. We raced about the seas of Addu, sometimes zooming in the direction of birds hovering in the sky, a sign of a possible shoal. Unfortunately, it was not a good day for tuna.

'Very low, just 500 kilograms,' said Hamad Dideed, who seemed stoical about it. He was short, with bushy eyebrows and a carefully maintained side parting.

'Why was it not so good today?' I asked.

'Not enough small fish,' he said. The full moon the night before had meant that the floodlights did not work as well as usual in attracting bait.

We ate spicy noodles with eggs and herbs for lunch. Hasan was a dab hand in the galley. Soon afterwards we arrived at a jetty belonging to the Herathera Island Resort, where a van was waiting and the catch was sold for 25 rufiyaa per kilo; a particularly good price. The haul had not been deemed substantial enough to take to the government boat as usual.

'They will serve it to the guests and the staff,' said Hamad Dideed, overseeing the weighing of the fish.

Each of the crew was then given a tuna; on better days they would receive two. They sat on deck back at the docks and filleted the fish, before crossing a gangplank and heading home. So went the life of a Maldivian fisherman.

On Police Patrol

I had arrived on Hulhumeedhoo a couple of days earlier and begun to get to know the local neighbourhood courtesy of Yamin Hassan, a twenty-something policeman, and his wife Azma-Alia. They were related to Ahmed, a local sports journalist whom I'd met by chance on Male, and Yamin had kindly arranged my fishing trip. I was quickly becoming used to this baton-passing style of travelling. There were so few visitors to the edge of paradise that outsiders had a curiosity value, and I was shown tremendous hospitality everywhere I went.

Yamin had a reserved disposition and carefully angled, gelled hair with a buzz cut at the sides. He was handsome in a Hollywood film star sort of way and proud of his job; I imagined that one day he could end up as head of police on Hulhumeedhoo or another island. During my stay he took me on patrol, either on the back of his moped or in a dented police car.

'Traffic issues, smuggling, marijuana and brown sugar,' he said, giving me a run-down of police concerns as we puttered along dusty lanes in search of criminals.

It didn't seem likely we would find any among the 6,500 inhabitants. With the sun beating down on palm-tree groves and sleepy neighbourhoods of neat single-storey houses with bougainvillea-filled gardens, the island seemed too perfect for crime. And too hot: at midday the temperature was well above 30 ºC.

During our first patrol on the Meedhoo side, we stopped at Kogannu Cemetery, where Yamin wanted to show me the island's most noteworthy spot. This was close to a beach and was said to be the oldest cemetery in the country, believed to date from the twelfth century. The graves were in a sandy plot behind a whitewashed wall. They were grey and made of coral, shaped like mini surfboards poking out of the sand. Those with rounded tops marked the burial places of women and those with pointed tops were for men.

They were carved with ancient Dhives Akuru inscriptions, connected to the centuries-old Brahmi script of central and northern India. Maldivians have an amazingly complicated mixture of ancestral roots, partly because the country is, obviously, a maritime nation, with Indian, Sinhalese and Arabic lineage coming from those who happened to pass by and stay. Some locals believed that the southern islands were converted to Islam earlier than 1153 AD, when Abu Barakaath Yoosuf Al-Babari impressed the sultan with his recitals of the Koran.

It was a restful place. There were no criminals around. I asked Yamin if he enjoyed being a policeman. It seemed such a well-ordered society, I sensed there might not be enough action to keep a cop busy.

'Yes!' he exclaimed. He wasn't given to great shows of emotion and this was as animated as I had seen him. 'To serve and protect the people!'

'What is the biggest crime?'

'20 to 50 grams of marijuana or hash,' he replied.

'What about alcohol?'

'I am glad we do not have it. Crime would be high if we did: fighting.'

This counted as a long discussion with Yamin. Mainly we drove in silence along paths lined with mango trees, keeping an eye out for wrongdoers. Once we stopped at a beach to investigate a lump of concrete that had been part of a Second World War gun battlement. Another time we went to the Koop

City Café, where Yamin drank a high-energy soda and smoked a Camel cigarette, while I sipped another Lavazza.

'Is the internet everywhere?' I asked to try to get some talk going. He was peering at his smartphone.

'Yes. Three Gs,' he replied.

I was surprised, but not that surprised. There we were on a tiny sun-drenched island in the middle of the Indian Ocean and I could, if I borrowed Yamin's phone, check my work emails.

We reverted to speechlessness. Yamin began flicking the screen on his phone once more.

'Do you get many foreigners here?' I ventured.

'Not really. Bangladeshi construction workers. Tourists only come on excursions.' Apparently a few visited from nearby resorts to take a look for an hour or so at a time.

'Do you worry about rising sea levels?' I asked, trying him out with a staple of Maldivian chatter.

'No, there is no time to think about it,' he answered. 'Crime.'

Similar enquiries uncovered that his favourite football team was Manchester United and he had once played as a goalie. Despite our stilted exchanges, we got on just fine. Sometimes it's best not to gabble.

Yamin and Azma-Alia lived in a single-storey house by a lumpy football pitch. They had a 3-year-old daughter named Yasha. Azma-Alia's mother and sister were usually around as well. We would sit in a lounge with a plastic orange coffee table, a fan and a picture of a waterfall on a wall. Maldivians like the idea of waterfalls, as they have none of their own. A creaky swinging chair with a metal frame and a seat big enough for two stood by the door. Azma-Alia's mother often sat here in pride of place.

Azma-Alia cooked excellent *garudia*, on which I was quickly becoming hooked. Pudding might be sliced oranges and bananas. Yamin was usually on the night shift, and I would be served my food alone in the spotless lime-green kitchen, as was the custom for male visitors. The rest of the time I either sat in the lounge or retreated to my room. This had a large double bed with pink pillows with a white flower pattern and an en suite bathroom. A tea towel with a 'Historical Map of Scotland' covered a side table on which a large bottle of mineral water had been placed with a glass. There was also a fan. It was like being in a little hotel.

Azma-Alia was more talkative than Yamin, and I began to understand why.

'He can't discuss politics,' she said. 'The police can't support any political party.'

That was why he was reticent to speak. He was being diplomatic, not wanting to cause a fuss. Azma-Alia, on the other hand, was a great fan of the Maldivian Democratic Party. 'Mohamed Nasheed was the best president,' she said brightly. 'Lots of good things for Maldives.' One of the former president's key aides was from Hulhumeedhoo, she added, and the ex-president had visited.

Often a political item would come up on the television, which was always switched on in the corner. Rallies would be shown with members of the MDP waving their arms frenetically on a stage not far from the artificial beach on Male.

'They are talking about tourism promotion,' Azma-Alia would chip in, or comment, 'It's all about the election.'

One item was on the launch of the DVD of a film entitled *The Island President*, a documentary about Mohamed Nasheed's campaigning to raise international awareness of the effects of climate change.

'There he is, Nasheed!' Azma-Alia exclaimed. 'Oh look, and there is Shauna. She's from this island.'

Azma-Alia missed her friends on Male, where she had once lived. 'There is nothing to do here,' she confided during a quiet moment.

I was an outsider, basking in the warm air, the tropical fragrances, the otherworldliness and the sense of peace that came from stepping off the hamster wheel of work for a while. I was enjoying meeting people, finding out about a way of life so alien to mine. On my daily commute back home I might pass tens of thousands of people via Waterloo and London Bridge stations, yet I was unlikely to engage in conversation beyond asking if a seat was free. On Hulhumeedhoo there were only a few thousand folk and talk came easily.

All that said, I did not have to live there. I was not confined to a couple of square miles of land on the edge of the ocean, watching the world on a smartphone and imagining what went on beyond the island's sandy shores.

The United Suvadive Republic

I n the early evening, women walked briskly down the lanes of Hulhumeedhoo, swinging their arms exaggeratedly and looking like uncoordinated soldiers on a march. This was for exercise, Yamin informed me. We were back on patrol again. It was a pleasant way to cool off after a hot day, bumping along on his moped between coral walls and along snaking paths through thick jungle foliage. We arrived at the southern end of the island, where the musky smell of mosquito spray reminded me of the picture of RAF mosquito killings.

The fumes were wafting out from the grounds of the Herathera Island Resort. This was connected to a remote tip of the island by a bridge across a channel. I hadn't known international travellers were so close at hand, although we never saw any guests venturing out. It was all slightly puzzling. Herathera means 'hideaway' in Dhivehi, so I suppose it was suitably named.

After a couple of loops of the island – no criminals, nor even the slightest hint of suspicious behaviour – Yamin and I went to the Café Wish Point in Meedhoo. Figures lurked at tables beneath rusting old satellite dishes, which acted as sunshades during the day. Several of Yamin's colleagues were eating tuna curry in the dark. There were no women at the tables. We joined Ibrahim Rasheed, a lance corporal in the local police force who was hungrily enjoying his food alone under one of the downturned satellite dishes.

After introductions, he too said he was concerned about the spread of drugs on the islands.

'Brown sugar. That's the problem,' he muttered. 'People smoke it. Very few inject. Hash. It's not grown here. Mostly it comes from Indonesia and Sri Lanka. Every day we take some.'

I still found it hard to believe that the island harboured hardened criminals, junkies and class A drugs.

Ibrahim Rasheed talked proudly for a while about Meedhoo's cemetery – it definitely was, he said, the oldest in the country – before gruffly adding that there were 'some problems with guesthouses, if they allow alcohol on the islands'. As he said this, he gave me a look. The cops of Hulhumeedhoo were not ones to have the wool pulled over their eyes. They had a hawk-like vigilance and I almost pitied the criminals, wherever they were hiding.

We were joined by a man wearing a purple shirt. His name was Hassan Shahid, deputy mayor of Addu City. The Maldives may be stretched almost 600 miles from top to bottom, but the country is a small place with a tiny population. The chances of bumping into a particular person were high.

Hassan Shahid knew about an appointment I had made to see the mayor the next day; I would be travelling back by ferry to the island by Equator Village. He sat next to me and placed an iPad on the table. Telling me that he caught the ferry between the islands to go to work, he let out a big sigh, although I soon discovered this had nothing to do with his commute.

'Things are not going well in the Maldives,' he said bluntly.

I could barely see his face in the gloom, but it was clear straight away that he was a plain talker.

'We had hoped for change but we are back to square one,' Hassan Shahid said, looking down at his folded hands.

He was referring to the 2012 coup. 'Since then we have had a struggle to run our budget. Central government has taken over everything. On Hulhumeedhoo there were plans for an inter-block road.'

I had seen dank piles of inter-blocks, concrete slabs that could be slotted together to form a driveable surface, covered in wild vegetation close to the docks. They were one day to be fitted on the dirt roads of the island, many of which suffered from horrendous potholes.

'This is now on hold,' Hassan Shahid told me. 'So are plans for 700-plus houses in Addu. We are in deep trouble in economic terms. The finance minister asked me to cancel all progress.'

He sighed again, which I suppose you might if you'd been asked to cancel progress. Yet again, more discontent in paradise.

The air was still and humid. Stars pricked the sky beyond the satellite dishes and palm-tree fronds. Yamin and Ibrahim Rasheed had begun furtively discussing police matters on their side of the table. Perhaps a brown sugar raid was in the offing tomorrow.

Hassan Shahid clicked on his iPad. There really was no way to escape the internet entirely. He went to a website with the address Maldivesroyalfamily.com. This turned out to contain a smorgasbord of information about Maldivian history, including essays on ancient kings, the place of religion in the country and the 'Arabisation' of the nation in ancient times.

He flicked to a page on the United Suvadive Republic. His eyes went misty as he scrolled downwards, as though imagining life in an independent Addu. The article described how the two main southern atolls, Addu and Huvadhoo, had been wealthy for many years running up to the 1940s. During this period locals had traded directly with India, Indonesia and Ceylon, bypassing central authorities in Male. This situation had deeply frustrated officials in the capital, who wanted a piece of the action. They were also disgruntled because the troublesome southerners, being so far away, could dodge taxes.

In short, Male had lost control. This lasted until the beginning of the Second World War, when British troops were stationed on Addu Atoll. To improve security in the Indian Ocean passports were introduced in the Maldives, as they were in Ceylon and other British territories. Because these were the principal trading posts, Adduans could not ignore this requirement: they needed the right paperwork. But as the passports were only issued in Male, they were forced to cooperate with the north. This led to the loss of direct trade, bringing a halt to the golden age in the south.

A militia, protected by the British at their base in Gan, was sent from Male to Addu in the early 1940s to keep an eye on things and prevent illicit commerce. In exasperation, locals eventually rose against them and the militia, who had quickly earned a reputation for violence, fled to the British barracks. However, when the initial uprising had calmed down, the reinforced militia went on the hunt for those involved in the trouble. Abdullah Afif Didi, the future leader of the short-lived United Suvadive Republic, was caught and flogged.

The website took up the story: 'Public flogging called *burihan negun* (literally, removing the skin off the back) involved being simultaneously beaten by two sets of cat-o-nine-tails until the victim was covered in blood, then chilli paste was rubbed into the wounds that covered most of the area of the back between the shoulders down to the lower legs.'

Such horrific attacks were not forgotten and must have influenced the rebellion of 1959, by which time the southerners were at their wits' end. The revolt created ripples around the world, with a letter by Abdullah Afif Didi even being published in *The Times* of London. I had not expected that. Hassan Shahid angled his iPad so I could take a closer look. He seemed full of admiration for the revolutionary hero.

The letter explained how Male's indifference to the south had meant a lack of food, clothing, education and medical supplies. In 1958 an outbreak of dysentery had led to many deaths. 'We appealed to Male for help,' Afif Didi wrote. 'They refused and very piously told us to go on reading the Quran!'

Meanwhile, all Addu's trade with Ceylon was going through Male and a trick was being played on the southerners. While they would be paid for their goods, mainly dried fish, in Ceylonese rupees, officials from Male would confiscate this cash and pay the traders in Maldivian rupees, worth half of those from Ceylon. Then the southerners would be made to buy any goods they wished to transport back at prices set in Ceylonese rupees. It was a double squeeze and the result was that 'for many years we have been reduced to serfs bled by extortionate taxes and levies'.

Hassan Shahid looked both sad and exhilarated. The light from the iPad showed a glint in his eyes. It was late in the evening and all the tables at Café Wish Point were busy. Who knew what plots were being hatched beneath the rusting old satellite dishes.

Reading a Book in the Rain

When it rained on Hulhumeedhoo it really bucketed down. I looked forward to these sudden storms as they would clear almost as swiftly as they had arrived, leaving the island refreshed. Yet their onset never ceased to surprise. The patter on the dust street outside Yamin and Azma-Alia's house would begin slowly, like a pianist tapping notes one by one. Then a symphony of rain would start, great torrents pouring from the Equatorial sky. Soon there would be two inches of liquid on the road with potholes filled to the brim, some shaped like murky versions of plunge pools at a five-star resort. It was as though Noah was on his way.

Every now and then a local would cycle by in a poncho, acting as if it were just a normal day; which I suppose it was. Some preferred umbrellas. Elderly women would wobble along delicately clasping stripy brollies while circumnavigating bigger potholes. Guys on mopeds, sometimes riding two at a time, would splash onwards through the temporary rivulets, umbrellas aloft. The sandy soil must have been incredibly saturated for the water to form puddles and streams so quickly. I wondered how much of a rising sea it would take to wipe out an island such as Hulhumeedhoo.

Inside, the splatter on the roof was accompanied by the leak and drip of gutters. After the deluge abruptly stopped, the sun would wake up and the waterlogged island would begin to steam.

During one of these 'down times', when you couldn't go anywhere by foot as the water was so pervasive, I read a thriller entitled *The Strode Venturer*, by the adventure novelist

Hammond Innes. Innes had been an anti-aircraft gunner during the Second World War and his RAF connection had brought him to the base on Gan. Aside from the racy novel *Beach Babylon* by Imogen Edwards-Jones and Anonymous, which describes various *Carry On*-style goings-on at plush resorts, it was the sole piece of fiction about the Maldives I had come across.

Much of the action takes place on Addu, and the plot is based on the period of revolt during the time of the United Suvadive Republic. The protagonist, Geoffrey Bailey, is set the task of tracking down the co-owner of a shipping company who has gone native and become involved in the rebellion, causing problems among the board of directors back in the City. The language captures 'velvet nights', 'frond-fingers stirring in the breeze' and air 'still and heavy with the day's trapped heat'. His descriptions gave me that sense of déjà vu that sometimes hits you when you read about a place you're visiting.

It was fascinating to get Innes's take on events at the time. In one section an RAF officer on Gan provides a briefing on the local set-up: 'You've only just arrived and you know nothing about these people – how they've always been different to the rest of the Maldives, how the little they're able to produce for export has always to be sold through Male. That's the sultan's capital … the Male Government doesn't give a damn for the welfare of the Adduans. Exploited, living near the edge of starvation, T.B. and elephantiasis rife – you've only got to look at the size of them. You see what you think is a ten-year-old boy and you find he's eighteen, possibly twenty. It's pathetic.'

In the book, the rebels are led by the shipping company director, who has become feverish in the Equatorial heat. They go off on a mad mission in search of what they believe might be a newly formed volcanic island somewhere out in the Indian Ocean. The island is said to be rich in minerals and the plan is that mining these will provide the wealth required to form a prosperous independent nation. The scheme fails, ending in a traumatic voyage on the high seas in *The Strode Venturer*, the name of the steamboat from which the novel gets its title.

I wondered how many copies there were in the Maldives. While the shelves near the old officers' bar at Equator Village had been stacked with modern-day thrillers by Lee Child and John Grisham, there had been no sign of Innes's enjoyable novel.

Hulhumeedhoo was perfect for reading in the rain, settling into the pace of island life and going for meandering walks in the shade of breadfruit and mango trees. The island had one guesthouse: 'Charming Holiday Lodge, Addu City: The Finest'. If I hadn't been staying with Yamin and Azma-Alia, this would have been my digs. It did indeed look charming, with air-conditioned rooms and a suite with a private courtyard and a hot tub. The owners could arrange watersports or whisk guests to the nearby Shangri-La or Herathera Island Resort should they wish to use the pools or have a drink. A note stated that 'consumption of alcohols are strictly prohibited on inhabited islands by the law of the Maldives. But alcohols are available in nearby resorts.' The Maldivian tourist industry clearly took a very practical approach to the matter of Allah and booze.

When I came to leave, I was sad to go, but I was ready to get back on the move.

Yamin and Azma-Alia would not accept payment for my stay, so I gave Yamin some Camel cigarettes. He took me on a final spin around the island – no law-breaking in evidence, as usual. Before catching the ferry back to Feydhoo, we stopped near the docks, close to a beach.

Yamin began to talk about iPads. 'You know they are very expensive here,' he said, sounding ruminative.

I nodded.

'But they are less expensive in Europe,' he continued.

I nodded once more, though I was unsure whether this was true.

'How about you buy me an iPad, you send it to me and I give you the money?' he asked.

I said I didn't know how much an iPad cost.

'Hmm, maybe you can find out for me?' he said.

'Email me,' I replied. 'And I'll look into it.'

But I never heard from him. I hope he got his iPad (at the right price).

'We are in a very strategic position'

I went for my appointment with the mayor of Addu City. The taxi driver taking me there was named Mohamed, and he turned out to be studying to become an imam. He was wiry, with a wispy beard with the moustache shaved short and hazel eyes that shot sideways as we slowly made our way to the mayor's office on Hithadhoo, barely breaking 15mph. It was as though he wanted to conserve petrol – the gauge was on 'E' – and talk.

'Prayers! Five times a day: 4.50am, 12.10pm, 3.25pm, 6.10pm, 7.25pm,' he said, as we crawled along. 'I am a *mudhim*.'

This was apparently the name for a trainee imam.

'In a month I will be an imam. It is good to be an imam when young.'

Mohamed was only 23.

'Older people won't have the stamina and strength. I like the routine.'

He moved to the side of the road to avoid a group of women walking down the centre.

'On my island, few people become imam. They think it is low grade. They think that a good job is wearing a tie and going to an office.'

He sounded aggrieved. His hazel eyes flicked my way and hardened.

'Do you know about Islam?'

'A little…' I replied.

He cut in. 'Being an imam is the best job in the world, I think. Our prophet says that the imam calls our people to prayer five times a day: five prayers is obligated in Islam. It is best thing being in mosque on time.'

He smiled smugly. 'So what religion are you?' he asked.

'I have none,' I answered.

'You have none,' he echoed, as though the act of repeating this was a winning point. He smirked and shook his head.

This was getting annoying.

'You have none,' he repeated, shaking his head some more. 'Have none...' He smirked again and then exclaimed, 'Ha!'

We were rolling along at about 10mph.

'Yes, I choose to have none,' I said, before adding something along the lines of: 'I believe in people making up their own minds about things and, unless they want to, not being required to go to prayers five times a day and for women to wear what they like and to be able to have the same jobs as men, such as being an imam.'

'I think you have the wrong information,' he replied sanctimoniously. 'I would like to discuss this with you.'

He seemed to want to convert me. After driving at a snail's pace for the last few hundred yards, we had finally arrived at offices that appeared to belong to the local government. A jogger could have overtaken us.

'Can women be taxi drivers in Islam?' I asked.

'There are no women taxi drivers,' he replied. 'They do not want to be taxi drivers.'

Mohamed seemed keen, but I wasn't ready for a long discussion about Allah. Besides, I had to meet the mayor. I jumped out. We had set a fare based on a return journey, so Mohamed would come back in an hour. I could hardly wait for the reunion.

Beyond a monkey puzzle tree I entered a building whirring with fans, ascended stairs to the third floor, and sat down on an aquamarine faux leather armchair in a waiting room. After a while, I was called through to another room with black chairs by a coffee table. Plastic daisies were clustered in a vase. Outside, a hawk flew past the window.

The mayor, Abdulla Sodhiq, entered wearing a purple shirt and a navy-blue tie. He was dapper, polite and incredibly open. His nickname was 'Sobe', which meant 'baby' or 'brother'. Within a few moments, he began to tell me how he had been beaten up in these offices two years before. It occurred on 7 February 2012, the day that Mohamed Nasheed, the former leader of the Maldives, had been overthrown.

'It was really frightening what happened that day,' said Abdulla, who is a member of the Maldivian Democratic Party. 'We had learnt that there were close to 1,000 people demonstrating in Gan. The police station was attacked. The police did not use force to defend the station. This surprised me. I got a call from the chief of police saying: "Can you stop it happening?" But what could I do?'

He sounded exasperated and had become animated, his eyes alight as he retold the story.

'I was on my phone outside the offices here. Six people got into the yard and they beat me up. They jumped over the wall. It was 8pm. My wrist still hurts from the attack. My elbow took two months to recover. I recognised those involved, as did the security guards and my wife and aunt, who saw what happened. We identified them. Yet we were not summoned to court. And the suspects were given not guilty. I was outraged. We are not going to get justice for this.'

His own verdict on the affair was: 'When a centrally elected government gets overthrown, people like these go to the streets. They were happy about it.'

We changed the subject and discussed Addu in general. The atoll had a registered population of 32,000, although 10,000 of this figure were 'moving about'. Like Abdullah and Captain Ahmed, Sobe praised the British during the time of the RAF base: 'Good health, good education, good food. After the RAF left, we were haunted. Our men went to Male.'

I asked him about the period when Addu had become the United Suvadive Islands in the late 1950s. Within a few days of being on Addu, I could tell that there was a big gap between here and Male, I told him. Addu was a separate place with its own distinct identity.

'Yes, we are different here,' he said, echoing the words of the Hammond Innes character. 'We are in the southern hemisphere: a different hemisphere to Male. Physically, everything is different. After the trouble, when I was attacked, people came to me and said: "Why don't you declare independence?" I answered that we don't have the means. To be independent we have to have a viable economy. A population of 30,000 does not make a viable economy. We need a booming economy.'

I asked him whether a foreign power had ever approached and offered financial support in return for creating an Indian Ocean base. After all, the US Navy was stationed in Diego Garcia, a British Indian Ocean Territory just 500 miles to the south. 'Have any Americans or the Chinese ever turned up with a cheque book?'

'No,' Sobe replied quickly, but the rest of his answer was slightly confusing. 'The American ambassador visited us, and before we also met the British High Commissioner. Afterwards, China, Sri Lanka and India. The talks were not in that direction.'

'But if you led them in that direction, what might have happened?' I persisted.

'If I had led them, perhaps they were of that thinking,' he answered. 'We are in a very strategic position.'

I later learnt that the Russians had in fact come very close to renting the base on Gan in 1977, after the British had gone, offering the government in Male US$1 million in a bid that might have opened up the Cold War in the Indian Ocean. The government had rejected the deal and the Asian *Wall Street Journal* reported that the Russians were furious: 'A Soviet diplomat complained angrily to a Western colleague that you could buy the whole country for a million dollars.'

Addu Atoll seemed full of intrigue.

Sobe and I shook hands and I went outside to find Mohamed. The taxi driver was waiting bang on time.

'I am sorry about earlier,' he said. He wanted to be friends. 'Do you have Facebook and a Twitter account?' Even trainee imams were hitting the social media scene.

He gave me his Twitter name and began to tell me how he had originally hoped to be an engineer and had applied for a scholarship, but was not accepted. We drove back chatting about cars. The taxi-driving imam-to-be had spent £1,950 on his motor, but was having trouble with the engine. This time we didn't discuss women or the Koran – and the journey was much faster.

The Search for a Boat North

E quator Village was the kind of place Graham Greene would have been in his element, meeting characters such as Sobe and Mohamed and piecing the fragments together into a novel.

When I got back the Russians had left. There were no more calls of 'Yuri!', no more *spacebas* by the bar. I checked out the old NAFFI shop, the Astra cinema, and a Second World War memorial flanked with canons close to the airstrip, which is now a small commercial airport. Then I had a game of snooker.

I had met a British couple, Phil and Jacqui, from near Maidstone in Kent. They were playing cards in the lounge, the only people about. Phil had a gravelly voice and was drinking a glass of wine (from one of the 'ALL-INCLUSIVE' shelves, so he hadn't had to pay). He had been a signal and telecommunications engineer in the RAF and had been sent to Gan to work in 1975. This was why they were there: he was on a nostalgia tour.

'I was a corporal when I came and this was the officers' accommodation,' he said, referring to the rooms at the hotel. He and his wife loved snorkelling, for which he had first developed a taste back in 1975.

'The world has changed an awful lot,' he said. 'It's not as abundant and colourful as it was in terms of fish and coral. It's still good, but not what it was like 40 years ago.' He blamed climate change for this and the bleaching of coral as the temperature of the ocean rose.

We played snooker and discussed the Russians. Phil didn't like them: 'They're an ignorant lot, I tend to find. The Germans have a bad reputation, not entirely deserved, for taking the pool benches, but when we first came across Russians in Sharm el-Sheikh we thought they were just so loud, totally self-centred and ignorant. Whatever they want: that's their goal. They'll push in front in the buffet queue.'

He asked if he could take off his shirt. 'You won't be offended, will you? This is getting serious.'

The snooker game was close. I left a ball hanging over a pocket. 'It's set up for someone, but it's me at the end of the stick!' said Phil, now shirtless. I came to realise that was his favourite snooker catchphrase.

The game went on for almost an hour. We clocked up our awful scores on an old wooden board formerly used by RAF officers. We were both equally useless. Eventually, as if lightning had struck, I smashed in the black from an improbable distance, grasping a last-ditch victory.

'You've been toying with me!' said Phil, who seemed genuinely devastated.

Reservations officer Abdullah with an 'h' and I became friends. He invited me to his house, where his wife, Aisha, cooked *garudia* and fishcakes made with onion, garlic and coconut, known as *boakiba*. Maldivian food is incredibly healthy and what with the alcohol ban on 'inhabited' islands, an island-hopping break is like going on an unintentional detox. Sure, you could get a drink without too much difficulty (not that I had, yet) if you went to a tourist island such as Gan and visited a resort such as Equator Village, but for the most part you were 'dry'.

After eating, Abdullah, Asiha and I sat on a red velvet sofa next to a giant Sony TV in his living room. His wife's brother, who worked at a nearby Shangri-La resort island, turned up and talked about his work for a bit. He said he had once been given a US$300 tip by the chief executive of Phillip Morris. This was his largest, although a colleague of his had been tipped US$1,500 by a Saudi prince. Tips were both incredibly important, helping to supplement incomes, and a source of much gossip. It was interesting to learn about tourism from the 'other side'.

'They are too rich,' he said, referring to the wealthiest holidaymakers, often from the wealthy oil states of the Middle East. 'Too rich for us: the normal people. Sometimes they spend US$15,000 a night for the presidential suite.'

I asked him if he ever became frustrated at the gulf between tourists and resort workers.

'Sometimes,' he replied cagily. He did not want to be drawn on the subject, which was fair enough given his position.

'Do you ever dream of what it would be like to stay in the presidential suite — of being a millionaire?'

It was a silly question, now I think about it.

'You can't dream like that,' he replied sensibly.

We drank our fruit juices and talked. Day by day I could feel myself adjusting to the Maldivian pace of life: less rushing, less fuss, more time to watch the world go by. Make up your own mind about things. Don't be hurried along. I liked it very much. Maybe I really was beginning to get the 'island thing'.

It was time to head northwards. I was planning to travel to Laamu Atoll. This would take me across both the South Equatorial and the One and Half Degree channels. On Laamu Atoll there was an island, Isdhoo, that was said to possess one of the largest remaining Buddhist *stupas* in the Maldives. This mini-hill acted as a kind of Maldivian Everest, one that pre-dated the arrival of Islam in the twelfth century. That seemed to be a good place to aim at for the next stage of my adventure.

Neither Abdullah nor the front desk staff knew boat departure times, so I went to a café by the harbour to ask. A few guys sat at tables beneath an awning. It had begun to rain. Water gushed from gutters into tropical plants in the café's garden. One of the men sat with his legs crossed and wore a broad-brimmed hat. I was about to ask a question when I noticed he was fast asleep, his mouth agape, wheezing softly.

After ordering a drink from a waiter, I asked a (conscious) cafe-goer if he knew of a ship heading north.

'The boat *Raadoo*. It left yesterday. So did the *Maadoo*,' he replied, or at least that's what it sounded like.

'What about the *Naza Express*?' I asked, hoping Captain Ahmed and his crew might be on one of the Addu islands.

'Left yesterday,' he replied, adding: 'Weather not good now. Rough sea.' His name, he said, was Chilli and he was a mechanic. He lived near the football ground by the causeway.

'Don't worry,' he said. 'Call Chilli.'

When I phoned him later, as arranged, he told me: 'Boat goes tonight – or tomorrow. Huvadhoo, then Laamu.' I was in luck. We went to the docks at 4.30pm, but the boat wasn't there.

'It comes at 7pm,' Chilli said, after conferring with a figure loitering on a bench. We returned at 7pm beneath a sky full of fruit bats. The creepy creatures were especially busy at dawn and dusk.Again, there was no boat.

'Maybe one week,' Chilli said with a shrug.

As it was shortly the onset of Ramazan, the Maldivian name for Ramadan, all the ships had gone to fetch goods from Male in preparation.

Island hopping by boat was not quite as straightforward as I had thought. I asked Abdullah what I should do. He was in his air-conditioned back office surfing the internet (as most Maldivians seemed to be doing most of the time).

'Is this you?' he asked. He was looking up my Twitter feed. 'I follow you … ha!' he said.

For a while we discussed the pros and cons of tweeting. Then he gave me his verdict. 'Fly to Kadhdhoo,' he pronounced, as though this were a self-evident solution.

'What about boats?' I asked.

'Fly to Kadhdhoo,' he repeated. 'A plane goes in three hours.'

Kadhdhoo was the main airport island for Laamu Atoll, from where I could catch a ferry to Isdhoo. Abdullah had already looked up flights on Maldivian, the national airline. He called the airline office, speaking quickly in Dhivehi and mentioning 'Mr Tom', not using a surname. 'It is booked! Just go to their office.'

Strictly speaking I may have planned to go on boats all the way, but a little hop by plane every now and then wouldn't hurt: I had never intended to turn into Robinson Crusoe, holing up on a remote island for weeks on end. I wanted to see different parts of the watery nation.

Abdullah and I said our farewells and I headed down Equator Way. A coconut farmer in a tractor indicated I could have a lift. I joined an overall-wearing passenger in the trailer, coconuts rattling on the metal floor.

Thus I arrived at Gan airport to the bemusement of two security guards. No one else was around. I hopped off the tractor and entered a hall with strip-lighting and a sign warning that 'CORRUPTION AFFECTS EVERYONE AND EVERYWHERE'. At check-in I was weighed on the scales along with my luggage.

'It is a very small plane, we need to know,' explained the assistant.

And not long afterwards we were aloft in tan leather seats in a Dash 8 300 series twin-propeller plane. Islands, reefs and resorts with water villas came and went below. Blinding light reflected off the sea. I imagined the *Naza Express* somewhere down there, the crew eating chicken curry, chewing on areca nuts or dozing. The journey was 180 miles to Kadhdhoo and almost as soon as we were up, we were going down.

I was north of the Equator again, about to land on my tenth island, ready to see some of the most ancient, and forgotten, sights in the Maldives.

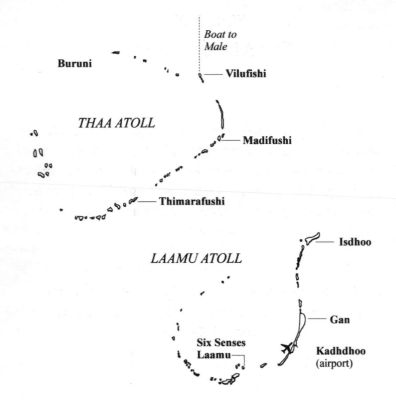

Buruni

Boat to Male

Vilufishi

THAA ATOLL

Madifushi

Thimarafushi

Isdhoo

LAAMU ATOLL

Six Senses
Laamu

Gan

Kadhdhoo
(airport)

PART TWO
The Middle Islands

A visit to the Buddhist *stupa* on Isdhoo on Laamu Atoll, followed by a stay on nearby Vilufushi, which had to be evacuated and rebuilt as a result of the 2004 tsunami. Afterwards, a stop-off at an island being built two metres above sea level, where many Maldivians may one day move for safety

'The sea has never been friendly to man. At most it has been the accomplice of human restlessness.'
Joseph Conrad

'On this beach we will allow the bikini'

Another day, another atoll. Travelling with no set plans in the Maldives gave me a fantastic sense of breaking free. I could just pitch up wherever I chose and another piece of paradise would be waiting.

Laamu Atoll is about five times bigger than Addu, but the population is less than half. About 14,000 people inhabit its 80 islands, aligned in a tear-drop shape around a lagoon. The result is that the atoll is even more low key. I felt as if I had the place to myself, though first I had to see off the Russians.

Luggage from the plane was pushed through a hatch into the tiny baggage hall, not much bigger than a suburban front room. A group of half a dozen Muscovites, two middle-aged men and four glamorous (younger) women, scooped up expensive-looking cases. They were led a few paces to their dockside ride. Their destination? Six Senses Laamu, the atoll's main resort.

How much were they paying each day, I wondered, as they shuffled off, all Gucci sandals and Prada shades. The answer was US$700 a night, plus 18 per cent for the service charge and government taxes in a 'lagoon beach villa'. A two-bedroom 'ocean beach villa' would be US$2,500 a night. These came with 'open-plan bathrooms with double vanities, tub and shower'. There were also 'outdoor platforms with loungers and over-water netting for a relaxing experience, panoramic upper dining deck and viewing platforms, plus aquarium dining decks with all-glass tables and sunken ocean view all-glass bathtubs'.

Nice. Their speedboat to the resort and back was a mere US$385 per person extra. A nifty little earner. How else were they going to get there, swim? I watched as the nose of their boat rose, skipping across the waves.

Once they had gone, I was alone with the Maldivians. I was aiming to get to 'Reveries', one of the new breed of guesthouses, on the inhabited island of Gan (this one without an RAF base). The island was connected to Kadhdhoo by causeways, but it was a few miles away, too far to walk in the 30 °C heat.

I contemplated what to do. Perhaps there was a bus, I was thinking. As I did so, a man with orange-tinted hair and an orange-tinted beard sidled up. He had a middle parting and when he smiled exposed thin, razor teeth that looked as though they had been sharpened with a metal file. These too were, very strangely, coloured orange.

His name was Hussein, he whispered, introducing himself.

'How much would it be to go to Reveries?' I asked.

He sized me up, his eyes swivelling like a lizard's. 'To Reveries?' he pondered thoughtfully, as though calculating the answer to a complicated equation. '300 rufiyaa,' he said, a little too swiftly, and shiftily.

'How about 150 rufiyaa?' I responded, applying the tried-and-tested 'halve it' approach in these situations.

'OK, 200,' he replied.

We had a deal.

It was then I realised we were being joined by four others, the last remaining passengers at Kadhdhoo Airport, who were holding cardboard boxes containing packets of rice. We all squeezed into a battered Toyota mini-van. I was given the front passenger seat, rice boxes between my feet.

We jolted along a potholed dirt road flanked with palms. I asked Hussein if Reveries was the only guesthouse, in case there were options.

'Yes,' he replied, but he sounded unconvincing.

'Are there any other guesthouses?' I pressed.

'Yes,' he replied.

'Could you take me to have a look on the way?

'Yes.'

'Do you know where they are?'

'Yes!'

We drove onwards, the yes-man and I, watching fruit bats lope between the treetops. On the island of Maandhoo, black soot wafted from a roadside bonfire. Ours was the only vehicle on the street and we wove from one side of the track to the other, avoiding the massive potholes.

A woman driving a moped appeared with torpedo-style gas canisters strapped to the back of her seat. She swayed and bumped nonchalantly along, dodging the many coconut husks that littered the few pothole-less spaces and were another obstacle.

'Do coconuts ever hit your car?' I asked Hussein.

'Yes, sometimes,' he answered.

'Do they cause damage?'

'Yes!' he replied, grimacing a bit.

We passed a beach strewn with palm fronds, a dusty football pitch and the 'Finest Taste' grocery shop. Then we turned down a side street where two of the passengers got out at a coral-stone house by a breadfruit tree, where 'WE BELIEVE IN FREEDOM FOR EVERYONE' was written on a wall. Rice boxes were unloaded before we continued back on the main road. As we moved along, a man sitting in the back seat gestured urgently to the driver to stop. When he did so, the passenger got out and was sick.

'Like the sea! Like the sea!' said Hussein. 'Waarh! Aaarh!'

We continued slowly and a woman wearing a purple scarf, sitting next to the pale-faced passenger who had been ill, told me about herself. 'I'm an interpreter for the hospital.

We have to make sure that doctors understand people as not everyone knows English,' she said. Many of the doctors were from India, apparently, and had English but not Dhivehi. We dropped her and the remaining passenger off at another coral house and Hussein drove me on to Reveries. He left me with an orange smile.

Reveries turned out to be a showpiece for guesthouses in the Maldives. I entered a minimalist reception with copies of English-language magazines on a table, next to an inviting café. 'Summertime' from the opera *Porgy and Bess* played on a stereo, merging into a Radiohead track. In the back garden a swinging sofa rocked in the breeze beneath a palm-frond sunshade.

Suresh Babu, the hotel manager, wore a yellow Reveries polo shirt, faded jeans and flip-flops. He was Maldivian-relaxed, with close-cropped hair and long ears that poked out like oyster shells. He was also eager to show off the guesthouse and seemed to regard me as a possible harbinger of planeloads of tourists.

'Much more than a guesthouse! Much much more!' he said, leading me to a plunge pool, a little shop selling sarongs and T-shirts, and a room with a pool table. 'More like a three-star hotel!'

Reveries had been open just over a year and had 23 rooms. The rate was US$55 a night, breakfast included. One guest had been Mohamed Nasheed himself, who had initiated the change of policy to allow accommodation on 'inhabited' islands in 2009. It was an important part of a Maldivian Democratic Party campaign to create a fairer society. In Male and on Addu Atoll, I had already seen many MDP posters advertising the newfangled guesthouses. They depicted idyllic beachside houses topped with climate-change-friendly

solar panels. White guests clutched surfboards and min-
gled with locals. The sun shone. Speedboats trailed smiling holidaymakers on parasails. Everything in the posters
seemed perfect and the message was clear: here is the future,
let tourism work for you, not just the big multinational hotel
chains.

Suresh led me through the back garden. We crossed a
road and stepped via a gateway onto a beach. The gate was
cut into a wall of plastic tubes that had been neatly aligned
into a long, tall fence to prevent anyone passing by seeing
the sand. There was a reason for this.

'It is a priv-it beach,' Suresh said. 'Priv-it. On this beach
we will allow the bikini.'

To respect Muslim sensibilities, bikinis were banned in
public places outside of tourist resorts. The pipe-fence,
which rose to about ten feet, was a way of creating a private setting and was apparently the only beach of its kind in
the archipelago. By barring the possibility of prying eyes, the
guesthouse was able to tiptoe around the regulations.

'According to culture, they don't like,' said Suresh, referring to the Maldivian attitude to bikinis. 'But actually people
do like. It's only human nature! Ha ha ha!'

He had a good chuckle.

'What about alcohol?' I asked.

'We don't have alcohol as we were not given permission.
Maybe in the future this will change,' he replied. Guests who
wished to have a tipple could travel by boat to the Six Senses
resort.

Suresh outlined some of the activities available at
Reveries. These included diving, volleyball, big game fishing,
and crab-racing on the plastic-pipe beach. We strolled back
to the guesthouse, where I took a room and then ate a spicy
tuna and chilli sandwich in the otherwise empty restaurant.

I was the only guest. As I was eating, I was joined by Abbas, the food and beverage supervisor. Aged 25, he was from the village of Thundi and was at a loose end.

After establishing I was enjoying my sandwich, he drew up a chair and told me a story.

'When the tsunami struck,' he said, 'I was on the beach and I could see what was about to happen. The seawater came up, up, up. It reached island level and seeped onto the land. I never saw any waves. I walked 100 metres from the shore and it followed me. I was working then in the power station. I ran to the power station and turned off all the generators. Then I closed the door and waited for the water to go down. I was holding the door like this.' He mimicked bracing a door with his shoulder. 'I could really feel the pressure. I had to wait seven or eight minutes. Then, after the water had subsided, I went to my house. There was no damage as we had a boundary wall, but all the houses on the beachside were affected.'

Abbas switched topic and talked about his career.

'I was at the power station for two years and then I got an offer,' he said. 'One of my cousins was working at a resort in the North Ari Atoll. I went there for two years and was earning 1,700 to 1,800 dollars a month including tips. I was once given 1,000 euros by a Russian. At the power station I had been earning just 220 dollars a month. I worked as a butler and I served some very rich people. Some were staying in villas and paying 3,500 dollars a night. But the management cut my wages to 660 dollars a month and a few of us who were working there decided to leave. I started a small restaurant in my village serving fried rice and fish and chicken dishes. That went well for a while and then I heard about this guesthouse. After the opening, we didn't have guests for eight months. It was because of the change of government soon afterwards, the coup. People were boycotting tourism. They were afraid to come. But we've started getting tourists.'

He was a fast talker. He paused briefly, as though considering whether to let me in on something.

'Recently,' he began, 'some US special forces stayed here. Seven officers.'

'What were they doing on Laamu Atoll?' I asked.

'Training – with the Maldivian army. They're coming again next month,' he said matter-of-factly.

'At the end of their stay, four of them asked for a speedboat to take them to Six Senses,' he continued. 'They wanted to go for a drink.'

It all sounded rather odd and I wondered what they had been up to, but before I could ask any more Abbas had moved on, telling me about the menu at the guesthouse and changes they hoped to make.

This went on for some time, at the end of which I asked about alcohol. It seemed a key part of the likely success of guesthouses – if they were truly to take off, wouldn't the authorities have to change the law and grant permission?

'We hope, we hope,' was all he would say.

Climbing Everest, Maldivian-style

A T THE docks near Reveries guesthouse I found the ferry to Isdhoo. It was a small white boat operated by Captain Mosa Rasheed, a wiry man in a crumpled green polo shirt. He was from Isdhoo and said he could arrange a room on the island. He also promised to show me the *stupa*. All of this was conveyed in a minimum of words via a ferry-hand. The captain had little English and was not given to gushing. Most of his communication came in the form of nods and unusual juts of his jaw.

So I found myself on the packed ferry to Isdhoo, sitting near a stack of boxes containing microwaves. I was seated next to a fellow passenger named Mohamed, who happened to be the former deputy atoll chief. He looked a little like the ex-West Indian cricket captain Viv Richards, and wore brown-striped slacks and a brown polo shirt with a tartan collar.

Mohamed told me we were going to stop to let passengers off at Mundoo and then Maabaidhoo on the way to Isdhoo (I wondered if there was anyone who actually knew the names of all the country's tongue-twisting islands). The journey would take an hour and a half.

He told me about the *stupa*, saying it was 'about 35 to 40 feet tall. We call it the *haitheli*.' That was the name given to a local cooking pot, which the *stupa* resembled. 'We cannot call it a mountain,' he added, 'as it is something we have created.'

'Is it the highest in the Maldives?'

'I think so,' he replied.

Mohamed was a theology lecturer. While this job focused on the teachings of the Prophet Muhammad, he did not believe in burying the country's Buddhist past. This, however, was precisely the goal of some Islamic hardliners. The previous year a group of extremists had stormed the National Museum on Male and smashed precious Buddhist relics. It had been an act of wanton vandalism designed to rid the country of the 'infidel' influence of Buddhism.

I asked Mohamed what he thought of the attack.

'Oh, I had not heard about it,' he said, surprising me; although on reflection, with much of the Maldivian press being in the control of powerful figures who might not want to stir up controversy, it was perhaps not such a shock. Maybe the smashing of Buddhist relics at the time of the recent political upheaval was deliberately overlooked by some editors. I explained what had happened, which I had picked up from a *New York Times* report.

'That is not something that we should be doing as it is related to the history of our country,' Mohamed said. 'We were not using them for prayer.'

When we arrived at Isdhoo, tying up by scrubland, Captain Mosa Rasheed jerked a thumb towards the interior and made off in the direction of a palm grove. I said goodbye to Mohamed and scrambled in the captain's wake, almost jogging to keep up. Down an alley, we came to what I took to be his home. There were four children playing on swinging *jolies*. They seemed shocked by their father's acquisition of a Westerner. The captain nodded at them in much the same manner as he had taken to nodding to me. Then he gestured towards a moped. I joined him on it and we zoomed off, taking a narrow track between palm trees.

The captain did not say a word. We hit the island's main street and picked up speed, passing nondescript single-storey houses and grocery shops.

'Just stay on the moped, don't fall off, it will hurt,' I was thinking.

At the end of this long road, we followed a path through jungle, arriving at a mound of stones partially covered by vegetation. Not one to hang around, the captain had taken me straight to the 'mountain'.

It was strange seeing this peak in this forgotten corner of this little-visited island in a nation that barely rose above the crest of the sea. Late-afternoon sunshine warmed its slopes and the captain began scurrying to the summit. He was soon at the top, where I joined him, crunching up the coral slope amid clumps of purple wildflowers.

The captain looked out to sea; we were close to the shore. Waves boomed beyond a concrete breakwater. Another smaller mound, also part of the place of worship, was inland.

We had reached an understanding that there was little point in trying to communicate, so we stood for a while enjoying the breeze.

Little has been written about the ancient history of the Maldives, but one of the main books is by Harry Charles Purvis Bell, a British Archaeological Commissioner in the Ceylon Civil Service, who came to the country on a series of trips between the 1870s and 1920s. He catalogued aspects of the islanders' lives under headings such as 'Meals', 'Habitations', 'Dress', 'General Character', 'Religion' and 'Social Distinction'. Before leaving the UK I had read one of his books: *The Maldives Islands: An Account of the Physical Features, Climate, History, Inhabitants, Productions, and Trade*. It offers rare insights into a long-lost way of Indian Ocean life, and was the first of a cluster of publications that culminated in Bell's posthumously released book (in 1940) describing his efforts to hunt down Buddhist relics, effectively 'discovering' the Maldives' pre-Islamic roots.

As he tramped across the islands in search of *stupas*, he had a sharp eye on the society around him. 'The ordinary dress of men consists of short drawers, a cloth wrapped round the waist after the Sinhalese fashion and a plain handkerchief twisted over the head,' he wrote. 'On board their vessels and when in foreign ports, some don a thin shirt, generally white, and Turkish waistcoat, which, with the peculiar coarse blue waist cloth edged with red, and the red handkerchief, mark a Maldivian at once among other races.'

Meanwhile, 'no Maldivian not of the priesthood now ventures to wear a turban in the royal presence … this headdress being retained by the Sultan exclusively'. Women wore 'a waist cloth, generally of native manufacture, coarse in texture, the ground of a rich chocolate colour, relieved by black and white stripes. The upper part of the body is covered by a loose-fitting red-coloured "jersey" reaching to the knees, short sleeved, and edged at the neck with silver tinsel lace … the tout ensemble forming a very becoming and picturesque costume.'

Bell did not visit the mound at Isdhoo on his main trip to find signs of Buddhism, though he did see other *stupas* on Gan in Laamu Atoll (these have since been largely destroyed by vandals, I was told). By the time of his 1920s trip he had become friends with the king, who leant him the royal schooner to ease his investigations. I found only one grainy picture of the archaeologist, who is notable for his walrus-like moustache. His hair is cropped and there is something doleful about his expression.

Bell came to the conclusion that mounds such as the one at Isdhoo were without doubt Buddhist. He also saw Buddhist influence in the names of some islands: one translated to 'City of the Delightful Buddhist Monastery' (which made matters pretty self-evident). He decided that it is 'abundantly clear that Buddhist missionaries ... departing "to intermingle among all unbelievers, teaching better things", carried their doctrine across the sea even to the despised and little known Maldives.'

The 'general character' of the Maldivians, Bell concluded, was that they were 'an inoffensive, timid, but – from their isolation – naturally suspicious people. This reserve seems to be the effect of a vague feeling of apprehension, lest information given to foreigners may be used to their disadvantage. When confidence, however, has been once restored, they exhibit in their intercourse with strangers an excess of inquisitiveness often positively embarrassing. Sober, fairly honest, and of a disposition naturally cheerful, they have but few wants, and are consequently inclined to be sluggish and lazy.'

It was going pretty well until that last bit.

Since Bell's digging about many artefacts have been destroyed, including the precious items ruined during the attack on the National Museum in Male. The remains of the Isdhoo mound, and others, were just about all that survived of this period.

It was a sad state of affairs. The recognition of the country's pre-Islamic past was a burning issue. Some believed that, unless a conscious effort was made, extremists could wipe out all such ancient heritage. Another writer, a Spaniard named Xavier Romero-Frias, who visited the country in 1979 and penned *The Maldive Islanders: A Study of the Popular Culture of an Ancient Ocean Kingdom* after learning Dhivehi, argued that the 'aggressive Islamization' of the country under the rule of former president Gayoom had threatened the 'fragile legacy of the ancestral Maldivian expressions' born out of Buddhism. He wrote that increasing 'arabization' had brought about a 'bleak, unsmiling, hieratic ideology'.

It was a lot to think about. These piles of old coral on the edge of Isdhoo signified much more than a mere lump on the land.

Cheap Eggs and Evil Spirits

Captain Mosa Rasheed and I clambered down the mound, during which one of my flip-flops snapped. Perhaps the gods were displeased with our mountaineering on a holy site.

We raced down the main street once more, stopping briefly at a shop to buy new flip-flops, like a pit-stop in Formula 1, before careering along to the island's 300-year-old Friday Mosque. This had a two-tier roof made of corrugated metal painted blue. The captain wanted to show me all the sights in one speedy go. I was invited inside and I removed my new footwear, entering a small room with a coffee-coloured carpet. A man sat on the steps cleaning the blades of an electric fan, eyeing me cautiously. We strolled about the weed-strewn graveyard and inspected the well.

That accomplished, the captain seemed to regard 'tourism' completed. We remounted the moped and hurtled back to his house, where he disappeared into a back room, leaving me by the swinging *jolies* and a child kicking a football in the street. The youngster had an incredible mould-like growth on his leg. It looked as though he was suffering the late stages of gangrene or some other horrific condition. Yet he seemed nonplussed and quite pleased to be booting the ball with his other leg. I asked if he was OK.

'Oh yeah,' he replied. 'Maldivian medicine.'

I later learnt that the mould was a form of herbal remedy and would easily pull apart and wash off. Its purpose was to help heal a wound; I bumped into the boy later on when the awful-looking 'growth' had been removed.

The captain had built extra rooms on his house for lodgers and seemed to be doing quite well for himself. Two of the lodgers were teachers from India, and there was a doctor from Pakistan. One of the teachers, Dhanaraj Gopal, was from Hyderabad.

'It took me seven months to get adjusted to the islands; sometimes I just felt like leaving, going home,' he said, after explaining he could earn more in the Maldives than in India. 'And the best thing is the cost of living: everything is so cheap!'

Half a dozen eggs, he quickly informed me as though letting me in on a secret that might persuade me to consider taking up permanent residence, cost 12 rufiyaa (46 pence).

Cini Nelson was from Kerala. She had a 9-year-old child in India and had come for the work; teaching jobs were in short supply back home. She told me that sometimes, if there was stormy weather or the ferry had engine trouble, you could get stuck on Isdhoo for days at a time. The previous month she had needed to go to Gan, but had had to wait a week. She had been on Isdhoo for four years and intended to live in Germany one day.

'I think the Netherlands is also possible,' chipped in Dhanaraj. He too was planning to emigrate to Europe. Despite what he had said earlier, it sounded as though he was still getting used to the Maldives.

'Yes. I'm not finding it easy. It's the privileges and the facilities in India: that's what I miss. Especially the food. It's 98 per cent vegetarian here and the preparation of the food is totally different,' he said. He curled a lip: he didn't seem at all keen on Maldivian cuisine.

What did he like most about the islands?

'One benefit is that it is a population-free country, that is one of the benefits,' Dhanaraj replied. He enjoyed the peace and quiet.

The sun was setting in orange and scarlet. Twisting palm trunks and a half-built *dhoni* were silhouetted against the light. One of the captain's children said he wanted to be a policeman, another a nurse. The teachers invited me to dinner the next day. Then the captain sprang out of the back room and headed off towards a café not far down the street. He eyeballed me and jutted his jaw a few times. I was to follow.

'Like a machine, a machine! Never stands in one place for one minute: click, click, click!' said Dhanaraj, watching the captain rush away.

I caught up and we dined on a selection of short eats. These were typical of Maldivian cafés and consisted of spring rolls, boiled eggs, samosas, and fried balls of tuna and chilli. Served in a plastic bowl, they were very tasty indeed. We were joined in the pistachio-coloured room by an elderly man with a stick and a navy sarong, who jangled his heavy gold watch, but said nothing. The captain held his counsel too.

A Bollywood film played in a corner, next to a poster advertising the previous year's Euro 2012 football tournament. Mosquitoes buzzed at our ankles. The meal, as delicious as it was and served with a coffee, lasted about five minutes. It was, I reflected silently, a very short eat indeed.

The end of dining was signalled by the captain rising, jutting and departing. He indicated I should get back on the moped and we sped on, passing a row of elderly men conversing on *jolies*.

'Where are we going?' I shouted over the engine.

'Room!' the captain yelled back.

After a short, rapid drive we pulled up. The captain gave me a key to a single-storey concrete apartment with three bedrooms. One of these was mine. No one else was in the building.

My air-conditioned room at Reveries had been spotless, the best I had stayed at in the Maldives. It had come with a power shower, satellite television, writing desk and a couple of black-and-white pictures of fish. This room was slightly different, with strip-lighting, bare walls and a double mattress on the floor. An air-conditioning unit whirred away with wires connected directly into the socket, but no plug. A sound similar to the plunging noise made by a submarine echoed from somewhere within the apartment. The room had royal-blue floor tiles and an en suite shower room with a 'WELCOME' mat. Occasionally a moped roared past, but otherwise all was quiet, save for the submarine sound and the purring a/c. I felt absolutely comfortable, tucked away in the heart of the Indian Ocean.

Isdhoo has a population of about 2,000, split between those who live near the port, such as the captain, and those dwelling closer to the *stupa*. The island is about five kilometres long and one and a half wide. The communities are linked by a long, wide road that is typical of streets across the country. I had been surprised at the size of these thoroughfares, and I was soon to learn, courtesy of reading Xavier Romero-Frias's engaging book in the flickering light of my apartment, that there was a story behind them.

During the 1940s many tracks were cut through the islands as part of a grand modernisation programme begun by then Prime Minister Mohammed Amin Didi. The idea was to bring the country into the twentieth century by updating the infrastructure, and the very look, of the islands, although some suspected an ulterior motive. Rather than being about progress, many believed that the new streets were in reality introduced to establish central control. The theory went that with good, broad roads, troops could more easily take charge during flare-ups. The roads also allowed government forces and police to go on parades, flexing their muscles during peaceful times. Mohammed Amin Didi had taken to wearing a military uniform and had carefully developed a cult of personality; portraits of him were mandatory in public offices and schools.

All of this deeply annoyed many inhabitants of the southern atolls, who were already suspicious of the north and could not see the point of the endless avenues. Sadly, though, there were three further consequences. The first was that there was great suffering during the compulsory, back-breaking construction of the roads. Secondly, because adult men devoted their time to the work, they could not go fishing and families went short of food; some children are said to have died of malnutrition during this period. Finally, the nature of the islands altered as in the past there had been an inward-facing social layout, coconut trees and vegetation acting as barriers to sea spray and high winds, helping to protect sensitive crops such as bananas, breadfruit and papaya. Long, straight, grid roads of the sort you might find in an American city opened up the interiors to the elements, altering the formerly cosy style of village life.

The backdrop to all this was the anti-colonial movement. Ceylon had gained independence from the British in 1948, just a year after India broke free of the empire. At the time, Britain's 'protected status' arrangement with the Maldivians left internal affairs to the islanders. Having stamped his authority through policies such as enforced road building and increased militarisation, Mohammed Amin Didi proclaimed himself president of the first Maldivian republic in 1953.

So the wide roads had a history that helped explain the foundation of the independent nation, according to Romero-Frias. He is however saddened by the effect they had on an aspect of island life I had not previously known:

'Traditionally, the paths within islands were winding and shady and according to the islanders it was a pleasure to walk on them. Those paths were also winding, not only to avoid the salt-spray, but also to hamper the movements of certain evil spirits that moved in straight lines, like the malevolent spirits of the dead ancestors, known as *kaḍḍovi*, and the feared *vigani* as well. This metaphysical dimension points at the relationship between the layout of the village and the need of sanctifying space.'

These evil spirits – the extra dimension – were countered by astrologers known as *nakatteriya*, who aligned houses in clusters of homesteads. The new roads meant that communities had come to be arranged in straight lines: 'All this had – and is still having – unforeseen traumatic effects upon the vitality of the Maldive island society and many of those adverse effects have not even been fathomed, for the traditional position of the house and the orientation of its door in relation of the cardinal points had a paramount influence on social organization and attitudes.'

Mohammed Amin Didi had become a divisive figure: regarded by some as the 'Great Moderniser' and by others as a troublemaker. Whatever the point of view, his legacy was the wide-open main streets of so many of the islands.

'Be peaceful and live simple'

During my stay on Isdhoo I would walk down the dusty boulevards, nodding 'hello' to men with machetes and women sweeping sand. I would stop at the café by the port for short eats, sit in a *jolie* near the docks reading a book, or go for a swim in the harbour. Graffiti on a wall by a football pitch at the end of one avenue said 'SMOKING CAN KILL YOU. EASY TO START. HARD TO END. EVEN IMPOSSIBLE TO FORGET!' There were flyposters for a Maldivian-style *X Factor* by the magistrates' court, and an inscription that read 'BE PEACEFUL AND LIVE SIMPLE'. I rather liked that. I had been going through a turbulent period in my personal life and the message hit home.

On one smaller lane I entered a mini-market, first removing my flip-flops as other customers had. Inside were aisles of powdered milk, bags of rice, notebooks, instant coffee, non-stick pans, showerheads, pasta, Adidas socks and packets of 'Fair & Handsome Advanced Whitening Cream'. Despite the incredible isolation, it was not all that different from a corner shop back home.

Ismail Shafeeu was at a counter in a striped pink and purple polo top and heavy-framed glasses. He asked me what I was doing on Isdhoo and I mentioned my trip to the *stupa*.

'Did you like our mountain?' he asked.

I said I did.

He dealt with a customer and busily wrote an amount in a ledger; people had accounts and did not pay cash on every visit.

'It is a very long time ago now,' he began, 'non-Muslim people come to this place in the night and they created these mountains.'

He paused to let this sink in and to mark the purchase of a packet of cigarettes in his ledger. 'During prayers the next day, they ran away to the sea,' he continued. 'While they were running they heard the imam and they froze and died.'

Another customer arrived and the price of a box of biscuits was scribbled down. 'I have never seen them myself,' he said, 'but very recently my father told me that he saw ghosts by the water.'

'Ghosts,' he repeated, scribbling down the cost of a tin of instant coffee. 'Ghosts on the water. He saw them.'

Yet more spirits in the air. Not many corner shop assistants come up with tales like that.

As it was time for his break, Ismail took me to meet his grandmother, who lived in a 'developed area' built by the Red Cross after the 2004 tsunami. We reached her home on his moped, driving down a narrow path cut between cucumber and chilli plants, papaya and breadfruit trees. Sanfa Ismail was sitting on a *jolie* in front of a little house and invited me to join her. She wore multiple gold bracelets and rings, plus a headscarf, and was clearly one of the island's movers and shakers.

She waved at a young man, who scurried away. He returned with a can of Sting With Ginseng Vitamin Energy Drink and a Snow Cake From London, along with some crunchy pieces of breadfruit. Sanfa Ismail handed these items to me, checking that I approved of the cake. It had a sugary white covering and had seemingly been given to me in case I was suffering from homesickness (I definitely wasn't).

'Have you ever met a tourist before?' I asked.

'Never,' she said.

She told me about her experience of the 2004 tsunami. 'Suddenly it happened, just happened: 15 feet high.

Everybody had to swim. In one minute it was like this. I had to swim and hold on to the top of a *dhiggaa* [cottonwood] tree and wait for 15 minutes. I thought the world was ending. For 30 minutes I did not see anyone else. Then I got to the jetty. They took me to Male and I stayed there for three months.'

Even though it was almost a decade on, I could sense her continuing shock at what had occurred.

It was prayer time, and Ismail Shafeeu and Sanfa Ismail disappeared. I finished my energy drink and wandered out into the streets, beginning to buzz with sugar. I was becoming used to these breaks in the daily routine. The roads, never all that busy, would empty. Allah was waiting in the mosque.

I went to the harbour for a swim. There were only a couple of boats: the captain's ferry and a small cargo vessel. Steps led down to the water and in effect I had a large saltwater pool all to myself. I placed my T-shirt, flip-flops and shorts in a pile and dived in wearing my trunks. I splashed about, drawing the attention of a solitary cargo ship hand, who watched impassively.

Then I noticed the crows. They were trying to take my shorts away – containing all my money, my Visa card and my passport. A murder of crows was pecking at my possessions. I yelled out. The cargo ship hand chuckled. The crows continued pecking. I swam at a great rate of knots to the steps, splashing upwards as I arrived. The crows got the message and reluctantly left.

What did they want to do: eat my flip-flops?

The crows gathered on broken lampposts and observed me. I did not want to give up the water because of them, so I swam close to the harbour wall. As soon as I was at a distance at which they judged they could attack my clothes, the crows would pounce and I would turn towards them and splash the water once again. They would return to their lampposts and regard me from on high, until they reckoned another assault was possible. I've never had a swim quite like it.

D r Mitholal, the captain's third lodger, was from Karachi and wore a pink-striped shirt with a couple of top buttons undone. Not one to miss a trick, he was 'making himself available' for the evening meal I had been invited to. The aromatic smell of curry filled the porch by the swinging *jolies* outside the captain's house.

'Are you an archaeologist?' he asked, before telling me he had previously worked in Lahore and the Republic of Ireland.

Dhanaraj and Cini regarded the doctor sharply, with the implication he was gatecrashing our gathering. He gave them a beady-eyed look and followed us into Dhanaraj's room, where a superb meal was laid out: curries and masalas and bhajis and lime pickle and papadums and salads and rice and noodles. What a spread. The doctor would have been a fool to miss out. We sat at plastic chairs beneath a sign on the wall that said 'ELCOME' and proceeded to demolish great bowls of spicy chicken and tuna. It was a fine last supper.

Both teachers had tsunami stories. The rising water had not apparently affected all parts of the island equally. Dhanaraj told me, 'Some people saw a huge tide come over the coconut trees. They were screaming and started floating and tried to catch the tops of trees. They can swim and most were not scared of the water, but there was so much of it.'

'A boy in my grade seven class,' Cini added, 'he was swept away and after two days he was found by a rock in a mangrove on Gan. After that he had mental problems. His studies are good, but he is slow.'

Other teachers came to join us, and they talked about the difficulty of living in the country as Christians. 'Living here, Christians are – how you say? – the enemy,' one of the newcomers said quietly. 'By God's grace, if I get work in a Christian country, I will go there. There is no religious freedom here. The Maldivians are very good, but because of the religion, it makes them very remote. They are not exposed to the outside world. They think that this is the world, that there is nothing greater than this island. When we teach something they say: "No, we don't want." Their mentality is confined to this island. We feel like outsiders ... a lot.'

The following day, both Dhanaraj and Cini waved me goodbye from the dock. Captain Mosa Rasheed was back at the wheel of the ferry, jutting his jaw and muttering in Dhivehi. Black crows fluttered busily by the water's edge. I had conquered the Maldivian Everest and I was heading north once more.

Getting to Vilufushi, on neighbouring Thaa Atoll, first meant the ferry trip to Gan, via Maabaidhoo and Mundoo. After that a taxi would drive me across causeways to Maandhoo and onwards to Kadhdhoo. I was then to take another ferry to Thimarafushi, one of Thaa's main islands, a journey of about 35 miles. Afterwards a separate boat would be required to move within the atoll, pausing at various islands including Guraidhoo and Madifushi. I believed I could get to my destination before nightfall. Those to whom I mentioned my intended journey gave me long, searching looks. I didn't care: I was going to give it a shot.

The ferry churned ahead through a vaporous early-morning sky. Little islands with yellow Maldivian Democratic Party flags came and went. The water oscillated and shifted colour: turquoise, aquamarine, indigo, teal.

When we arrived at Gan I walked to Reveries, collected my bag and went to find a taxi. Hussein was outside and he drove me to Kadhdhoo for a 'special fare' that I have forgotten but seemed like a lot at the time.

Outside the airport was a dock and there, amazingly, I saw a green and red ferry. A couple of guys were on board, including a teenager with a massive afro. I asked him if I could catch the ferry to Vilufushi.

'No,' he said, nodding.

'Ah,' I said. 'Can I get to Thimarafushi from here?'

This was the island where I would have to change ferries.

'Yes,' he replied, shaking his afro.

Eventually, through this process of affirmatives, negatives, shakes and nods, I worked out that in an hour the ferry would depart for Thimarafushi, a journey of three and a half hours. I sat down, not taking the risk of leaving the vessel. A mother with a son aged about 10 sat on the opposite bench. The child had eyes shaped like poker chips and spent most of the voyage staring at me (slightly disconcertingly). Two teenagers boarded and climbed a stepladder for a smoke on the boat's flat-top roof.

We began to move, heading towards towers of cumulus clouds. Ferry 503 was a real chugger, an old wooden *dhoni* with chipped red paint and a gravelly engine. I paid my 30 rufiyaa fare and watched the dolphins as they flipped past.

I was re-reading a rucksack-battered copy of *A Time of Gifts*, the first part of Patrick Leigh Fermor's story about walking from the Hook of Holland to Constantinople when he was 18. His eccentric perambulations in 1933 involved much boozing at inns and country mansions – not many of those in the Maldives – but in the passage I read on Ferry 503 Leigh Fermor speculates about a historical moment that felt relevant to my trip.

'What if the Turks had taken Vienna, as they nearly did, and advanced westward?' he wrote. 'And suppose the Sultan, with half the east at heel, had pitched his tents outside Calais? A few years before, the Dutch had burnt a flotilla of men-at-war at Chatham. Might St Paul's, only half re-built, have ended with minarets instead of its two bell-towers and a different emblem twinkling on the dome? The muezzin's wail over Ludgate Hill?'

It was an interesting perspective. If the Turks had taken Vienna, my current trip might have been quite different. Would there have been tourist islands with sommeliers, cocktail bars and dancing? Or would I have been joining the 5am crowd and kneeling in the direction of Mecca?

Maybe the sun and the salty air were getting to me.

We arrived at Thimarafushi harbour on Thaa Atoll at 2pm. I did not go to the mosque by the boat-building yard. Instead, I visited a tangerine-coloured café by the quiet waterfront, where I munched on vegetable samosas and drank coffee quite happily. I was conscious that the day had gone suspiciously well so far.

I watched a cyclist wheel past. Thimarafushi, population 4,250, had precisely 164 bicycles, according to an article I'd read. Two of the bikes were owned by the local government. Somebody, it seemed, had counted and categorised them.

The ferry arrived. It too was tangerine; everything in these parts appeared to be citrusy. Many passengers disembarked. They had been on day trips to Veymandhoo, the capital of the atoll, and were clasping shopping bags, while a few held pizza boxes aloft.

On board, I relaxed on a tangerine sofa with a coffee table. This was the plushest boat yet, though it was about the same size as all the others, perhaps 50 or 60 feet in length. I could hardly believe it was so comfortable.

A man with red-rimmed glasses sat down on my sofa with a sigh of contentment, as though he'd had a long day. He was Chandra Kumar, another Indian teacher. He began to talk about Vilufushi, where he lived and worked. Of all the islands in the Maldives, Vilufushi had been the worst struck in the tsunami, he told me, with 19 deaths out of a population of about 2,200 and almost all the buildings destroyed. An evacuation had been required during the reconstruction of the village.

'People went to refugee camps on Buruni, a nearby island,' Chandra said. 'Steel and sheet tents: temporary accommodation. Hot. All of it was horrible. People had fear. They had lost everything. They didn't have a rufiyaa in their hands. Before the tsunami, they had had no savings. They were in the refugee camp for four years. Their minds have been disturbed. They think that any time it could happen again.'

Vilufushi had been wiped out. 'Three or four bodies, they are still missing,' Chandra added.

The engine of the *Spirit of Kolhumadulu* rumbled loudly. We lapsed into silence, as shouting over the cacophony was too much effort. Chandra had told me there was a guesthouse on his adopted island and that he would take me there.

After a couple of hours, stops at Guraidhoo and Madifushi completed, we arrived at Vilufushi. It was still daylight – Maldivians generally prefer not to travel by sea in the dark – and I had made it, despite all the doubters on Isdhoo.

The guesthouse was more like a self-catering apartment. It stood by government offices next to the largest mosque outside of Male, funded by a wealthy benefactor from the capital. My digs were a two-minute stroll from the docks; you could easily walk around Vilufushi in less than an hour.

Guesthouse owner Mousa Musthafa, a local councillor, had been at the waterside when we arrived. He was a bit of a smoothie, with designer stubble, baggy chinos and a yellow Puma T-shirt. He had been energetically overseeing the unloading of buckets of tuna and wheelbarrows full of breadfruit.

'You can stay there but you will have to pay,' he had said.

That was how I found myself in a small house with three rooms, a lounge with faux leather sofas and a kitchen with a fridge on which a bossy note said: 'MILK: PLEASE PUT IT BACK. USE IT OR IT WILL GO OFF AND IT COSTS: BRITISH RED CROSS.' Volunteers from the Red Cross had stayed at the guesthouse while overseeing the rebuilding of houses and schools on the island. My room came with two single beds, air-conditioning and a ceiling fan. A bookshelf in the lounge, which had a television and DVD player, was stocked with Charles Dickens, Paul Theroux and Agatha Christie. I opened the copy of *Great Expectations* and a bookmark fell to the floor. It was a quote on a piece of card, the type left on pillows at plush hotels during turndowns.

'It is time to begin to live the life you've imagined' read the auspicious words of Henry James. I tucked the card carefully into my rucksack.

Mousa and Chandra arrived to take me to see the island's chief. I wasn't in any trouble, they assured me – quite the opposite. I hopped on the back of Mousa's moped and we buzzed along to a shady café where men were playing checkers and chewing on areca nuts. Here I met Ahmed Adam, the bearded island chief (president of the council), who told me via Mousa's translation that I was the first tourist to visit the island and how glad the islanders were to be back on Vilufushi after their evacuation to Buruni. We nibbled on spring rolls and spicy coconut balls with tuna that had been caught by the local fleet. Fishing, I was told, was the sole economic activity.

Chandra invited me to address the local school in the morning (outsiders, now that the volunteers were long gone, were a rarity). Then we went for dinner at the chief's house. The hospitality of islanders was something else. Away from the golf buggies, spa treatments and infinity pools of holiday-brochure paradise, I was discovering a parallel existence in which courtesy, good manners, gentleness and civility came to the fore. Strip everything away (every penny, all your possessions), wash it into the sea and find yourself sent to a refugee camp for a few years: I wondered how we would deal with that back home. Would we be quite so calm and welcoming?

Mousa, Ahmed, the latter's charming wife Aishath Dhiyana and I tucked into steaming bowls of rice and curry, with yet more *garudia* and grilled fish with chilli and garlic, plus a coconut milk sauce and a salad of chopped onions and *lunboa* or limes. *Garudia* was becoming firmly established as my favourite Maldivian dish. We ate heartily and drank *lunboa* juice, sitting at a table next to a living room with a foreign football game playing silently on a gigantic TV.

Mousa gazed at the screen and told me he had studied for O-Levels on Male, where he had had a trial for the under-16 squad of a professional football team. Brazil and Spain were playing in a match the next day and he was rooting for Spain, he said. Most Maldivians were obsessed by the game.

The chief described the islanders' time on Buruni. All was not so courteous and perfect back then. 'There were not big problems, but there were a few. Mostly it was because some Vilufushi boys tried to go with Buruni girls. The Buruni boys were not happy.'

The temporary shelters were uncomfortable. It had been a 'bad time'. The people of Vilufushi had finally returned to live in 250 new homes constructed by the British Red Cross in 2009, after much land had been reclaimed from the sea to bolster the island and wave defences added. These homes, built to be earthquake resistant, came with electricity and 'rainwater harvesting tanks'. The islanders were impressed and pleased with them.

The chief had been on Male when the tsunami hit the capital. 'It was about 5.30am and after praying I went fishing,' he related. 'Then at 7.30am I went home and at 9am I was outside my office smoking a cigarette. Then I started noticing that people were shouting. They began running around. That was when I knew something was happening. I jumped on a bench and I saw the waves. So I climbed a mango tree.

I saw the sea coming down the road. I saw a small bus that was being washed along in the current. There was three feet of water in the street. I was shocked.'

Just like Sanfa Ismail back on Isdhoo, fear and disbelief showed in his eyes. For a nation that lived so close to the water, the tsunami had been the ultimate nightmare come true.

'They think it might come again'

The tiny island of Vilufushi had come to symbolise the low-lying Maldives' fragility in the middle of the vast ocean. In the aftermath of the tsunami the battered landscape was visited by United Nations Secretary General Kofi Annan, who had wanted to see for himself what it was like to live on the water's edge during increasingly unpredictable climatic times. I wanted to try to understand this too, though I had not come to gawp. This visit was not about voyeurism. Sure, there are other parts of the world that are often flood-struck, but the possibility of disappearing altogether was on another apocalyptic level. I was intrigued at the different mentality, a natural resilience, required to live in such a place.

I had covered the 2004 Boxing Day tsunami for *The Times* on the day it happened, and recall the shock of realisation that the undersea earthquake and resulting waves were likely to be the biggest natural disaster of my lifetime. The death toll eventually reached more than 280,000. My task at the time had been to find out how many British tourists were in the affected region: about 10,000, with well over 1,000 in the Maldives. The disaster had struck during the peak 'winter sun' holiday period and my story on December 27 was headlined 'ALTERNATIVE BREAKS WILL BE HARD TO FIND'. The travel section followed up with a special edition on the tsunami in which I interviewed Tony Wheeler, the founder of Lonely Planet guidebooks, who urged people to return to the countries affected swiftly, as tourism was so important to their economies: 'Go sooner rather than later. They will be very glad to see you.' According to the World Travel and Tourism Council, tourism at the time accounted for 64 per cent of employment in the Maldives. Over the next few weeks the paper ran many further articles, including one under the headline 'EXPERTS ONLY PLEASE; UNSKILLED VOLUNTEERS MAY HINDER RELIEF EFFORTS'. An army of 'tourist volunteers' had been heading to the region and aid agencies had been concerned that well-meaning amateurs could interrupt the efforts of trained aid workers.

At the time of Kofi Annan's visit, he commented: 'Assistance to those who have been traumatised, particularly the children, should be given priority.' His advice had been taken on board, thanks to the financial backing of international aid agencies, with the British Red Cross especially important in the Maldives. A shiny, state-of-the-art school had reopened on Vilufushi in June 2009. Many of those who had previously lived on Vilufushi had moved to Male, so while the population was officially more than 2,000, the actual population on its return had become more like 1,400. The school had about 250 pupils aged 6 to 17.

In the morning after dinner with the chief and a good sleep in my Red Cross apartment, I was introduced to the smartly dressed school captain and deputy captain. The captain, who wore a blue and gold sash, told me: 'I was seven years old when it happened. My father held me. I could not swim. I thought that the world was going to end.'

'Did you think you would die?'

'Yes,' she said. 'Within five minutes all the island was destroyed. We couldn't see houses, just the sea.'

She said this so plainly that the statement seemed quite normal, as though she was speaking of a childhood holiday rather than the annihilation of the place she called home.

I followed the captains into the auditorium. The pupils wore pristine white uniforms and the girls had yellow ribbons in their hair. I was positioned at the front of the hall and spoke a few words about my visit, though my principal job was to hand out gold star-style awards for homework. Then Chandra and Abdulla, the head teacher, showed me round.

The classrooms had smartboards onto which information from the internet could be projected; I had never seen anything like them before, anywhere. In one room a teacher wearing an orange top was highlighting the 'Characteristics of Money'. These were that it was 'generally acceptable: no one denies money. Everyone is ready to accept money. It is scarce: it should be earned with hard work. No one gives it freely. It is not easy to get money.' The hard facts of life delivered at an early age.

The school was built around a courtyard with a cluster of tropical trees at the centre. Many slogans were written on the walls. These were catchy, if a touch gloomy: 'LOST TIME IS NEVER FOUND AGAIN … FAILURE IS SUCCESS IF WE CAN LEARN FROM IT … MEMORY IS THE MOTHER OF ALL WISDOM … EDUCATION BEGINS IN THE WOMB AND ENDS IN THE TOMB … THE WORLD IS A STRANGE AND WONDERFUL PLACE'. There was also a notice referring to the school's ban on plastic bags and other non biodegradable materials (what a great idea), and another warning pupils about the danger of befriending strangers online. The internet creeping into everyone's lives, yet again.

In the staff lounge, Chandra and Abdulla talked about the continuing effect of the tsunami on the children. Many had not recovered fully and still had a fear of water, they said. Some of them would not swim; a few were in counselling. It was hard to imagine what they had gone and were going through. This was nine years after the event, although only four years since the return from the refugee camp.

'They think it might come again,' said Chandra, softly repeating what he'd said on the ferry.

I had a feeling of travelling full circle, from breaking news almost a decade ago to lives beginning to be pieced back together again. I was truly seeing the parts of the Maldives that few tourists reached.

Rain clouds were rising to the west and it was a sticky day. Crows were making a racket by the roundabout that led to the docks. I looked inside the grand mosque, where a man was vacuuming a field of gold-brown carpet as light filtered through jade windows. Empty pink hammocks hung between palms by the government offices. A teenager wearing shades wheeled past on a custom-made bicycle with a large front tyre and a small back tyre, plus widened handle bars: a pedal version of a Harley-Davidson. He fooled around, spinning in a circle for my amusement.

I bought a few provisions – cans of tuna, bread and limes – from a shop made of battered corrugated metal. A couple of old CDs attached to a string had been hung by the entrance to deter troublesome crows. I took the food to the guesthouse, which I had to myself, and set off on a circuit round the island.

By the docks, I came to a Buddhist relic that had been discovered bobbing in the sea by fishermen the previous day. The unusual structure was about ten feet tall and had a pagoda roof. I wondered where it had come from and if it would soon end up as firewood, given the mistrust of non-Islamic icons. I kept on walking along a scraggly coast to a two-storey concrete building on the sea's edge. Crabs scuttled on the broken tiles of a downstairs space leading to a terrace that had collapsed into the water. Lampposts had toppled like trees felled in a storm.

As I wondered what was going on, Mousa buzzed up on his moped. 'This is the fish market. We think it is of no use now. Such bad luck: we think that we are the unluckiest people in the Maldives,' he said.

He explained that the market had been completed in 2010 as part of the redevelopment of Vilufushi. The idea had been to create a new fish-processing plant at this end of the island and to sell produce at the market. Sadly, planners had underestimated the strength of the sea battering against the post-tsunami reclaimed shoreline. More than 50 feet of land had disappeared in three years and in all Mousa believed that the island had lost about five hectares since the population had returned from Buruni.

We left the sorry mess and drove across an empty plot to the old fish-processing area. When we arrived, I could hardly believe my eyes. It was as though we had stepped into the pages of a Dickens novel.

Smoke rose from an encampment of rickety wooden and corrugated iron sheds, where a handful of figures huddled. A few attended to long tables made of metal and chicken-wire that on closer inspection turned out to be stacked with tuna. The fish had already been boiled and had been lumped, ready to be deboned, in a rusty metal container. A tiny woman wearing a purple shawl was slicing the tuna, peeling away bones and then placing the fish on the table, which was about 15 feet long. Once it was full of tightly stacked fish, a tarpaulin would be pulled over so they could dry out. The cover also acted as protection against attacks by the many crows that perched on a nearby fence, cunningly considering their options. In five days the fish would be ready for the next stage of preparation.

There were many chicken-wire tables in this scrubland, well away from the island's houses. Metal buckets filled with old fish bones were strewn here and there. The smell of burning wood and fish rose from across the yard. This was where some of the tuna would go instead of being dried, to be turned into *garudia*. Creating my favourite dish, I was told, took eight hours of simmering in water and salt in a blackened metal vat with the circumference of a lorry wheel. Coconut husks and palm fronds were used to stoke the fire beneath the pots. This job was dealt with under a sloping shelter by a pot-bellied man in a sky-blue sarong. Beside the vat of bubbling *garudia* there was also a cauldron of gurgling *rihakuru*, a copper-coloured concoction that was used as cooking stock.

At any one time there might be six tonnes of tuna being processed at the ramshackle plant. At the far end I came to the starting point of the job, where men and women in aprons smeared with blood sliced open the tuna to remove the innards and behead the fish, sliding the results across a slithering table to a man who collected them ready for the next stage. They did this beneath another shelter with a tatty yellow flag flying above. 'Don't you know, we like Nasheed a lot!' exclaimed a woman in a red shawl, brandishing a dripping knife. The Maldivian Democratic Party was evidently popular among the tuna processors.

The wood, fronds and husks were collected from uninhabited islands. This fuel was used in a tumbledown 'hot room' constructed from stained wooden boards, where the fish would go after being dried on the tables. I was given a piece of the finished product by Hussein, who ran this section. It was almost as tough as wood, but salty and full of flavour. Hussein said that Sri Lankans loved this tuna and were important customers.

Mousa, who had been translating on my behalf, added in an aside to me: 'There is a certain job that this man also does for Muslim boys in this area. He is the only one on the island who does it. It is a specific job that he does...' From his gestures I gathered that Hussein was the one who performed circumcisions on Vilufushi.

We made our way back to the track, leaving the Dickensian smoke, toil and stench. A van had pulled up with four swordfish slumped on the back. They were magnificent creatures with razor-sharp elongated bills, from which they gain their name. Their eyes were silvery and the size of fried eggs. The largest was three metres long and had taken half an hour to land. They were valued at 850 rufiyaa each, about £33.

Beyond the van and down the track I was staggered by what Mousa brought me to next: another Maldivian mountain, but bigger than the one on Isdhoo.

This one had nothing to do with Buddhism, however. It was a pile of crunched-up coral and sand that was to be used in land reclamation as and when required, although as one islander had already told me, 'This was the plan but it was not implemented well.' Had things gone as intended, the fish market would not be falling into the ocean. Vegetation was growing on the chalk-white slopes, which appeared almost snow-like. If I blurred my eyes a bit, I could have arrived at Mount Fuji.

We scrambled to the top, about 60 feet up, high enough to see the curve of waves breaking on the reef encircling the island. 'Vilufushi was built as a "safe island" concept,' said Mousa, 'but we don't think the concept is so safe.'

Two Castaways – the Doctor and the Teacher

I was getting insights into island life that I had not expected, and I was about to learn more, courtesy of two local characters: the doctor and the primary school teacher.

Mousa had said I should go and talk to Musthaq Ahmed, the island doctor, as he was especially opinionated. This seemed to be the style of doing things on these remote outposts: just turn up and talk.

When I arrived at his compact Red Cross home, Dr Ahmed was wearing boxer shorts and nothing else; not that he seemed perturbed at talking to me in this state of undress. His wife, fully clothed, went to fetch coffee and breadfruit crisps. Dr Ahmed had a wide, open face and an extremely hairy body. He sat down on a sofa by a cabinet with an aquarium full of multi-coloured fish, looking a bit sleepy and hugging a pillow to his chest as a nod towards modesty.

'Mostly viral fever or diabetes,' he said, discussing his work. 'Those are our biggest challenges. People eat too much sugar or salt from packaged food, which brings on diabetes. They do not do enough exercise, because of the fishing, which is so draining due to the long hours. A few play football, but mostly they just sit about in their *jolies*. Another problem is kidney failure, which comes from not collecting rainwater properly. They are not boiling the water, just drinking it. I have had six cases: we sent them to Male for dialysis.'

Dr Ahmed, like so many professionals here, was Indian, from Kashmir. He seemed exasperated by the Maldivian lifestyle, which until then I had thought rather perfect.

'Not good diet,' he said. 'They are not getting enough vitamins in general. They are only getting vitamin A from fish. Skin diseases are a problem. It is because vegetables and fruit are expensive. There's also hypertension. This is because there is not enough physical activity combined with the salty diet: high blood pressure. It is possible to get fruit from Male, but still the islanders don't want.'

He had been in the Maldives for nine years and was on call 24 hours a day, the only doctor on Vilufushi. After the tsumani he had worked for a non-governmental organisation at the camp on Buruni, where he treated people for mental problems brought on by the shock of the tidal waves. He was outspoken and world-weary.

'Maldivians are a very lazy people,' he said, echoing H.C.P. Bell's opinion. 'They have a problem about time. They say: "I'll come in an hour" for a consultation and they'll turn up ten hours later.'

He turned dreamy-eyed. 'I miss Russia,' he said, out of the blue. He had been posted there previously. 'St Petersburg. The money was good. Here it is too stressful.'

He lit a cigarette. 'This is a good country for tourists, a bad country for living. Come here for a while, enjoy the tour, but live here a long time?' He let the question hang in the air.

My second meeting was down a dirt track not far from where Dr Ahmed lived. In another Red Cross house, the door was answered by another foreigner, this time from Zurich in Switzerland. Maya was a former tour guide who had come to the archipelago on holiday in 1986 and had switched to teaching a decade ago. She had married a local man, who was a supply boat captain and a mechanic. He was living on a different island in Meemu Atoll with his second wife. It was common for Maldivian men to have more than one wife. Of her husband, who she said was 14 years younger than her, she quickly told me: 'God, he is such a good person. Such a good person.'

When Maya came to the Maldives, the highest building on Male had been two storeys high and there were a 'couple of cars' and sandy streets: 'Every time it rained it was like little Venice. There was no crime. You could walk about at two in the morning with bundles of dollars in your pockets, a single woman with blue eyes, and nothing would happen.'

She was blonde and in her 40s. She had a ginger cat and a young daughter named Saya, who briefly and shyly came into the book-lined living room. 'I fell in love with the people and the nature. I love it, I love it. But I don't want to be in Male any more. I lived there up to 2000, just when the crime first began,' Maya told me. The capital apparently had a reputation for 'trouble', although I hadn't come across any.

Before moving to the Maldives, Maya had been a label manager at a record company in Switzerland, selecting LPs and singles for Warner Brothers. Her talk came in great torrents, as though she hadn't had anyone to tell her stories to for a while.

'I used to be the "nose" for what would sell. I'd arrange radio interviews for artists as well: Seal, Rod Stewart, the Pointer Sisters. I met them all. That was a different lifestyle. So many backstage passes for concerts. It was complicated: filing tax returns, sorting out how many days you are paid. Your life makes me laugh. Mine is so free.'

She said all of this with such an unembellished delivery, a tone of 'this is just how it is', that it was impossible to take offence. She didn't mean any.

We discussed politics for a while and she had some interesting views, although the following morning I found a note under my guesthouse door. It read: 'Dear Tom, I need to ask you to do me one big favour: please do not mention anyone in any political statements. Foreigners living in this country are forbidden to make any.'

Maya served me short eats of crispy fried tuna balls. She told me about the horror of the tsunami, describing how the wall of her house had crumbled and she had been swept outside into a neighbour's garden as the rest of the structure collapsed. She and Saya had had a lucky escape, though they were left both passport-less and cashless. 'The shock stays with you,' she said.

Maya took a call from her husband and told me more about him: 'He's a wonder. He's almost totally uneducated. He left school at grade six to get a job as one of the boat crew for one of the tourist resorts. He spent his wages sending 50 kilogram bags of rice for his parents. He's almost illiterate but he's an amazing mechanic. The most honest person I ever met.' She had had a previous Maldivian husband who 'betrayed' her.

'My parents and I financed his first ship,' she continued, referring to her current husband. Of his other wife, Maya said: 'She has a job in a regional hospital. She's not jealous or possessive at all. They have two boys.'

It was quite a rollercoaster of a life story and by the time she had finished darkness had fallen outside. There had been a power cut and I walked back to the guesthouse by the light of a torch beneath glittering constellations. Vilufushi was a magical setting. Yet as much as I was enjoying my tour of the remoter islands, I could not imagine staying there for good.

'Everything had gone into the sea'

My glitch-free journey to Vilufushi had been a fluke. When it came to travelling back to Thimarafushi in search of a boat northwards, there was a problem. A small group had gathered at the docks in anticipation of the arrival of the *Spirit of Kolhumadulu*, but there was no sign of the sofa-filled tangerine vessel.

An elderly woman in a yellow polka-dot shawl was exclaiming 'Netti! Netti!' I later looked in a dictionary and found that the Dhivehi word *nethikollun* translated as 'terminate'. Another woman with a red butterfly brooch on her lapel said: 'Engine trouble!' A guy I'd seen in the café added: 'There is no ferry! No good! Come back tomorrow!'

All of this was communicated with much joviality. There was no ferry: hurrah! The Maldivians really are a super-chilled people. News of the crippled boat had come via someone's mobile phone. The other passengers shuffled back to the village with their bags.

I, too, had almost given up worrying. I briefly attempted to see whether the sole cargo ship at the dock was about to leave, but a member of the crew shook his head. As he did so, the sailors suddenly leapt into action, attacking a hornet that was buzzing their boat. They took off their flip-flops and began flapping wildly, attempting to swat the insect. It was like a Native American dance. I watched in wonder as they gleefully pursued their prey. The hornet eventually buzzed away.

This constituted an 'event' on Vilufushi. It really was a sleepy place.

I returned to the guesthouse and pondered my predicament. In theory I was stranded on the island for the time being. Who knew when the *Spirit of Kolhumadulu*'s engine would be fixed? I went to the council office, where a member of staff informed me there was a 'speed launch' the next day. This was a kind of 'wonder ferry' that was actually a rigged-up speedboat. The council member kindly called and booked a ticket. The boat would go to Male, halfway on my journey to the very north of the archipelago. The journey would take three and a half hours and the fare was 850 rufiyaa, the same price as a swordfish.

By any means necessary, I was learning, was the rule when it came to travelling in the Maldives.

I returned to the guesthouse. Having finished *A Time of Gifts*, Vilufushi seemed an appropriate place to begin *The Drowned World* by J.G. Ballard. This dystopian novel imagines a future when the globe is flooded by a rising sea, and describes London under water with a few remaining citizens living in the top storeys of old buildings; the protagonist takes a penthouse suite at the Ritz. Temperatures have risen to 130 °F thanks to melting icecaps. Iguanas and crocodiles rule the roost, while crazed pirates loot what they can. Humanity has migrated to the poles and most of the planet is submerged in a 'luminous, dragon-green, serpent-haunted sea'. It was not, perhaps, the cheeriest of reads to recommend to the denizens of Vilufushi.

I hung out at the café with the checker players and ate dinner as a guest at Mousa's house – another terrific meal. I heard more tsunami stories too: 'I was taken in the heavy current, crashing into walls and trees, I was injured badly: wounded legs, arms and feet, I could not even think of my son, I was overwhelmed … I was sleeping when it hit, the water rose to four feet, my mother was trapped in her room, I smashed the door and took her hand and we were swept away … I thought we were finished, we could not see any

land, everything had gone into the sea: phones, water tanks, televisions, possessions ... there was a lot of noise, like a big flight coming over the island, then the waves came, the first house by the seaside was smashed, we were swept away ...'
The day was etched in the memory of every islander.

The rigged-up speedboat turned up on time, engine in order. We surged beyond the harbour wall, soon bouncing along at 28 knots (32 miles per hour). I knew this as, unbelievably, my neighbour on the packed vessel checked using a smartphone app. The launch had a blue artificial turf floor and deckchairs in the gangway so that every possible space was filled. The passenger sitting opposite me wore a T-shirt with a logo that said 'SOUL POWER. DAILY ADRENALIN. NOBODY CAN DESTROY'. Next to him a gaunt man with a mobile phone tucked in his pocket quietly muttered to himself and a woman in a burqa hummed a tune as she gently rocked a baby. We stopped at Meemu Atoll to squeeze in yet more people and in an hour or so turned in at a breakwater on the north of Male.

I was back in the Big Smoke.

The Divorce Capital of the World

Country music played at the Sea House Café by the ferry port on Male. Willie Nelson was singing 'On the Road Again' and the lyrics matched my mood, even if the way ahead was on water: 'Goin' places that I've never been, Seein' things that I may never see again, And I can't wait to get on the road again.'

Soft yellow light illuminated choppy water beyond the harbour. Oil tankers and cargo ships were clustered on the horizon, like giant insects conducting a meeting. In the foreground, foaming waves broke on tiny Petrol Island, known as such due to its fuel tanks. Staff in orange shirts scooted between simple wooden tables delivering high-energy drinks and coffees to a terrace busy with smokers. The smell of fried food, curry and spices filled the air and a breeze came through open windows overlooking the ferry terminal below.

Speedboats buzzed helter-skelter past Petrol Island. There was a chaotic impression of boats tearing here, there and everywhere, skipping over the sea, veering and careering past slower vessels, which bobbed and swayed and stayed steady. All that horsepower; all that motion. It was easy to see that mishaps might occur.

And apparently they often did. Before leaving the UK I had read stories of several recent accidents on the website Minivannews.com, which claimed to be the only reliable source of 'independent' news in the Maldives (*minivan* translated as 'independent' or 'free' in Dhivehi). By this it meant it was unconnected to wealthy owners with vested interests in businesses or political parties. One piece was about the tragic death of a telephone operator working at the Four Seasons resort on the island of Kudu Huraa, about 20 minutes from Male. Aishath Safa had been struck by a speedboat propeller while on a diving excursion on her day off. Earlier in the year an Italian tourist had been killed in Thaa Atoll, while a German honeymooner had suffered serious leg injuries from a dive boat's propeller at the Reethi Beach Resort.

A group of three guys who needed a place to sit joined my table. They were dressed in shirts with the sleeves rolled up and two of them had sunglasses hooked into their shirt necks. They were workers from a nearby office and we soon got talking, though I won't give their names as I would not want to land them in any trouble.

They wanted to give me an insight into the Maldivian social set-up. 'I have little option but to marry if I want to be with my partner,' said one. He was talking about sex. 'So there are many frustrations. The common Maldivian is quite Westernised, but the laws don't allow a Western way of doing things. We are constantly trying to juggle – to strike a balance between Islamic sharia law and common law. We have not been able to strike this balance yet.'

He had a shaved head, a shiny purple shirt clashing somewhat with his red tie, and a no-nonsense manner. 'I think this is related to the high divorce rate,' he went on. He believed that because people could not be with one another before marriage, problems could arise later.

This definitely seemed to be the case. According to the latest United Nations figures – and the *Guinness Book of World Records* – there were 10.97 divorces per 1,000 inhabitants per year in the Maldives, making it the divorce capital of the globe. The next most problematic country for lasting romance was Belarus with 4.63 divorces per 1,000 people and the United States with 4.34. The Maldivians were twice as fickle in love as anyone else; or so the stats suggested. Whatever the truth, they were startling numbers for an international honeymoon haven.

'There is a lot of sexual abuse. It's all connected,' the first man added, before his heavy-set friend cut in.

'A gentle tap,' he said, his hands folded neatly before him on the table. 'Just a gentle tap. We don't follow strict Islamic law.'

He was talking about the 'lashings' handed down as punishments for women who had engaged in premarital sex. Two months before my visit a 15-year-old rape victim had been sentenced to 100 lashes, prompting condemnation around the world. Amnesty International had described the ruling – which was eventually overturned – as 'cruel, degrading and inhumane'. The charges had come after accusations that her stepfather had raped her and killed their baby. This man did not face trial. The judicial change of heart had happened largely as a result of a petition launched by the global campaigning group Avaaz, which had attracted two million signatures and put pressure on the Maldivian government. Not wanting to jeopardise tourism, politicians had intervened.

During its work to overturn the decision, Avaaz had conducted a survey that found that 92 per cent of Maldivians wanted a reform of the law to protect women from assault. The group also revealed that one in three women aged between 15 and 49 had suffered physical or sexual abuse, and pointed out that no one had been convicted of rape in the previous three years. The subject was a hot topic.

'I saw a lashing,' the heavy-set man continued. 'It was by the government building, but it was just a gentle tap on the upper thigh. It would sting but nothing else. Nothing compared to Saudi Arabia. It is more like a humiliation type of thing. You repent in this life so you do not carry your sins into the next.'

His friend, who had a wide oval-shaped face and a ready smile, disagreed: 'I have seen a lashing twice. It was painful.'

The heavy-set man, turning to him, retorted: 'We are Islamists, we should follow sharia law.'

The man with the red tie piped up: 'I think that's really open to discussion. A lot of punishments do not fit the crime.'

The heavy-set man looked me in the eye. 'In the Western world, sharia law is very misunderstood.'

The Sea House Café seemed to have a secondary role as a debating society. The next subject was five-star tourism. One of them had seen the Portuguese footballer Cristiano Ronaldo during his visit the previous year, another had laid eyes on former England striker Alan Shearer. Pedro Rodriguez of Barcelona, ex–Real Madrid manager Carlos Quieroz and Sam Allardyce, the manager of West Ham United, had also been spotted. As much as the Maldivians adore football, footballers seemed very fond of the Maldives.

'We have not benefited from upscale tourism. Most of the people here would not have gone to a resort,' said the oval-faced man, talking about the locals. 'If you go for a swim at the artificial beach you may find a condom in the water: that's the situation there.' It was the only beach on Male.

The man with the red tie added: 'We are renowned across the world for our beaches, but what's crazy is that more than half the population has this artificial beach. That really sums it up. We are not resentful, we just feel a little let down by government policies. Nearly every business is monopolised. Nearly everything is owned by government ministers: hotels, catering, supply/imports. Five or six big people, mostly politicians. They control. It's not a level playing field.'

He paused to sip his coffee. He had come to life and, although he claimed not to be angry, he was doing a decent impression of being pretty annoyed. He explained how, if someone wanted to start up a retail shop on Male, they would have the choice of about six suppliers, but: 'I guarantee you would not make a profit unless you had an affiliation with a politician.' Kickbacks, he said, were par for the course: 'It's sad but true.'

The man with the oval face told me: 'Up to 2004, if you wrote anything like this – if you were critical – well, you would go straight to Dhoonidhoo.' This was before the aftermath of the tsunami partially led to a political shake-up that brought about democracy.

Dhoonidhoo was just to the north of Male and was where some British representatives to the Maldives stayed on official visits back in the days of British influence. It was now the site of a prison. 'My former boss was held there for five days,' he said.

His boss's crime, apparently, had been to speak out about corruption. 'After he had been there did he ever say things again?' I asked.

'No. He would only ever write what the president wanted.'

The heavy-set man did not look as though he approved of much of what was being discussed. He stared into his folded hands, raising his eyebrows now and then.

The man with the red tie ignored him and looked squarely at me: 'Up until 2004, Dhoonidhoo. Then democracy came, with the help of Mohamed Nasheed and the international community.' Since the coup, he said, many were worried about whether freedom of expression would last: 'Let's face it, football clubs are owned by politicians. Media outlets, television stations, restaurants, resorts, big retail shops, commercial flats, speedboats, yachts … everything is politicised now.'

On Emergency Island

I caught a 20-minute ferry to Hulhumale. It was, by all accounts, a peculiar place. Until 1997 it had been no more than an area of reef at the far end of Airport Island. In the years since, more than US$30 million had been spent on land reclamation to create a new island. The purpose was twofold: to provide an area of overspill housing for Male, one of the most densely populated places on the planet, and also to have a higher landmass than the capital should waves rise as climate change scientists foresaw.

Hulhumale was 2 metres above sea level. This may not sound like much, but in the Maldives it was a big deal. The country, as I'd already found from visiting its 'mountains', is incredibly low-lying. With most of the land at about 1 metre and a highest natural point that's not a Buddhist *stupa* or otherwise man-made of 2.4 metres, the nation only just manages to poke above the waves.

No other country is so low. Even the Netherlands, so famously flat and at risk from sea surges, rises to 322 metres at Vaalserberg, a hill nicknamed 'Mount Vaals' by the Dutch, while parts of Denmark scale 170 metres. The natural peaks of the Maldives were tiddlers by comparison, below the rim of a basketball net. Hence the need for Hulhumale, effectively the country's 'Emergency Island'.

One day, planners believed the land could house as many as 100,000 people. It represented a possible future for the Maldives, although another extreme vision was that the entire population would have to evacuate to another nation, with India and Australia mooted as possible homelands. Given that scientists were confident that the world's seas would rise by about half a metre by the end of the twenty-first century, these had become serious propositions. I had only to think of the crumbling fish market on Vilufushi, wrecked so soon after being built on reclaimed land after the tsunami, to understand the enormity of the potential situation.

A fact file on the Maldives compiled by the Union of Concerned Scientists, a group founded in 1969 by students and staff at the Massachusetts Institute of Technology to raise awareness of pressing environmental problems, describes it this way: 'After looking closely at the volume of water that could come from glacial and ice sheet melt by the year 2100, scientists estimate that sea level could rise by 80 centimetres, and that as much as two metres is possible, depending on the pace at which heat-trapping emissions are released. Given mid-level scenarios for those emissions, the Maldives is projected to experience sea-level rise on the order of 50 centimetres by around 2100. [In such an instance] the country would lose 77 per cent of its land area by the end of the century. If the sea level were to rise by one metre and the Maldives did not pursue further coastal protection measures, it would be nearly completely inundated by about 2085.'

Without wishing to sound melodramatic, I was in a country that could disappear in the not too distant future.

The ferry passengers quickly dispersed and I found myself rolling my bag towards a little customer-less café next to a picnic area with a lawn. A man was slumped half asleep on a chair behind the counter. Birds cooed in wide-leaved trees by the picnic tables. The café attendant roused himself when I ordered a Holsten, which looked like a beer from the famous brewery but was in fact fizzy apple juice. Then I asked for directions to the Fuana Inn guesthouse. The attendant mumbled something and pointed vaguely in the direction of a junction where there was a choice of three empty, tree-lined roads. Hulhumale was only half finished and had a ghostly quality.

I sipped my Holsten. 'What is life like on Emergency Island?' I asked the first resident I had met.

The attendant mumbled something more, and in English added: 'This nice, but more nice: home.'

He was from Bangladesh and had lived in the Maldives for seven months. In two months, he said, he intended to go to Italy or England, although he did not say how. 'Not good money,' he muttered, referring to his wages.

After wishing him well, I took off down a long road beyond a sign that warned 'DRUGS DISRUPT FAMILIES'. I kept to the shade beneath tall fir trees I had not seen elsewhere in the country. Camel cigarette packets and plastic bottles were scattered in the verge and on the other side of the trees I glimpsed deserted plots of weed-filled land. The air smelt of herbs. Other than the sound of the birds, all was silent. I was, I soon realised, totally lost.

I retraced my steps and tried a second road. A man walking towards the ferry port appeared and I asked him the way. 'I don't know, I'm from Male,' he said.

A seaplane buzzed above. A fly-poster on a tree near a plot with a half-built structure advertised a 'BANGLA MUSIC CONCERT NIGHT'. Another walker materialised. He too was unsure of the hotel's whereabouts. I was beginning to wonder if I'd made some sort of mistake.

After a while I came to a row of shops in a modern two-storey building with a pharmacy, a mini grocery market, a computer service centre and the Cappuccino Café. At the latter Indian cricket was playing on a television and a few men sat chewing areca nuts. This stretch turned out to be the island's epicentre, with a hospital on the opposite side of the street and the headquarters of the development company behind Hulhumale in a tower connected to one end of the shops.

Two teenagers near the café made a beeline for me and said they knew the way to the hotel and would take me there. One was named Nawal and the other was Zimaam. Nawal was spindly with a bouffant haircut, a bead neck-chain and a T-shirt with a slogan saying 'ROCK'. Zimaam had a deliberately ruffled hairstyle, rolled-up jeans and looked as though he could handle himself in a fight.

When I asked why they liked the island, Zimaam said: 'The beach, the weather, the girls.' Sometimes Western women would stay at my guesthouse and another one next door while waiting for flights. An Airport Express bus linked Hulhumale with Airport Island. 'The ventilation,' he continued. 'Better air than on Male. You can breathe fresh air. You can swim…'

Nawal cut in. 'Too much emotion,' he said, nodding towards Male. 'Too much traffic. This is peaceful. So much space…'

Zimaam took over: 'Crime is low here…'

Nawal stopped him in his tracks: 'It is a good island…'

Zimaam stepped in: 'Here the future is in our hands.'

If you ignored the bit about girls, they sounded as though they worked for the Hulhumale branch of the Ministry of Tourism.

After passing a bus stop with a notice advising locals to 'TAKE A STEP MORE TO LEARN ABOUT OUR PROPHET', we turned down a street and arrived at an empty beach with a bank of white sand sloping to lapping water. Women in burqa swimsuits splashed in the shallows, looking like sea lions. Beyond, waves rumbled on a reef. Rows of palms rose along the shore and a few multi-coloured sunshades clustered outside the Ripple Beach Inn. Apart from the sea lions, hardly anyone was around.

The Fuana Inn was next to the Ripple Beach Inn. It was a teetering affair with rooms the size of regular double beds. In mine, a miniscule wardrobe unit had been fitted into a low-level desk, as though they belonged in a children's bedroom. A sideboard with a piece of beige carpet on its surface was next to a narrow mattress and a shoebox bathroom with a curtain-less shower. The sound of tapping came from outside. I looked through a tinted window to see workmen hammering beside a concrete mixer in a yard full of rubble. I was on the top floor, facing inland. On buildings opposite, satellite dishes cupped upwards amid rusty metal spikes left as though mid-construction. Hulhumale, it was clear, was very much a work in progress.

I had two days on the island before heading to the far north of the archipelago, 500 or so miles from Addu. Once I got there I would be at the top of my figure-of-eight of the country. On Hulhumale I was in the middle of the eight, if you like, swerving upwards with the bottom loop complete.

The following morning I went to the offices of the Housing Development Corporation. I was soon sitting in a shiny reception with a blond-wood floor flicking through a brochure for Coral Ville. This was a housing project that offered a 'unique opportunity to buy your own dream home'. It was a 'concept of living inspired by the deep blue sea' based in a 'secure and healthy environment'. The brochure asked: 'Are you ready to own your dream home and attain a better quality of life for you and your family?' It answered this question on potential buyers' behalf with its slogan: 'CHOOSE YOUR NEW HOME, START YOUR NEW LIFE!' Inside pages showed pictures of living rooms with muted colour schemes, glass-topped coffee tables with bowls of fruit, and flat-screen televisions on which footballer Cristiano Ronaldo was captured raising an arm in celebration of a goal.

Ahmed Varish, Senior Marketing Officer Corporate Affairs, Marketing and Business Development of the Housing Development Corporation, was relaxed and friendly and in his late 20s. He wore a striped white shirt, well-polished shoes and a navy tie with polka dots. His hair was ruffled in the same style as Zimaam's. I had not made an official appointment, yet he kindly agreed there and then to show me round, taking me down from the third-floor offices to a room with pictures of the island in various stages of construction.

'Welcome to our exhibition room,' Ahmed said. 'All this started back in 1997. Gayoom: this was his project. He realised that Male was getting congested. People were running out of room for houses, so Hulhumale was built.'

We were in a dimly lit chamber with pictures of Hulhumale taken from above at various stages of construction. A photograph from 1997 showed an area of shallow water and sand, the airport runway visible on the neighbouring island.

'Oh yes, it was water: three metres to six metres deep,' said Ahmed. 'What we did was take sand from the rest of the lagoon to build it. Some parts of the lagoon are now 12 metres deep. It took about five years to build the island as it now exists.' The project had begun slowly due to limited funds, but had accelerated thanks to a loan from a Belgian bank.

We came to a picture from 2003 showing an anvil-shaped mass of land in the space formerly occupied by fish. Where we were standing had not so long ago been the domain of crabs, sharks and moray eels. Since 2003 water-purification depots, power plants, sewage-treatment sites, roads, residential buildings, schools, mosques and hospitals had sprung up. That was just the beginning. Models revealed plans for grand boulevards, marinas, skyscrapers and hotels that made me think of the early days of development in Dubai.

From Ahmed I learnt that a checkpoint existed between Hulhumale and Airport Island, and that to reach the terminal you had to cross the runway. He told me that the beach by the Fuana Inn had a base of bags filled with sand and concrete. Fortunately, 'nature helped us create the beach'. The tide had covered the concrete bags with sand from the ocean floor. A 150-metre gap had been left between the beach and the reef.

'We had learned the lesson of Male,' Ahmed explained. 'Male used to be a small island. But we realised that if you cleared the water so there was land up to the reef, then you needed a protection wall against the problem of the waves.' This was why the capital's tetrapod defences were required.

During the 2004 tsunami the airport had been flooded, but water had washed off Hulhumale 'as it was on higher land'. Ahmed's previous boss had described the day to him: 'He said he was pretty scared. He thought "Oh shit, we're going down".'

Ahmed told me that the highest building currently planned would be 16 storeys and that the island would eventually reach 230 hectares, with an optimum population of 60,000, although that might increase. He said that the population of Male, although officially 105,000, could be much more. The capital consisted of 190 hectares, so the amount of land available to Maldivians living in the vicinity of Male was effectively doubling. This was creating a new breed of Maldivian commuter, travelling to work by ferry – Ahmed himself crossed from Male to Hulhumale and back each day.

Properties were only available to locals, so I could throw away my Coral Ville brochure. A swanky 250-room Radisson Blu hotel was to open shortly; I had seen the building site when I got lost from the ferry port.

During my visit, 20,000 people were living on the new island. The target date for the completion of 'phase one' was 2020. This would be the first 188 hectares of the island, with work continuing to bring the total size to 230 hectares.

There it was, in numbers and dreams. There was a sense of science fiction about the Hulhumale project, a foretaste of what the Maldives may have to wake up to in the future.

'Good money? No money!'

I went for a jog around Hulhumale without coming across a single vehicle on the perimeter road. Lizards scuttled in the scrubland where mixed-income housing would one day stand. Women in headscarves carrying groceries looked away as I passed. Concrete mixers rattled on the edge of the soon-to-be Radisson Blu. As I came full circle, I stopped for a coffee at the Cappuccino Café, where I met two security guards and a trainee policeman.

One of the security guards worked for the Housing Development Corporation. He wore a pistachio uniform and had once been in the merchant navy. He said he had been round the world seven times, but he preferred his life now. 'Too rush, too windy, too rainy, too snow,' he said, referring to his previous existence. 'I like this island. Too peace, no noise, no crowded, very peace.'

The other security guard had worked for the former president Mohamed Nasheed. 'I went with him to Addu. Very dangerous. Always there must be people around him,' he told me. He said that his brother had been arrested five times under the regime of former president Gayoom, picked on as he had been involved in industrial action. He had been taken to the dreaded Dhoonidhoo.

'I hate him,' he said, speaking of Gayoom.

The trainee policeman was an evacuee from Vilufushi. 'We lost our house and all our possessions. Sharks and eels were on the island. It was a big shock.'

Almost everyone in the Maldives seemed to have a tsunami story to tell.

From the café, I walked to the island's first school. On the wall by the entrance was an enormous slogan painted in red: 'OUR MISSION IS TO PROVIDE THE STUDENTS AN EXCELLENT EDUCATIONAL EXPERIENCE, TO BE HONEST, RESPONSIBLE AND MORALLY PREPARED CITIZENS TO FACE THE CHALLENGES OF AN INCREASINGLY COMPLEX SOCIETY.' A lot to take on board when you're 11 years old, I couldn't help thinking.

Beyond was a mosque with a green-and-gold carpet and a wooden partition separating men and women. Fans blazed in the high ceiling as if the whole building was about to lift off into the sky. I continued along avenues of almost-completed apartment blocks, whitewashed though parts of each block were painted lime green, orange or blue. They looked like Lego houses, as if they'd been taken from the model in the exhibition room and somehow blown up to full size. The roads were empty and taped off to prevent vehicles entering.

This really was the stuff of Aldous Huxley or George Orwell. And just like in *1984*, I was soon to come across the proles.

Huddled beneath a tree by the road to the airport, a group of Bangladeshi construction site workers watched me approach. They were by a building that would soon be an office of some sort. Their faces were glum and they were stick thin. The eldest must have been 35, though the average age was probably mid-20s. I went up and said hello. After some hesitation on their part, we had an impromptu discussion.

The best English speaker, who wore a purple polo shirt, was pushed forward. Under a fierce afternoon sun, I asked if they made good money.

'Good money?' he replied, sounding disbelieving. 'No money! No pay for three months.'

His eyes moistened and he spoke passionately. He told me that his team worked ten hours a day for six days a week.

Their passports were with a foreman and they had signed up to three years of employment. Their wages, when they were paid, amounted to 4,000 rufiyaa a month (just over £150). Most of this would be sent home to relatives in Bangladesh. He added that they lived ten to a room, sleeping next to each other like sardines on thin mattresses.

'Sometimes I feel very down. I just want to go home,' he said. Next year his stint would be up and he hoped to return. There were about 40,000 Bangladeshis in the Maldives working on construction sites for projects such as Hulhumale or at hotels.

What did they do for fun?

'On Fridays, we go to the mosque,' he said. 'Sometimes we play cricket or go to a café.'

He suddenly became frightened and backed away, as did his friends. He seemed to realise that by talking to me he might be putting himself in trouble. Their movements were crab-like, edging into the recesses of the building they were diligently constructing without pay.

'Please don't worry, I won't use your name,' I said.

'Oh thank you, thank you so much,' he replied, his anxiety momentarily easing. Nevertheless, that was the end of our discussion. Before I knew it the road was empty and the workers had disappeared into the shadows.

'Macbeth in the tropics'

I caught the Airport Express to Airport Island, or Hulhule, to give it its real name. I had a meeting with a journalist from *Minivan News*. For his sake, though he subsequently left the website and the country (as did his colleague), I'll call him X. He was from Europe and had come to work in the Maldives as a travel writer concentrating on 'high-end resorts'. He had switched to *Minivan* after this work 'fell through'. He was young and enthusiastic, and wore a T-shirt and flip-flops, like an Australian about to attend a barbie.

I had wanted to talk to someone who had got to know the country as an outsider and who had an independent voice, although X was quick to put me straight on how his website was regarded by some locals.

'We're seen as a kind of Zionist front,' he said, in a manner that suggested he found this so crazy it was funny. 'Oh, they hate us.' By 'they' he was referring to the traditional establishment in the Maldives. All was clearly not (all that) well for some journalists in paradise. 'They think we are just a mouthpiece for the Maldivian Democratic Party. The other day someone came up to me and called me a "colonial arsehole". He was obviously a government troll.'

Minivan promised unbiased reporting and claimed to be 'internationally regarded as the Maldives' most reliable news source ... the country's first fully independent platform for free expression'. Stories about subjects such as gay travellers (homosexuality is illegal), political corruption, 'vote buying', public lashings, climate change, drug use, environmental waste and abuse of foreign workers had got up the noses of officialdom. X monitored keenly the fate of Bangladeshis such as those I had met earlier in the day.

'There's the most heightened sense of the haves and the have-nots,' he said, talking about tourist resorts as we strolled into the drive of the Hulhule Island Hotel, the only hotel on the island. It was where many stayed before or after flights; much more upmarket, and pricier, than the guesthouse on Hulhumale.

'In resorts there is this incredible segregation,' X continued. 'Tourists are happy just to turn their heads away from the lives of staff. They don't need to concern themselves. It's almost Victorian. There are almost Dickensian parallels. The haves and the have-nots; the growth in religion; the morality of it all. When I came I just thought: "This is very odd."'

We were heading for Champs Bar, the only place to get a drink close to the capital if you didn't catch a speedboat to a resort. The bar, which had a pool table, air-conditioning and cricket on television screens, was 'kind of infamous' among expats, said X. We sat out on a wooden deck with a view across the water to Male, sipping Heinekens.

X began telling me how politicians often swap sides and 'usually they have a silver BMW the next day'. He said people had begun referring to elections as 'buy-elections'. As he did so, a colleague from *Minivan News* paced up to the table.

I'll call him Y. If X was a chatterbox, Y was more like a chatterstorm. He pulled up a chair, ordered a beer and began to hold court. He too was a Westerner and was dressed casually in the style of a tourist. He was a bundle of energy: Hemingwayesque, pugnacious, sweating and ready to let loose.

'There is no distinction between businessmen, politicians, criminals and resort tycoons,' were almost his first words to me. He followed this by declaring that the recent ousting of Mohamed Nasheed had been 'Macbeth in the tropics'.

He swigged his Heineken, pausing for a split second. 'Elections here are like the football transfer market,' he pronounced, before saying that money earned by the big resorts 'goes straight to Singapore', meaning rich hotel owners rarely paid proper tax and tourism did not benefit the country. The Maldives was, he said, a 'wild west nation state run for the benefit of a couple of families'. He questioned why so much alcohol was sold to Maldivian-owned tourist resorts: 'It's prohibition era, Al Capone stuff.'

This was not, according to X and Y, an easy time to be a journalist in the Maldives. Amnesty International had recently reported frequent attacks by security forces on reporters. There was a fear of 'a man with an iron bar in the hall'.

Had they been attacked?

'They leave us alone for the moment,' said Y. 'Deportation is more likely for us.'

However, one reporter they knew had received death threats. There had also been a horrific case involving a Maldivian blogger named Ismail Rasheed, who had written about gay rights and had been targeted by a gang who had slashed his throat in Male in June 2012. The knife missed an artery by millimetres and he survived, but had fled the country for safety. The freedom of expression group Reporters Without Borders said that Rasheed had been picked on for his writing. Amnesty International believed that campaigners for religious tolerance in the country were under threat. An outspoken colleague of X and Y, the Maldivian *Minivan News* journalist Ahmed Rilwan Abdulla, was later to go missing in suspicious circumstances, prompting great fears for his safety.

It was not the kind of stuff you read about on the message board in your five-star hotel. Yet again, I was learning of another side to paradise, from two of the nation's most outspoken, and bravest, journalists.

'Echoes, ticking, text delays: that's common,' said Y, describing oddities he had noticed when using his mobile phone. He assumed he was being bugged. 'You ring someone and say hello and you hear an echo – it's completely silent. I described this to a reporter from Reuters who said that these were all like a checklist of signs that your phone is being tapped.'

Their news service, partly financed by advertising and figures who (sensibly) wish to remain out of the limelight, was later subject to an undercover investigation by the Maldives National Defence Force. The journalists only learnt of this thanks to a leak from within the secret police. They expected that they were being followed and feared that the state was searching for excuses to close down their website.

We ordered more buckets of ice-chilled Heinekens and eventually made our way back to the docks. As we passed through Champs Bar, a group of men sitting at a table stared directly at X, Y and me, prolonged eye contact that we could not mistake. We had been 'observed'.

Then, on the ferry back to Male, a man approached us. We were sitting on a bench to one side of the ferry, enjoying the breeze off the water.

'Can I take a picture of you there?'

'Why?' asked Y.

'Can I take a picture?' he repeated.

'Why?' Y asked again, then turned to me. 'Do you want him to take a picture?' he asked.

It all seemed quite odd, so I said no.

The man sat down right by us, within earshot. I whispered to Y, 'Is he police?'

'Something like that,' was all Y would answer.

Hangover Cures

In the morning I ran twice around Hulhumale to clear my head. Locals stopped what they were doing and watched with frank astonishment as I passed by. In a short space of time I appeared to have gained a reputation for eccentricity on Emergency Island. When I returned to the Fuana Inn, I realised why: my face had turned bright red in the heat. Even at 8am it was scorching. No wonder I almost never saw any joggers.

After cooling down, I went to a neighbourhood workers' café and bought a Maldivian breakfast of *roshi* (flat bread), *mashuni* (tuna, onions and chilli) and *kulhimas* (another version of spiced tuna, served with coconut milk). The idea seemed to be to wrap the *roshi* around the pieces of tuna. With a cup of black tea, this healthy meal came to 15 rufiyaa (58 pence).

I was so hungry I not-so-healthily ordered another, and sat in the shade of the red-brick building alongside Bangladeshi construction men listening to an Indian soap opera involving doctors. I had brought a few printouts of cuttings about the Maldives with me and was steadily getting through them in idle moments. I flicked through some in the cool shade.

One *Daily Telegraph* report was about extraordinary plans for floating islands, including one with an 18-hole golf course and an underwater clubhouse. Apparently a Dutch company that claimed to be a 'global leader in floating developments' aimed to build this island, complete with a 250-room hotel, in India or the Middle East and tow it to the archipelago. The aim was to conquer the threat of the rising sea. Meanwhile, Ian Belcher, a travel writer for *The*

Times, had visited a resort in Dhaalu Atoll to see the world's 'only sub-aqua dance floor', wryly commenting that it was no particular surprise after the planet's first sub-aqua spa, which opened at a hotel named Huvafen Fushi in 2004, and an undersea restaurant at Conrad Maldives Rangali Island. These underwater attractions were, Belcher said, 'a rose-tinted glimpse of a nightmare future'. The journalist and television presenter Kate Humble had visited a resort close to Hulhumale to report on the state of the coral reef, which was under threat from global warming. 'Rising sea temperatures,' she wrote, 'pollution, ocean acidification - all have a detrimental effect on coral which ultimately will have a devastating effect on we humans.'

Cheery stuff. For some reason the Maldives seemed to attract a wide press that often, quite rightly, highlighted the danger posed to the country by climate change, yet the matter of the country's politics was frequently overlooked. Travelling around the fringes of paradise, I was slowly becoming attuned to the undercurrents of local life. I was not to experience echoes, clicks and text delays on my phone, but a bigger and more complicated picture was emerging.

Not everyone sang from the same hymn sheet, nevertheless. Though the journalists I had met the previous night were largely in favour of the Maldivian Democratic Party and its ousted leader, the owner of Ripple Beach Inn supported the other side. After breakfast, we had a long talk. He believed that Mohamed Nasheed had correctly 'resigned' after breaking constitutional rules by jailing a senior judge. He also believed that the ex-president had threatened to block development on islands where people did not support him. He claimed Nasheed had used the issue of climate change as a vehicle to enhance his own popularity.

'Some scientists believe in the rising sea, some don't,' he told me. '90 per cent of Maldivians do not over-think about this. We know we have to be careful and look after the beach and to be careful about beach erosion. All of that we respect. Maldivians have been here for 3,000 years, so we are not worried. Why are so many businessmen investing in resorts if they think that in 20 years' time it will all be under water? They're not stupid.'

He had a point.

With that, I rolled my bag back towards the ferry port. I'd soon be in Haa Alifu Atoll, almost seven degrees north of the Equator, level with the southern tip of Sri Lanka many miles to the east. Here I would learn much about the ancient history of the country, just as full of twists and turns as the modern past.

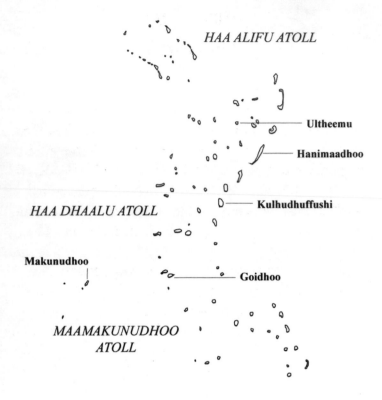

HAA ALIFU ATOLL

Ultheemu

Hanimaadhoo

HAA DHAALU ATOLL

Kulhudhuffushi

Makunudhoo

Goidhoo

*MAAMAKUNUDHOO
ATOLL*

PART THREE
Up North

After a flight to Hanimaadhoo, a speed launch to the island of Ultheemu, where lived a hero of Maldivian independence, before travelling to a series of islands so remote they are used for official banishments and haven't seen outsiders for as long as 20 years

'I must go down to the seas again, to the vagrant gypsy life.'
John Masefield

Home of the Hero

Not far from Ultheemu island on Haa Alifu Atoll, the engine on our speed launch failed. We had been shooting across the metallic-grey sea when a gurgling sound took over and the bow of the boat dipped. The engine made a few dying splutters and we came to a standstill.

I had been enjoying the ride on a blue-cushioned sofa. I had the boat to myself, chartered for the 45-minute journey from Hanimaadhoo for 1,000 rufiyaa (£38), the cost of two nights at a Maldivian guesthouse. It was the only way to reach the island I wanted to visit without waiting for a supply *dhoni* that was perhaps, or perhaps not, leaving the next day.

One of the two men in charge of the vessel wore a T-shirt bearing the inscription 'STAY REAL'. Following an inspection, he hammered the Yamaha V6 200 engine, bashing at the spot where the fuel fed into the motor. After a while, he called out to the captain 'Noo rang-allu!' or something like that, and sprang back to the front of the boat.

The sky was a canopy of high grey clouds veined with thin blue streaks. Heat haze rose from the choppy ocean. Stay Real returned with a petrol can and some pliers. He attached the can to a pipe then crouched, delicately holding the pipe aloft.

'Mee-haru! Mee-haru!' he yelled.

The captain fired the engine. It grumbled to life and for the rest of the journey Stay Real stood at the back of the boat manually pouring petrol into the Yamaha.

'Sorry, sorry!' he would shout from time to time.

In this manner we bumped along until we were approaching Ultheemu, where the water in the shallows gleamed aquamarine and a welcoming committee was gathered on a white sand beach. Men were dressed in lime greens, reds and yellows, and women in purple shawls with children in pinks and aquamarines at their feet. From a distance they looked like colourful confetti strewn on the sands. As there was no harbour, the speed launch aimed straight for the shore and we scraped to a stop.

I leapt off the bow into water that went up to my knees. My bag was passed from Stay Real to a local, who balanced it on his head until he reached land.

I had made it to one of the country's most revered historical spots: Ultheemu, home of the hero, about whom more later.

First, I watched as a grimacing young man with his legs wrapped in a sarong was carried towards the boat. A carpenter, he had cut his leg badly in an accident constructing a *dhoni*; boat-building was an important part of Ultheemu's economy. As there was no hospital on the island, he was catching my launch back to Hanimaadhoo for treatment. So the 'welcoming committee' was not for me, but his family assembled to see him off. If I had not booked the 'water taxi' he would have had to wait longer. For once, I had proved useful.

Thanks to the Maldivian grapevine, I had a contact on the island who was arranging a room. Abdullah Nuhaadh stepped forward wearing gold-framed aviator shades. Aged 22, he worked as a security guard at the island's magistrates' court, although he intended one day to study tourism and hospitality in Male. He led me a few yards down the beach to a lemon-yellow house with a corrugated metal roof and an immaculately swept sand yard behind a pistachio wall. Inside, I was taken to a room with a pink bed and a long, tubular pillow. Gold-framed calligraphy from the Koran hung on the pastel walls.

Abdullah left me to attend to his court business. He would come back at an appointed time, he said, then we would 'go roaming'.

In my new digs, I stretched out the blue laminated map of the country that I'd bought at a souvenir shop on Male, attaching it with a book to the top of a wardrobe. I marvelled at the great distance between Addu and Ultheemu. To reach the north of the Maldives I had caught a last-minute flight on a plane with dolphins painted on its fuselage from Male to Hanimaadhoo, from where I had booked the water taxi. I counted backwards. Including my latest port of call, I had been to 17 of the country's 1,192 islands.

Dwelling on this, I lay back on my pink bed in the lemon-yellow guesthouse. Even though it was still morning, I was struck by a sudden languor. Above the soft whirr of the air-conditioning I fancied I could hear the crash of waves beyond the palm grove on the beach. The map rustled, disturbed by shafts of cool air. I fell into a deep, dreamless asleep.

These unscheduled catnaps were becoming a regular part of my Maldivian days. I would go exploring, often in the mid-day sun (in true Englishman form), return and snooze. It was, I had come to discover, a pleasant way of conducting life and I was slightly disturbed by the thought of returning to a place where it would not be possible to doze at all hours of the day.

I was woken by a rap on the door. Not for the first time, I raised myself from a bed wondering where I had washed ashore. I shook myself awake. The rap came again. It was Abdullah.

'Roaming!' he said, smiling broadly at the sleepy Westerner who emerged.

He had the physique of a solid top-order batsman in cricket, short and bulky, though he told me he preferred to play football. His square jaw was covered in stubble that had almost become a beard. When he removed his aviator glasses – which was rarely – he revealed playful, happy eyes. He was the son of a major *dhoni* maker and the family had a house on a prominent lane near the main mosque. Ultheemu's population was about 900, making it the smallest of the islands I had yet visited.

We went for a ride on his cherry-red motorbike, traversing grid-shaped roads clearly dating from the Mohammed Amin Didi era. As we did so, Abdullah jabbered on about his court work.

'Last ten years: no crime on this island!' he said. 'Very, very peaceful.'

That seemed immediately evident: there was hardly a soul about. I asked him whether a court was required if the people were so well behaved.

'Yes, yes – every inhabited island must have a magistrates' court,' he replied, crime or no crime.

I inquired about his work as a security guard.

'I protect the computers and the building,' he said.

Had he ever come across anyone acting suspiciously?

'Oh no,' he answered. 'Very peaceful. I'm sure of it.'

When was the last crime?

'I would have to look into that actually. I would have to check,' he said. He wasn't entirely sure whether it was ten years ago or longer. Ultheemu was quite different from Hulhumeedhoo, with its (supposed) hives of criminals lurking behind every palm tree.

We turned into a crimeless, twisting lane and rattled along, arriving at Abdullah's house. We had been heading to the palace of the hero, but Abdullah had had a sudden change of mind. 'It is too hot for palace and I am very busy,' he said cheerfully, before dropping me off at his family home, where

I was soon reclining in a *jolie* placed before two women, whom I took to be his mother and sister. With great concentration, they were slicing pieces of breadfruit into tiny pieces with a large curved knife. Abdullah disappeared once more. The mother nodded at me and continued her task.

Then Abdullah's wife Shuzna ushered me into the kitchen. She told me that she and Abdullah had been married one month and had met in Male, where she had been a travel agent for Villas Travel. Shuzna, who had sparkling eyes that matched her husband's, was from the island of Makunudhoo and wore a T-shirt over a stripy top bearing the message 'HAPPEN EVERY DAY'. She served me magnificent spicy tuna curry and fried tuna, slices of lime, salad and *roshi*, leaving me to eat alone.

I already knew a fair bit about the local hero whose home this island had been. His name was Mohamed Thakurufaanu and he had lived on Ultheemu in the sixteenth century. This was the golden period for the Portuguese in the Indian Ocean, after Vasco da Gama had set up his trading post at Calicut in Kerala. The Portuguese had dominated the waters close to the Maldives and in the mid-sixteenth century they had turned their attention to the islands. They were already the subject of hatred among Maldivians for their frequent piratical raids, looting and bullying. After a failed attempt, the Portuguese took their aggression a step further by launching a successful full-on attack on Male, home of the sultan, in 1558.

Their aim was to take control of the plentiful natural supply of cowry shells, which were used far and wide as currency in the Indian Ocean; it was at this time that the Maldives were known as the Money Islands. The invaders were also seeking coir, the fibre from coconut husks that was used to make rope, of which there was also an abundance. Other

attractions were the islanders' famous dried fish (probably processed in much the same manner as I'd seen on
Vilufushi), tortoise shells and ambergris, a waxy substance
produced in the intestines of sperm whales that could be
used in perfumes and medicines.

During this period Maldivians 'used no firearms and were
timid, but very ingenious and great sorcerers', according to
H.C.P. Bell. Yet despite the first repelled attack, sorcery and
ingenuity were not enough to keep the Portuguese at bay.

They were assisted by the inside knowledge of a former
Maldivian sultan who had fled the islands at the age of 20
and converted to Christianity in India. This ex-sultan, whose
new Christian name was Don Emanuel, did not return to the
Maldives. Instead, the Portuguese appointed a local governor and maintained control with a garrison at a fort on Male,
nominally acting under the rule of the new Christian king
back in India.

This was where the hero enters the story. After about seven
years the Maldivians had had enough. They were an Islamic
people being controlled by a Christian king who even before
the invasion had impudently and unsuccessfully called on
them to convert to Christianity. They had foreign troops in
their capital. The Maldivians began to engage in skirmishes,
adopting guerrilla tactics. Mohamed Thakurufaanu and his
two brothers, one of whom was beheaded after being captured during a raid, bravely led the resistance. They would,
they said, rather die than change their faith or be ruled by a
Christian king.

These encounters culminated in a famous assault in
July 1573: 'The pride of their race would never submit to
the Portuguese yoke ... getting word that the captain of the
fortress and the island of Male was gone to Cochin with a
goodly number of Portuguese soldiers, they could not miss

the opportunity, and resolved to attack the fortress: which project they carried out so well, that one night they surprised it by escalade, and made themselves masters of the place, putting to death upwards of 300 men that were within, and taking prisoner the native governor who was set there by the Portuguese.'

This is the account of Frenchman François Pyrard, who was shipwrecked on the islands in 1602 and based his description on word-of-mouth stories he later published in a journal.

In this manner, Thakurufaanu became the hero. After 15 years of submitting to rule by another nation, the Maldivians had beaten off their invaders. It is the only time in the islanders' history they have been administered from afar – even during the British period from the late nineteenth to mid-twentieth centuries, internal affairs were in Maldivian control.

I was pondering all this on a *jolie* after my enormous lunch when I heard the buzz of a motorbike. It was Abdullah. He indicated to me to hop on board and we sped to the 'old mosque' along sandy streets, flashing past a modern golden-domed mosque by a football pitch and an elderly man sauntering along clutching a massive golf umbrella. The temperature must have been close to 40 °C.

Beyond a yard full of coral-stone graves (the hero himself is buried on Male), we came to a building with a three-tiered terracotta-tile roof. Kandhuvalu Mosque, which had been redesigned in the nineteenth century, was deserted. A few tourists would come on speedboats from nearby resorts to take a look, and a sign said that this was where Thakurufaanu 'resolved to begin his campaign to liberate the Maldives after he and his associates offered prayers in this mosque and made a supplication to Almighty Allah to grant them victory in their struggle'.

It was interesting to see how closely entwined nationhood and religion were in the Maldives. Coming to this site helped me understand the reticence of many to the infiltration of Western ways, the reason tourists had been banned from visiting non-resort islands until 2009. Islamism, it was clear, was not just a religion here; it was more complex than that. The faith seemed to be an expression of national identity that had somehow come alive in the popular imagination with the defeat of the Portuguese and the shadowy Christian traitor Don Emanuel all those years ago.

Non-Muslims – infidels such as myself – were not allowed inside the mosque. However, Abdullah offered to take a few snaps on my behalf. So I know that there are tight rows of rust-red wooden columns, polished to a shine. Passages from the Koran are inscribed on roof beams to which fans are attached. Latticed, open-sided window frames allow in a breeze, but the central area of prayer is blocked off by whitewashed interior walls so no one can peer in.

Outside again, amid the coral graves, Abdullah put into words the meaning of Thakurufaanu to Maldivians: 'Oh yes, we are very proud. Because now we have our own power, not depending on others. We have our own government. Independent. Everything is free.'

Flag-waving came naturally on Ultheemu. We scooted down another series of sandy lanes, taking in a school displaying the slogan 'EDUCATION TO ALL FOR A PATRIOTIC AND HARMONIOUS SOCIETY', and stopped outside a memorial centre dedicated to the hero. I paid 25 rufiyaa (97 pence) to enter through an archway to a musty room with a few ancient oil lamps, boxes and coins on a couple of shelves.

'Old stuff,' commented Abdullah helpfully. We both stared at the old stuff for a while, as though expecting some kind of revelation. None was forthcoming, so we walked across a big sandy square to the palace, where Thakurufaanu had lived. As we did so, I asked Abdullah how many tourists came to Ultheemu.

'Some, some,' he said. 'Many rich people. A few every day.'

Why aren't they here now?

'Because of the weather. We don't have a jetty.'

This made it difficult for some tourists to get from boats onto the beach. Did many fall into the water?

'Yes. This season the sea is very rough and it is difficult. Usually we provide a ladder. People now are too afraid to come: they are afraid they lose camera and mobile. The resort people, they don't want to take the risk,' Abdullah said. 'We thought you were falling,' he added. Apparently my ungainly leap from the speed launch had had a few people holding their breath. I sensed that watching pale-skinned foreigners toppling into the sea was something of a local spectator sport.

My 25 rufiyaa also gained me access to the palace, built between 1512 and 1528. We stepped through a gateway cut into a long, whitewashed wall and made our way into a compound of single-storey constructions with terracotta roofs. The official tour guide almost fell off his chair when we arrived, yet he was dapper in a white shirt and purple tie, always prepared should a holidaymaker somehow drop from the sky. He was a heavyweight in size, with a bulging waistline and huge hands. His hair was slicked to one side and he wore shades: a Maldivian mafia museum man.

His name was Ali Hafiz. Despite his tough-guy look, his behaviour was gentle. He took me into the hero's bedroom, telling me that some days no tourists turned up, while on others – when it is high season and the sea is calm – as many as 50 people visited. He removed his shades and squinted, pointing at a hole in the wall that Thakurufaanu had cut to catch anyone trying to steal food supplies (there was evidently crime on Ulthccmu many years ago). Beyond was his sister's bedchamber.

'This door was shut 445 years ago,' said Ali, pointing at an old wooden door. It had not been opened since then, he added, for some reason I was unable to make out.

The hero's sister slept on a swinging bed and white flags were hung by chairs in a corner. 'They mean "peace",' said Ali, indicating the flags and gazing at the room lovingly.

We examined some ancient, painful-looking wooden flip-flops with heels at the back. Then we checked out a 3.3-metre-deep well, used when there has been no rain for a long stretch; a man wearing an Arsenal football shirt was digging out the bottom when we visited. We also inspected Thakurufaanu's meeting hall, consisting of four teak columns, coir rope, wooden pegs and a clever natural ventilation system. Then Ali quietly said: 'I proudly come from this island.'

His simple statement, echoing Abdullah, spoke volumes. Thakurufaanu had not been of royal or of high birth. He was merely a brave islander who had taken on the Portuguese with the help of his brothers. The skyscrapers and bustle of Male, with its cacophony, overcrowding, teeming life, mobile phones, juice bars and mayhem, was all a long way from Ultheemu. This island seemed to offer an insight into the past that was elusive in the overflowing, 24/7 capital. Ordinary people from an ordinary island had saved the nation in its time of crisis.

The Extraordinary Life of François Pyrard

Abdullah sped off on business. Maybe someone suspicious had been spotted attempting to steal the computers at the magistrates' court.

I rested in the shade of a gnarly old tree watching the world go by. There wasn't much of it. A few boys scrambled across the square in front of the tiny palace. A couple of likely lads inspected a motorbike near the town hall. The elderly man with the giant umbrella returned from the direction of the main mosque.

I turned to my copy of *The Voyage of François Pyrard of Laval to the East Indies, the Maldives, the Moloccas and Brazil*. This tells the extraordinary tale of the man who in 1602 joined the crew of a ship named the *Corbin* in St Malo, travelling in tandem with another vessel, the *Croissant*, all the way around the Cape of Good Hope heading for India, following Vasco da Gama's spice route. As the ships had approached the Maldives, there had been a disagreement between the captains about the best passage to avoid the already famously tricky channels and dangerous reefs. The *Corbin* and the *Croissant* took slightly different courses and, after sunset, disaster struck.

Pyrard's description is gripping. Even though his captain had chosen a sensible route, his instructions were not followed and there was a reason: 'Everyone was fast asleep that night, even those on watch. The mate and the second mate had been carousing and were drunk. The light usually kept on the poop for reading the compass was out, because the man at the wheel, who had charge of the light and the hour-glass, had fallen asleep, as had the ship's boy that attended him ... What was worse, the ship was steered to the east half-an-hour or three-quarters at most too soon. So, when we were thus all asleep, the ship struck heavily twice, and as we started with the shock, she suddenly struck a third time, and heeled over. I leave you to imagine the condition of all on board – what a pitiful spectacle we presented – the cries and lamentations of men who find themselves wrecked at night on a rock in mid-ocean and await a certain death. Some wept and cried with all their might; others took to prayers; others confessed to each other ...'

This early example of the dangers of drink driving was also a vivid insight into the terrors these waters held so many centuries ago, before depth readings on sonar displays and other digital gadgets. Pyrard refers to 'the impetuosity of the sea ... it is a fearful thing, even to the most hardy, to approach this reef, and to see the billows from afar come on and break with fury all around; for I assure you, as a thing which I have seen an infinity of times, that the crests and foam of the breakers rise higher than a house, of the whiteness of cotton, so that you see around you, as it were, a wall of exceeding whiteness, chiefly when the sea is high.'

Things got rapidly worse after they struck bottom. The ship held together on the reef, but there was no pinnace, a smaller vessel usually kept for reconnaissance missions; theirs had been lost in heavy seas after rounding the Cape of Good Hope. They were too far out to swim to shore since the water was so treacherous. In the morning, locals approached on a boat but would not come close.

Many of those on board believed they were going to be killed by the natives. Some began to 'consume the ship's victuals even beyond the necessities of nature, saying to the others of us who remonstrated, that we were all as good as lost, and that they preferred to die in that fashion'. There was swearing, fighting, robbery and a lack of acknowledgement of the captain, who was ill. Pyrard was horrified: 'I have seen but too many, leave their souls and conscience on land, so irreligious, demoralised, and insolent have I seen them to be.'

They were shipwrecked on Goidhoo Atoll, between Male and Ultheemu. Eventually they were rescued by locals, who took them to separate islands so they could not join forces and revolt. On the orders of the sultan in Male, the half-sunk *Corbin* was stripped of its merchandise. Meanwhile, the crew of 40 were held hostage, slowly dying either of illness or of hunger. Some of Pyrard's fellow seamen were found dead with grass desperately stuffed in their mouths – hellish last suppers. Others ate rats to survive. The islanders believed that the shipwrecked had hidden coins on their persons (as a few had), so they sweated out as much cash as they could, only offering proper food to those with coins.

Pyrard was lucky enough to be on an island with a benevolent chief, who appreciated that he had begun to learn Dhivehi. This brought him to the attention of a high-ranking lord who was visiting from Male and who took him to the capital, where he soon ingratiated himself at the court of the sultan. He was in his mid-20s when he was shipwrecked and stayed on the islands from 1602 to 1607. The sultan, for reasons of his own and because he was angry that a handful of those from the *Corbin* had escaped on a stolen boat (perhaps reaching India), did not allow Pyrard free passage onwards. The Frenchman managed to leave the Maldives only when he seized the moment to flee on a vessel during the confusion of a Bengali raid on Male.

Because he had access to the higher echelons, Pyrard, who was deemed to be of high standing back in France (a notion of which he did not disabuse the Maldivians), heard many stories from the royal court's great and good. As well as learning of the attack on the Portuguese, he was told of the aftermath, when Thakurufaanu was crowned sultan along with his brother. He writes that the pair ruled together peacefully for 25 years, marrying wives of 'the best houses of the country', and goes on to describe the backlash from the mighty colonial power they had defeated: 'As for the Portuguese, they were indignant at the rebuff they had received at the Maldives, and were resolved to avenge it; so the next year they sent an army to the islands, and carried on the war for a long time; but the two kings defeated all their forces.'

The conflict lasted three years. All did not, however, end so well for the brother sultans. Thakurufaanu had married the daughter of the king slain by the Portuguese, while his younger brother Hassan had married the daughter of a noble family. His sister-in-law's brother was apparently planning an assault on the throne, which he considered to be held by a person of low estate and not worthy of kingship. Thakurufaanu had him executed. Hassan was ill at the time and 'swore that if God should give him his health again, his brother should rue it'. Nevertheless, Hassan died of his sickness and Thakurufaanu passed away not long afterwards, whereupon his own son became king and soon had a close childhood friend murdered and dumped in the ocean for posing a perceived challenge.

Ruthlessness obviously ran in the family; though in those days, I suppose, the trait must have been part of the job description. Paradise had a rather bloody past.

I stayed a few days on Ultheemu, reading Pyrard and eating superb evening meals prepared by Shuzna and her mother at Abdullah's house. I watched Abdullah play football on the lumpy pitch by the mosque. On remote islands in the Maldives there appeared to be no offside rule, as far as I could tell at least. He scored two goals and was highly pleased, even though his team lost.

I was asked by a podgy man in the street if I was Muslim and when I said 'no', he refused my handshake, diverted his eyes and disdainfully grunted 'Eh!'

I watched women playing cards at a circular table under a breadfruit tree at sunset. I met Abdullah's father at his *dhoni* building shed. He was in the middle of constructing the 'largest dive boat in the Maldives', at 130 feet long. I met the island chief, Askar Adam, president of the local council, who told me he used to be 'senior butler' at the Island Hideaway resort. From butler to chief was pretty good going, another example of the vast void between tourists and islanders. How many other Maldivian island chiefs, I wondered, have delivered room service?

'I used to check for names with lots of *v*s. Most of the butlers were checking,' Askar Adam said. A lot of *v*s meant Russians and a lot of dollars. 'I got US$1,800 for ten days' work once from Andrei Molchanov. I went on the internet, he was worth US$4 billion.' Molchanov had made his fortune in the construction business and other websites I looked up later suggested his net value was a mere US$1.68 billion.

Askar Adam told me he wanted to raise average wages for locals. He hoped that leasing land for a resort and encouraging more guesthouses on Ultheemu would be a step in the right direction.

One evening Abdullah confided that he would like to be a dive instructor on a 'safari boat' once he had acquired his tourism qualification. Safari boats came with overnight cabins and were licensed. They took hardcore divers to otherwise inaccessible reefs and surfers to brilliant breaking waves. Abdullah already had some experience on one such boat and as we relaxed on *jolies* under a sky full of stars, he showed me pictures of 'Danish girls' he had met and Maldivian co-workers who had enjoyed a surreptitious drink every now and then.

Floating Bars and Shifting Clouds

I was fortunate to catch a speed launch back to Hanimaadhoo, where there was a place I wanted to see that was internationally famous. First, though, I went to the Asseyri Tourist Inn guesthouse. Asseyri means 'by the beach' in Dhivehi. I had called ahead and was whisked from the docks by a driver named Hussein in a Rover 620 SLI with cream leather seats and tinted windows. We lurched dramatically to avoid what must be some of the biggest potholes in the Maldives (and that's saying something), arriving shortly at a low-level building with a jade-coloured roof.

Owners Mohamed 'Arifi' Ali and his wife Fathimath Rifga were in their late 20s and had moved from Male to escape the rat race of the capital. They were taking a chance on the country's new tourism with a nine-room guesthouse in what had previously been a townhouse for visiting government officials. Self-confessed workaholics, they had thrown all their energy into their new business, taking great care with the decoration, which had an abstract art style and used many natural materials found on the island, such as old palm-tree trunks, pieces of broken coral and coconut fronds. They had begun a successful open-air restaurant on a terrace at the back, which would one day overlook a pool. Behind the perimeter wall by the entrance, a few electric-blue leather sofas and armchairs had been arranged in a peaceful 'chill-out area' with a shelter.

Guests had included professionals and expats from Male as well as a few international holidaymakers who had stumbled on their website, attracted by the well-designed, air-conditioned rooms and organised watersports. Rooms began at US$85 for a single up to US$220 for a family suite.

The couple were buzzing with enthusiasm and ideas. Arifi was thin and muscular with a wispy beard and a Timberland polo shirt, while Rifga wore an emerald headscarf, emerald top and faded jeans.

'It's been a big challenge,' said Arifi. 'People said: "Are you crazy? Who will come here?" Now that we've opened this and shown them how it works there are two more guesthouses locally.' They were considering launching a site called maldivesbudgetstay.com – somebody, I later noticed, had reserved this domain – and they wanted eventually to establish a 'mega-guesthouse' with a dozen more rooms, a diving centre, private beach, speedboats and a *dhoni*.

'We've suggested a floating base with a bar,' said Arifi. This would be offshore and a way of keeping tourists happy without upsetting local sensitivities, he believed. 'It is being considered. The current tourism minister is my classmate,' he added.

Arif and Rifga seemed pretty well connected and had left high-end jobs in IT before 'moving to the country'. Arifi's father owned a boat company. 'We would need the floating bar to have cabins on it to qualify. We've already designed a circular one with a pool.'

'We like to be creative,' Rifga chipped in. 'We want Westerners to come. In the past there were no Westerners here. Now they come and say hello.'

They were ahead of the curve, dreaming up schemes that were likely to affect future government plans for guesthouses. These, I subsequently discovered, included taking uninhabited islands and selling spaces to people such as Arif and Rifga who wanted to rent land to set up in business. Yet shiny new Asseyri was not the sole reason for my visit to the island. There was another local 'attraction' – one that does not usually draw any tourists at all.

Hanimaadhoo was home to the Maldives Climate Observatory. This was one of approximately a dozen such observatories dotted across the planet that are part of the United Nations Environmental Programme to monitor levels of 'Atmospheric Brown Cloud'. The project is coordinated from afar by two eminent scientists: Nobel Prize-winning Dutchman Paul Crutzen, whose analysis of the hole in the ozone layer earned him his award in 1995, and Dr Veerabhadran Ramanathan, renowned Indian professor of climate sciences at the Scripps Institution of Oceanography at the University of California. If you were picking a 'world eleven' football team of global warming scientists, you might put Crutzen up front in the striker's role with Ramanathan employed as a crafty winger.

Atmospheric Brown Cloud was first recorded in the Maldives in 1999. ABC is the term given to the brown haze that hangs over south and southeast Asia resulting from carbon emissions from burning fossil fuels and biomass (mainly wood used for home fires), the combustion of diesel, as well as nitrate emissions from vehicles. During the dry season, lasting between four and eight months, there is a build-up of haze as there is no rain to flush out pollutants. When the Indian summer monsoon begins, the water in clouds disperses across the brown particles carpeting the sky, which have grown in number as India has become more industrialised and wealthy on the back of its burgeoning middle class. This causes the average size of droplets to reduce. The knock-on consequence is that showers take longer to form, with clouds drifting further than usual before depositing their precious loads.

The bottom line? Rain was not falling where it was meant to. Some of these clouds were ending up as 'dirty snow' in the Himalayas. That, in turn, was causing the accelerated melting of centuries-old glaciers and altering delicate eco-systems (plus making ascents of mountains such as Everest riskier than ever). Dirty snow reflects less – and absorbs more – solar radiation, thus contributing to global warming. Add to this scenario the fact that carbon dioxide was trapping heat inside the earth's atmosphere, the greenhouse gas effect, and brown clouds were causing all sorts of trouble.

Hanimaadhoo's observatory was at the cutting edge of research into the big potential problems that many other nations in the region faced in the not too distant future. In a country as vulnerable as the Maldives to rising seas brought about by climate change, its scientists were unearthing important information about a potential nightmarish future.

Arifi and Rifga were curious about the observatory too, and offered to take me over. We bumped along a madly pot-holed road before picking up momentum on a lane with a better surface.

'I like speed!' declared Arifi, putting his foot down as we zoomed along in the Rover. He'd bought the car in Male, but had no idea how it had found its way from the UK to the middle of the Indian Ocean.

We turned down the worst track yet, juddering and creaking, and came to a halt by a sign that said: 'BURNING ANY MATERIAL AND ENGINE EXHAUST FROM THE VEHICLES WITHIN 500 METRES OF THE MALDIVES CLIMATE OBSERVATORY INTERFERES WITH THE AIR POLLUTION MONITORING PROGRAM. TO AVOID THIS REFRAIN FROM SUCH ACTIVITIES WITHIN THE AREA.'

Fruit bats flapped between the palmtops and mosquitoes stung as we followed a long path to a gate with a security hut. A guard told us we would have to wait half an hour because 'he is on his break'. Who this was, we were not sure.

We had not made an appointment. We were doing things Maldivian style.

To give us some respite from the mosquitoes, the guard let us into the observatory, where we were invited to sit at pink leather sofas positioned around a conference table. The guard stood to one side and watched us like a hawk. Computers cluttered every available worktop and book-shelves were crammed with titles such as *Aspects of Climate Variability in the Pacific and Western Americas*, *Air Quality in the Mexico Megacity: An Integrated Assessment* and *The Atmosphere: An Introduction to Meteorology*. Test tubes, flasks, pipes and monitors filled any available space not taken by screens and tomes with long titles. It was as though we'd stumbled from the jungle into a secret laboratory where plans were being made for an illicit bomb.

After a short while, we were greeted by Dr Krishnakant Bubhavant, an 'atmosphere scientist' from India with a PhD in cloud physics. He wore grey slacks and a checked shirt with a red dragon in place of the usual crocodile or polo player. He had a two-day beard and was cagey. 'I have to take permission from my HQ in Thailand,' were his first words after we asked if we could be shown round.

When he, quickly and astutely, realised we were not rival scientists coming to steal data nor about to launch a hit-and-run on the computers, he shrugged and smiled. He began telling us about his previous jobs working in South Africa and Antarctica: 'It's like a white desert: no trees, no humans, some penguins. Minus 30 °C, minus 40 °C. Horribly cold.'

'Does it glow like a diamond?' asked Rifga, who was inter-ested in all the ice and snow. 'Is it beautiful?'

'At first, but after the first three months, you get used to it,' Dr Bubhavant replied. He said it was the perfect place for scientists to research climate change, as they could literally 'see the ice caps melting'.

He paused and sighed. The experience had been 'amazing and unique for me in my life'. As well as half a year in Antarctica, he had also spent six weeks at a base in the Arctic. Dr Bubhavant gazed happily at the monitors and wall charts, looking slightly dreamy, before inviting us into a chamber full of wires and pipes.

'Air particles,' he said, snapping back in the Maldivian present. 'We check them in the filter system. Black carbon, we monitor.'

We were shown a condensation particle counter, an aethalometer and an aerodynamic particle sizer. Dr Bubhavant was completely at ease, as though taking us round his living room. He told us about the trouble the scientists had with locals burning rubbish close by, which occasionally skewed results and meant they would frustratingly have to cut the affected data. The observatory opened in 2004 and was a multimillion-dollar concern.

Dr Bubhavant took us outside to climb an observation tower. As he did, I asked what ABC and climate change meant for the Maldives. What was his own view? On the first steps of the tall blue-framed structure, he turned to Rifga and me. He had put on a pair of Blues Brothers shades, so we could not see the expression in his eyes.

'Yeah, the sea is definitely rising,' he said. 'No one can predict at exactly what rate. But some say, in the journals, that in 50 years' time half of the islands could be under water. If it continues I personally think that small islands will go under water. There will be more tsunamis and natural disasters.'

He believed that developing countries were to blame. 'They are not following the rules about carbon emissions: China and India, a large amount of pollutants.'

From the top of the tower there were marvellous views across Hanimaadhoo. The observatory was in the midst of thick jungle with a luminous green canopy that tumbled towards the sea. I had yet to see an island from this perspective. If you discounted telecommunication aerials and Male's skyscrapers, there could not have been a taller structure anywhere in the country. From the top, the ocean had three distinct bands of colour: a brilliant aquamarine by the shoreline that disappeared into a line of deep lilac. As the water spread towards the horizon the lilac darkened, turning jet black and merging into a milky-white sky. Squint your eyes a bit and nature's version of a Rothko emerged.

'Are you worried?' I asked.

'Yes! This is the future of the planet. Antarctica is melting!' He paused and wiped sweat from his brow. After the perfectly calibrated air-conditioning of inside, it was sweltering. 'It is not good for the human body either: fine particles stay inside people. That is hazardous!'

Islands squatted in the distance, looking like submarines that had risen to the surface. One of these, to the northwest, was Ultheemu. Dr Bubhavant showed us various pieces of equipment attached to the railings, including a sun-tracker radiation monitor.

'Every five minutes we are sending data via satellite to NASA from here,' he said. There were also machines measuring vapour, ozone, aerosol and photosynthetic radiation, plus a method of checking pollution levels in rain. Much of the information was 'collected and sent to the US', where it was turned into scientific reports. These reports became the basis on which we understood the extent to which the world is heating up.

Results from the lab had been a background reference in a recent speech given by President Obama on climate change, Dr Bubhavant told us. Obama had pointed out that the 12 hottest years on record had occurred in the last 15 years, and declared his intention to tackle greenhouse emissions and introduce more renewable energy. 'As a president, as a father and as an American, I am here to say we need to act,' he had said. 'I don't have much patience for anyone who denies that this challenge is real. We don't have time for a meeting of the Flat Earth Society.'

Standing on the flattest country on Earth, his words had a certain irony.

A Bust-up with Mr B

After a speed launch to Ultheemu, I took the weekly ferry to tricky-to-spell Kulhudhuffushi. The women shoppers of Ultheemu and I climbed a rickety ladder from the beach, squashing onto a narrow deck and clinging to splintered railings. It was like being on a rush-hour Tube train, with an outside possibility of a dip in the ocean thrown in (a very watery 'mind the gap').

My co-passengers wore bright headscarves and were conversing animatedly all the way. An ancient sputtering man was propped in a safe spot at the centre of the bow, protected like a precious egg. He was going for hospital treatment and had been hoisted on board by four lads. The shoppers gabbled and babbled, their bags flapping gaily in the Equatorial breeze. One of them, whom I took to be the chief gossip, said something to me in Dhivehi, causing much merriment among the other women. I grinned and she grinned back. It was a jolly journey.

We arrived at the Kulhudhuffushi docks after an hour and a quarter on the old jalopy of a *dhoni*, the smallest yet. In good spirits, after collectively admiring a crystal-clear double rainbow, we disembarked. This island was a big deal, the largest in population size in the north of the Maldives with about 9,500 inhabitants. The concrete dock ran for a hundred metres, at the end of which there were tall, rusting corrugated shelters within which *dhonis* were constructed. A dusty lot scattered with rubbish spread out from the docks to tunnel-like streets leading between thick vegetation. Of all the stop-offs so far, first impressions were the least appealing. And this unprepossessing place was where I had my first bust-up in the Maldives.

The taxi driver Mr B and I got off to a rocky start. In case he was just having a bad day, I won't give his name or even his correct initial. He was in his 50s with a chunky, bald head and inscrutable eyes that were so misty-brown I could not detect the pupils behind his heavy-framed glasses. He had a faintly bullying manner and reminded me of Robert Mugabe, minus the moustache. He was waiting by the docks and I asked him if he knew what ferries were departing that day. He wasn't sure, but speedily suggested I stay in a house on Kulhudhuffushi instead. Then, before I knew what was happening, he was on his phone arranging sleeping quarters.

After explaining I had not made up my mind yet, my 'order' was cancelled. Mr B was not pleased. His expression said: 'Typical tourist. Typical Westerner.' He raised his eyebrows and shrugged. From others nearby, however, I gleaned that a ferry to Makunudhoo would be leaving in a few hours. I knew this was the island Shuzna, Abdullah's wife, was from, so I thought I might as well go there.

With time to kill, I returned to Mr B. He gruffly agreed to show me round Kulhudhuffushi in his taxi for an hour at a rate of 200 rufiyaa (£7.70). I accepted without haggling. We drove across the dockside wasteland and down roads where the buildings had damp, cracked walls. Occasionally we would come to a pink-coloured municipal structure and Mr B would provide a succinct commentary: 'This is uni' or 'Family and children service.' I asked if there was a cashpoint nearby and he took me to a corner by a garage. A longish queue snaked to the ATM and Mr B, after indicating he would return, surprised me by disappearing with my luggage in the boot. I hoped I would see him again.

Machinery from the garage grinded and shrilled. The queue inched forwards. Although there were only about ten people ahead, each seemed to be scrutinising their bank statements in minute detail, as though investigating a fraud. Mopeds tore past. Drills screeched. The air smelt of smoke. A neighbour in the queue resignedly explained: 'It's because one person has three or four cards: they are doing it for their family. It is the only one on the island.'

After about 40 minutes, the money machine spat out some rufiyaa and I waited for Mr B. He eventually returned, with all my possessions. The hour was almost up and we speedily stopped at a knife-maker's yard, where a furnace was ablaze beneath a chimney of old oil drums. Workers squatted on stools bashing metal. Sparks flew as machetes and tuna-slicing knives took form. It was reminiscent of Vilufushi's ramshackle fish plant. Next door a couple of women were crafting rope the old way, twisting coconut husks into coir. They looked a bit startled when Mr B and I poked our heads into their doorway.

We raced back to the docks. Because of the delay, the taxi driver and I had been together for about 20 minutes out of a total period that was just over an hour. But Mr B was twitchy. He wanted 300 rufiyaa, not 200. Now, I realised that this was by no means a fortune, but irrationally or not I felt short-changed. I hadn't needed the ATM cash to pay the fare; I could have queued later and had no idea it would take so long. I gave him 500 rufiyaa and asked for 300 back. He was furious. Livid. He grabbed the note and paced away, saying he would have to find change as he did not have any.

He was gone for some time. To my surprise, though, he returned once more, whereupon he launched into a tirade.

'I know mafia!' he said, coal eyes burning. 'Mafia!'

He glared at me, looking as though he'd like to take a swing. His body had tensed and his hands tightened.

'Are you threatening me?' I asked, perhaps unhelpfully – he clearly was.

Mr B did not answer. He was enraged.

'Big mafia! Police!' he repeated.

I gave him a look to suggest: 'Go on then, get them.' He had lost it with me, why couldn't I with him? I should never have got in his cab in the first place. What is it with some taxi drivers, even the ones in paradise?

I began to walk away.

'This is bullshit!' he hissed. It was the only time I was to hear a Maldivian swear in anger.

'Bullshit! I know big mafia!'' he continued, veins seeming to burst in his neck. 'You watch out! Watch out! Mafia!'

I gave him another glance to recommend that he went and got them.

More veins emerged on Mr B's neck and a few began popping on his forehead. As they did, I left him cursing by the roadside.

Not in My Guidebook

I joined the orange-and-blue ferry to Makunudhoo, avoiding any mafia hitmen who might be lying in wait. From one of the crew I discovered I could book a room on the island for 250 rufiyaa a night, while the ferry ticket would be 25 rufiyaa (that put my taxi-driving friend in perspective). The boat rocked gently through the harbour with a few passengers and many boxes of curry-flavoured instant noodles, chocolate biscuits and packets of spaghetti. A breeze hesitated off the sea and Arabic music tinkled on a stereo as we rolled ahead. I was becoming addicted to the motion of the water.

A spindly, pensive man sitting opposite on a bench won the competition for the longest, and maybe strangest, T-shirt slogan in the Maldives: 'YOU'RE NOT YOUR JOB. YOU'RE NOT HOW MUCH MONEY YOU HAVE IN THE BANK. YOU'RE NOT THE CAR YOU DRIVE. YOU'RE NOT THE CONTENTS OF YOUR WALLET. YOU'RE THE ALL-SINGING, ALL-DANCING CRAP OF THE WORLD.' Well, well – that was a new one on me. The spindly man didn't speak English but posed for a picture, straightening his prize-winner so all the words could be read. I have never visited a country with so many messages pinned to its citizens' chests.

Waves bulged on the surging ocean. A blue tarpaulin was yanked across one side of the *dhoni* to keep out the spray. A crew hand offered sick bags round. White caps appeared on the indigo water. Another member of the crew began to work the bilge pump. The captain skilfully controlled the rudder using his feet, staring forwards with reptilian eyes beneath a baseball cap.

We paused at the island of Neykurendhoo, where many passengers disembarked. Then it was just me, an ancient fellow in a sarong, a family, the crew and the boxes of instant noodles. The water became rougher still. Afrad, who had passed out the sick bags, approached me. 'The weather is very bad. We go to Goidhoo,' he said.

He was 29, broad, dark-skinned and with a large, open face. It was his first day as a ferryman. He had previously been a yellowfin tuna fisherman, but had switched jobs so his home life would be easier. Yellowfin tuna fishing, as opposed to fishing for skipjack tuna as I had witnessed in Hulhumeedhoo, meant longer stretches at sea using pole-fishing techniques as well as hand lines.

Goidhoo wasn't mentioned in either of my guidebooks. Arriving to a 'WELCOME TO GOIDHOO' sign decorated with a leaping yellowfin, we stepped off onto a sleepy dock. A teenager dressed in purple was idly riding a purple bicycle in circles and a man was napping on a *jolie*.

Afrad and I walked to Café Kanmathi (or Corner Café), where we met the island chief, Ismail-Rasheed, and his associates. They were drinking coffee and fidgeting on mobile phones at an octagonal table beneath a palm-frond shelter. A mix of ages, some were bearded, some clean shaven. They told me that Goidhoo was famous in the Maldives for its agriculture – chillies, watermelons, cucumbers, cabbages, papayas and bananas – while fishing for yellowfin tuna and red snapper was the other main industry. The island was 160 hectares, the population about 700, even smaller than Ultheemu. There were two mosques.

'Are you a tourist?' asked a council member named Ramezz.

'Not really,' I replied, wondering how many tourists ran about with notebooks talking to island chiefs, tsunami survivors and exploited Bangladeshi workers.

'Are you a backpacker?'

'Not really,' I said; strictly speaking, I had a roll-along bag.

'Did you come by ferry?'

'Yes,' I answered. I felt as though I were going through an immigration check of sorts, although a very casual one, accompanied by Lavazza coffee, areca nuts and Camel cigarettes.

My answers, such as they were, seemed to satisfy the areca nut committee. We talked idly for a while. They had been discussing plans for Ramazan when I arrived. One of the council members said: 'After two or three days we get used to it. We feel very comfortable and fit. Some people lose weight. Some people feel faint. It is a time of much spiritual thinking...'

As he said this another council member emitted a large burp, a pronouncement that appeared to signify the end of immigration control. I was handed the key to a room around the corner to which Afrad led me (price 200 rufiyaa a night, or a taxi ride with Mr B in Kulhudhuffushi).

Golden light bathed the island. All the ferry passengers and the crew were to stay overnight on Goidhoo in the hope that the sea would be calmer in the morning. I left my room at 'Noovilu', which seemed to translate as 'Blue Villa' although it was painted green and white, tucked behind a damp coral-stone wall. I was in a family home, though there was no sign of the family apart from a few toys in the television room. The sandy street ended abruptly not far away and I found myself in what looked like a massive allotment.

Trees had been cleared and every patch of land was divided into neat, fenced-off squares and rectangles. Some of the allotment borders were marked by breeze blocks, others by sacks nailed to branches. Bent-over women in shawls tended plots of low green plants. With the help of gestures,

I asked one what she was growing. She wore a black head-scarf that must have magnified the sun's heat. Her body was covered by a leopard-print shawl and black leggings. She held a two-pronged metal earth prodder as though it were attached to her hand.

'*Karaa*,' she said, revealing purple teeth. She ushered me energetically into an allotment where there was a tall, thin scarecrow wearing a ragged robe and pointed to a basketball-sized watermelon.

I looked around the allotment and its hunched workers. How many of these dusty green basketballs were destined for the country's five-star resorts, I wondered. Were these gardens of Goidhoo where the breakfast buffets began?

She showed me a tray of white vegetables that I took to be butter squashes of some sort. They were neatly piled on a piece of blue tarpaulin. Everything was meticulously ordered.

I continued down tidy narrow lanes between allotments. Hosepipes had been plumbed in, so that just about every yard of land was irrigated. In some of the plots shiny CDs and DVDs hung from strings on sticks poking out of the rich soil, deterrents against birds. In others, I noticed odd sheets of plastic wobbling from posts above the plots. On closer inspection these turned out to be the results of X-rays. Snapped bones and dodgy knee joints waggled and twanged in the breeze. What with the scarecrows, who looked like a strange tribe of elongated Maldivian women, the CDs and the scans, it was all quite bizarre.

A shrivelled man tugged at my arm. 'Makunudhoo: *dhoni*,' he said, winking knowingly. Somehow he had got wind of the diverted ferry.

National flags rustled on poles. A half-moon smiled in the soft blue sky. Long shadows spread among the *karaa* allotments. There was a sense of well-being, contentedness and community. Had I stumbled on a utopian existence of harmony, honest work and oneness with nature, some kind of agrarian socialist dreamland?

Not quite. Beyond the allotments I came to a lane leading to a gorgeous mangrove-lined strip of beach. It was as perfect a spot as I had seen anywhere in the Maldives, with iridescent water breaking softly on sloping white sands. As I stood marvelling at the accumulation of tropical Equatorial images, a Man Who Lived on Goidhoo joined me with his child. The mangrove by the beach was made up mainly of magoo plants, he said, noticing my interest. These tangled bushes were common throughout the islands and came with clown's hand-shaped leaves. We talked about life on the island, and what he told me shattered the notion that all was blissful togetherness.

'Sex out of marriage, we have had one case this year,' he said. I'm not sure how we had got onto the subject. 'The woman was punished: flogging and one year's house arrest. She was flogged in front of the island court. Many people came to watch. It was painful. She cried. She was aged 20 or 21 years old. She was ashamed. One of the members of the court staff flogged her.'

He said all of this matter-of-factly. It was all part of sharia law, known as *sariatu* in Dhivehi, so it was proper and correct. But there was a seemingly happy ending for the woman involved: 'She married the man. The delivery of the baby happened. They were married two months later.'

How common were floggings of this sort?

'Women who have sex out of marriage, there are cases like this about once a year on average. The women are almost always aged 19 to 20,' he said.

Are the men punished?

He just shrugged his shoulders at that.

The Man Who Lived on Goidhoo was a good source of local controversy. He was short and well balanced, wearing lime-green flip-flops. Large areas of beach had disappeared and some of the coast had eroded, he said. 'Actually, this is caused by man not nature. The sand is used for construction. It is illegal.'

Violence had flared during a recent football match. Hooliganism and 'crowd trouble' had even reached the gardens of paradise. 'There was a fight during a game and four or five people were arrested. They spent ten days in prison each.'

He told me that although agriculture and fishing were important, 80 per cent of the island's income was from tourism, and 80 per cent of those aged between 18 and 40 worked in tourist resorts. Out of the population of 700, at any one time 350 to 400 people were away at resorts or else studying on other islands. In reality, most of the time the population was halved.

The Man Who Lived on Goidhoo gave me a lift on his moped back to the Corner Café, where I ate tuna, fried egg and rice under a fluorescent light. Then I returned to Noovilu, where there was still no sign of any other inhabitants, although the television had been mysteriously switched on. Someone had kindly placed a bottle of Bon Aqua mineral water on a side table next to a vase of plastic tulips. The ceiling fan clicked. Apart from that, there was silence.

Goidhoo felt like the back of beyond. I found it hard to believe that not so very far away, perhaps 60 miles as the crow flies, millionaires were clinking glasses of Cristal champagne at spa resorts in their water villas with wi-fi, hot tubs and 'senior butlers' (who might one day be island chiefs). The Oscar-winning actress Hilary Swank had recently holidayed at Soneva Fushi, 100 miles or so to the south. 'Staying here felt like I'd stepped back in time,' she had commented to a magazine. 'And it's so rare to experience that any more. Our days were spent lounging, then playing tennis and going on bike rides. I'm a big foodie and everything was exquisite: Japanese, Mexican, Italian, elixirs and fruit juices. It really hit the spot.'

There were no sushi bars, Italian restaurants, tennis courts or spas with elixirs on Allotment Island. I fell asleep listening to the steady flicker and hum of the ceiling fan, wondering if we'd make it to Makunudhoo in the morning.

On Banishment Island

The muezzin woke me at 4am. By now I was well accustomed to the strangulated, dying-cat cries. They had become, if not exactly comforting, strangely reassuring: dawn was breaking, a new day awaited.

A shower thudded on the roof of Noovilu, adding to the sense of the exotic. Water poured in torrents along gutters and down drains, sloshing, dripping, trickling, slopping. After the downpour, at 5.30am, I gathered my possessions and made my way between puddles in gloomy light to the docks. From an early-opening grocery shop, I bought Afrad and his crewmate cartons of chilled Nescafé Mochas. Then I reached the ferry, where everyone had already assembled.

All was rush, rush, rush. Five minutes later we departed, earlier than scheduled, and quickly found ourselves in heavy water. High waves enveloped the *dhoni* and the front doors to the cabin were bolted to stop water gushing in. Up and down we went, with an occasional crash on a big swell. The sun was a burning orange orb, turning the horizon flamingo pink. Yet while the heavens may have been heavenly, our matchbox ferry did not feel that way. Salt water lapped at my feet. Passengers looked anxious. Crew rearranged luggage so it would not slide into the sea. A child was sick.

An hour passed, perhaps more. Makunudhoo was separated from the rest of the Maldives by a channel and was the nation's most westerly point. The sea settled, slightly, as we approached a narrow passage flanked with flags on posts. For a moment I imagined what must have gone through the minds of François Pyrard and the crew of the *Corbin* when they heard the crunch of hull on reef. Looking out it was clear: you wouldn't stand a chance thrown into the sea out there.

The ferry threaded into the harbour, passing moored *dhonis*, one of which, I noticed, was named *JIHAD*. Contemplating the implications of that, I arrived at one of the remotest spots in the country.

Traditionally Maldivian sultans would banish their enemies to distant islands from where they could cause little nuisance; when they chose not to dispose of their bodies at high sea, that is. During Pyrard's time in the early 1600s the practice was commonplace. Many of the favoured islands for such banishment were in the south, across the One and Half Degree and South Equatorial channels. The extremely isolated Fuvammulah Atoll was a particularly good place for a foe. Another, in the north, was Makunudhoo, famous for its isolation and feared reef that worried the skipper of the ferry so much that we had stopped over at Goidhoo to wait out the storm.

Banishment to remote islands was still used as an alternative punishment to incarceration in the Maldives. Goidhoo as well as Makunudhoo had been selected in sentencing; those who were sent could move freely within the islands but not leave them.

Former president Gayoom had been banished to Makunudhoo in 1973 by his predecessor, Ibrahim Nasir. At the time, Gayoom was something of a bright young thing. He had recently returned from university in Egypt and was working in the government fishing department. The 1970s were years of great change as tourism was just beginning in the country. Spies working for Nasir allegedly overheard Gayoom discussing in private his dissatisfaction with the president's handling of the new influx of foreigners. The question of where all the tourist cash was going was much on people's minds (as it still was). It was also the time when there was concern that hippy backpackers and other such undesirables with little money to spend would come from India and Sri Lanka, upsetting Muslim sensibilities. Gayoom, who had gained a degree in Islamic Law and Studies in Cairo, was put under house arrest before being sent to Makunudhoo, where he stayed for four months.

'It is a very nice island,' he said in an interview. 'True it is cut off from the rest of the country, but it is a very clean island. People are industrious; it's a fishing island. People are good.' He had his clothes washed for him and meals cooked by a local family, and he admitted that his banishment had been 'almost like a holiday'. This enforced break had, ironically, stood him in good stead. While an amnesty after Nasir's 're-election' for another term in office meant that Gayoom's visit was brief, his time as a banished rebel increased his popularity, partly leading to his eventual rise to power in 1978 (Nasir escaped to Singapore after being nudged from high office, never to return, having the main international airport posthumously named after him in 2011).

Both Pyrard and H.C.P. Bell had also stopped by in Makunudhoo for single nights. Pyrard said little other than that the sailors feared continuing in the dark through the notoriously treacherous waters. Meanwhile, Bell noted: 'According to native information many ships have been lost on its barren reefs with all hands, scarcely a vestige of the wrecks remaining after a few hours, from the violence of the surf and the perpendicular sides of the reef.'

The island was the only one inhabited in the Makunudhoo Atoll, which was 15 miles long and 3 miles wide and had once been known by the British in the Admiralty Chart as the Malcolm Atoll, named after Sir Charles Malcolm, superintendent of the Bombay Marine in the 1800s.

I felt a little as though I had been banished myself as I jumped onto the dock. Great slabs of concrete with bits of metal poking out were stacked next to a Maldivian Democratic Party poster showing plans for a new harbour. From the cartoon-style drawings, it appeared as though a perfect new world was coming soon with well-organised moorings, fishing farms, processing plants and cheerful guesthouses with sunshades and waiters.

A solitary mechanical digger was scraping at rocks on a breakwater. Otherwise, there was little evidence of the coming transformation, apart from the bright poster and the slabs of concrete.

My ferry friend Afrad had phoned ahead to a contact with a spare room. Mohamed Shakir was wearing a crisp white polo shirt with the label of an upmarket resort and chinos. He had an efficient, organised air and a steady gaze. He had worked at the five-star resort advertised on his polo shirt for ten years and was now aged 39. I was soon balancing precariously on the back of his moped as we puttered beyond a silver-trunked tree decorated with pink and blue plastic flowers in the yard of the succinctly named Income Café.

Down dusty, deserted streets we went, Mohamed Shakir bellowing: '55 million rufiyaa! The new harbour will be very expensive! Democracy is very new! It will take a long time for people to understand it!' We made a sharp turn, my bag almost flying off.

The island had nine fishing boats, Mohamed Shakir boomed, as we zoomed down a coral-stone alley. Yellowfin tuna was the main catch. Makunudhoo's council consisted of five members, two of whom were from the conservative religious party Adhaalath, two from the Progressive Party of Maldives led by Gayoom's half-brother, Abdulla Yameen Abdul Gayoom, and one from the Maldivian Democratic

Party. The population was 1,634. All of this was conveyed above the putter of the engine. The last tourists Mohamed Shakir could remember visited in 2010: 'Two Russians came on safari boat! They went for swim on beach!'

His house was aquamarine with sky-blue window frames and a zigzag pattern of tinted and clear glass panes. It had a well-brushed sandy yard and was on a corner not far from the lime-green and canary-yellow Income Grocery Shop. Makunudhooians seemed switched on about the bottom line; they also appeared to love vibrant colours. I was led to an *undoli*, a swinging bed under a lilac awning fluttering with pink PPM flags. I sat on this and rested for a while.

Mohamed disappeared and a woman in a scarlet outfit with a crescent moon and flowers pattern came to regard me. She stood, hands on hips and staring at the *undoli* with a puffy, quizzical expression. I nodded hello and wondered what she was thinking.

As she continued her inspection, Mohamed Shakir returned. 'My mother, my mother!' he explained. Her eyes flickered 'hello' and she departed. Mohamed joined me on the swinging seat.

'Very very peace here. Our geography is very separate. Very very happy life. No drugs. No fighting,' he said, before adding. 'But not available, jobs.'

Mohamed Shakir had been an electrical engineering supervisor at his resort. He had enjoyed the lifestyle among the tourists and had had good food and accommodation. He had, however, missed his wife. Such absences were common among Maldivians. Cash from resort jobs was welcomed but the price, invariably, was a disjointed family life. That was just the way it was on these remotest of paradise islands.

We walked to the beach, where we hung out (literally) on *jolies* jangling from plastic cords attached to banyan trees.

Mohamed Shakir told me that we were on the south side of the island and that there were two communities: one on the south, the other on the north. Because it was so isolated, imports were expensive. In case someone fell suddenly ill and needed treatment, there was an emergency speedboat for trips to the main hospital on Male. Where we were sitting looking out to the horizon, there had once been 200 feet more of land. He remembered playing football on the disappeared sand when he was a child. Now it was 'gone, gone'. The island had, luckily, been unaffected by the 2004 tsunami.

As we swung gently in the wind, I learnt that his grandmother and mother had gone on *hajj* in Saudi Arabia: 'It was 72,000 rufiyaa for one person!' That's about £2,800. 'For one person!' He turned his head in his *jolie* and looked at me with raised eyebrows that suggested a pilgrimage to Mecca was on the pricey side.

I asked him if he'd been abroad himself.

'Sri Lanka,' he replied.

'Did you like it?' I sensed he was a fan of all things Makunudhoo and a little wary of life beyond the reef.

'I found it hard to eat,' he commented, pulling a face and then laughing: 'Ha! Ha! Ha! Ha! Ha! Not clean and bad smell. Things are very dirty. Dogs and these kind of things,' he continued. 'Ha! Ha! Ha! Ha! Ha!'

Mohamed Shakir found it amusing just thinking of the Sri Lankans with their strange ways.

'Do you not like dogs?' I asked, to see what reaction this would draw.

He shook his head and cackled: 'Ah! Ha! Ha! Ha! Ha! Ha!'

We were getting on fine. Mohamed Shakir always seemed to be in a good mood.

In his chinos and white polo shirt, he reminded me of a golfer. We paced around what there was to see of the island as though searching for a ball on a fairway. I felt a bit like his caddy. There was the garish red-green-blue Ummeedhee (Dream) School, a derelict fish-processing plant, and a group of athletic islanders on the north side of the island playing volleyball to an extremely high standard. Rallies would last 30 shots and there was something mesmerising about watching the players' skilful, elastic leaps to flick up the ball. Cries of jubilation rang out at each point won.

A handful of boys in their early teens were playing in the surf near the docks. They appeared flabbergasted to see a Westerner and came over to the 'white man'.

'I cannot remember another one like you,' said one of the boys. 'Not here.'

Another said: 'Twenty years ago. I heard that others came. They went to uninhabited island and cooked sea cucumbers.'

They peered at me as though counting my arms, legs and fingers to check everything was the same beyond the Makunudhoo reef.

Mohamed Shakir said that although I was unusual, I was not a 'total freak as they understand now as they watch television'.

I was glad to hear this. I asked the boys what they wanted to do in life and one said he hoped to be a dive instructor, another a resort 'front office manager', the third a fisherman, and the last a policeman. I tried to put myself in their shoes, living on an island on the edge of a big blue sea filled with swirling currents and razor-sharp reefs. I'd probably have wanted to be a resort dive instructor or work the front desk at a plush resort, if fishing for yellowfin or keeping the peace wasn't for me. I'd have had the same dreams too.

'The illusion of omniscience'

On the death of Patrick Leigh Fermor in 2011, Ben Macintyre, a colleague of mine on *The Times*, had mused about the place of travel writing in an age when it was so simple and affordable to jet around the globe. I had the cutting of this article with me; I'd used it as my bookmark for *A Time of Gifts*. On the one hand, Macintyre argues, the facility of getting about meant that old-style travel-writing adventures were a thing of the past.

'The world is simply too small, too fast, too well trodden to admit of such leisurely, civilised wandering,' he writes. 'The jumbo jet enabled any traveller to reach the four corners quickly and cheaply. The internet brought the world to your room. There are no spaces on the map to be filled in, no place that Google Earth has not seen already. The empty quarters and forbidden cities are full of tourists, and open to all.'

All of this was true. I later checked and, unbelievably, there was Makunudhoo on Google Earth. I fancied I could make out the aquamarine roof of Mohamed Shakir's house. You could also catch a cheap flight to visit the Maldives. I had done just that, with a few rocky ferries at the other end to get to where I was now.

Macintyre continues that literary travellers such as Leigh Fermor, Eric Newby, Norman Lewis, Jan Morris and Wilfred Thesiger had been followed by adventuring scribes in the 1970s and 1980s such as Bruce Chatwin, Paul Theroux and Jonathan Raban, who had taken advantage of the early days of easier methods of getting about. Yet as budget flights and greater disposable income opened up the globe to almost all, an era of travel for the sake of travel had begun. This had led to temporary disillusionment in American travel writer Theroux, who complained of hackery and 'literary self-indulgence, dishonest complaining, creative mendacity, pointless heroics and chronic posturing'.

In his most recent book, *The Last Train to Zona Verde* about an overland journey from Cape Town to Angola, Theroux goes further. I had brought the book with me and was enjoying his description of his dusty and difficult passage northwards: tussles with border officials, scrimmages for seats on early-morning buses, breakdowns in the depths of the bush. In his 70s, Theroux is contemplative about his continuing urge to explore wild frontiers, wondering: 'what perverse aspect of my personality was I indulging?'

His conclusion, after a lifetime on the move, is memorable. 'Reading and restlessness – dissatisfaction at home, a sourness at being indoors, and a notion that the real world was elsewhere – made me a traveler,' he writes. 'If the internet were everything it is cracked up to be, we would all stay at home and be brilliantly insightful. Yet with so much contradictory information available, there is more reason to travel than ever before: to look closer, to dig deeper, to sort the authentic from the fake; to verify, to smell, to touch, to taste, to hear, and sometimes – importantly – to suffer the effects of this curiosity.'

This struck me as spot on. And Macintyre is of the same opinion. He believes that the 'illusion of omniscience' offered by the internet makes visiting far-flung corners of the world more rewarding than ever.

I rocked on the *ungoli* in Mohamed Shakir's garden thinking about Makunudhoo. Being on such an isolated island had made me analyse why I had chosen to go to the peripheries of paradise in the first place. After all, this atoll had been until recently, and in theory under Maldivian law still was, a place of banishment. What had motivated me to come all this way?

The answer was simple: I wanted to follow my nose, to let loose ends lead the way and take me to places with stories and experiences that only travel could bring. Sure, there were Google spies in the skies, lurking even above this remotest of places. Let them lurk. They weren't down by the rumble of waves on the reef, listening to the birdsong in the magoos, feeling the salty, humid air in the shade of a breadfruit tree.

Well, not yet, at least.

Party Time

I was about to go to a party. The Maldivians, as I was soon to discover, know how to throw a bash. I was staying on a mattress on the floor of Mohamed Shakir and his wife Nageeba's lilac-coloured spare room, and he had casually mentioned an event was planned that evening. His manner suggested a few neighbourhood friends might be popping round.

At dusk Mohamed told me the get-together was about to begin, although there seemed to be no one about. Where were the guests? He led me outside and I put on my flip-flops. In the yard, Nageeba and the couple's 2-year-old son were playing. Nageeba had dressed in a dark outfit with a double stripe of electric-blue fabric, her hair wrapped in an elegant black headscarf. The boy wore chino shorts as though he was preparing for the day he could put on full-length golf-style chinos like his father.

'Tom-be,' said Nageeba, introducing me to the boy. 'Tom-be.'

It seemed as though my name had been adapted to a Maldivian version.

The party began a short walk away at a crossroads of two dirt lanes where pink Progressive Party of Maldives bunting was festooned from trees and lampposts. The lanes had been cordoned off with more bunting, and a building with pink walls had been opened up to reveal the office HQ of the PPM. Everything seemed to be the colour of seaside rock candy.

Tangerine plastic chairs had been placed at the centre of the crossroads. To one side, two trestle tables were loaded with a steaming array of well-charcoaled fish speared with wooden sticks and placed on wide green leaves that acted as a tablecloth. The smell of red snapper, grouper and jack-fish infused the humid evening air. The fishermen of the neighbourhood had put aside much of their day's catch. Party-goers gravitated towards the trestle tables, as though drawn by the tempting aromas.

Nobody touched the fish.

The sun had fallen and spotlights illuminated the junction. I was led to a row of roadside plastic chairs, occupied by elderly men and women. I sat there and a woman brought me a glass of juice. I was told by a neighbour that I was at a *ma hefu*, an event organised in the run-up to Ramazan. Each visitor to the party had contributed a gift of bottles of juice or water, or jellies for pudding, steamed rice, casseroles and salads. Bongo and drum music with a melody sung by a man with a happy, wobbly voice played noisily on a stereo. Distinguished gentlemen with sticks and sarongs, and women wearing glittery brooches, nodded to me. Then, like jockeys positioning before a big race, they moved towards the tables.

Nobody touched the fish.

I talked to another man named Mohamed who said he had two wives; Maldivian men may by law have as many as four wives, though most have just one. He said that one of his wives, who was in her mid-40s, lived in London where she worked in a hospital. His second wife lived on Makunudhoo and was aged 36. He smiled contentedly, looking pleased by this set of circumstances. A chattering crowd now hovered at the crossroads. I could feel the sense of anticipation.

Nobody touched the fish.

Then, responding to some signal that had passed me by, everyone did indeed touch the fish... with gusto. There was a great deal of fish touching.

The method was either to grab a stick with the whole fish attached and claim it as your own, or to tear chunks of flesh and add the fish to plastic plates. There were no implements provided for cutting; you merely ripped flesh from the bones using your hands. Two-wife Mohamed showed me how. The occasion was a free-for-all and that was the joy of it. There was jostling and use of elbows. Hesitation was punished: the grouper would be gone! Slabs of red snapper were snatched. Haunches of Napoleon fish were hurried away. Bulbous creatures I had never seen in restaurants disappeared in the blink of an eye.

Then it began to rain. Not a drizzle, not steady rain, not even a shower: a torrential outburst. The fish-eaters, myself included, were taken by surprise, soaked in seconds. We dived for shelter and I ended up in a nearby house with two strangers, an elderly couple. The husband was an imam, waif-like with a gimlet eye, goatee and gold watch. He offered me some rice to go with my damp, steaming fish. He told me he had once been a fisherman and that he was pleased with the day's attendance at the mosque; 150 people had turned up. His wife remained silent and gave me some noodles. We were standing in their kitchen; they seemed to have planned to make an escape, whether it had rained or not. The table had been laid for the two of them.

The downpour ended and I returned outside where there was a muddy pond-sized puddle at the junction. The men had simultaneously lit up and a fug of smoke hung in the air. A few dabbled with puddings of jelly, but the main eating was over. The spinal bones of tropical fish glistened on the otherwise empty trestle tables.

And that was how a *ma hefu* went.

I relished my time on Makunudhoo; not quite off Google Earth, but definitely on its outer edges. I would go for long walks, read on a hanging *jolie* by the beach, or take dips in the remarkably calm water off white sand beaches. This was Robinson Crusoe with an en suite room and the occasional feast.

One day Afrad joined me for a swim. We walked a long distance down the soft sand, hermit crabs scurrying into holes where they would peer out with claws raised like boxers putting up a defence. We reached what Afrad described as a 'nice zone, eh?' It was, he said, the best beach on Makunudhoo.

It was perfect. The water was cool with rippling eddies. Schools of green tiddlers led to beasts with black spots and purple streaks. Flickers of yellow sped among clusters of coral with spiky appendices. The sound of crunching tinkled in the calm blue sea – fish nipping the coral. I swam in a crawl out in the direction of the reef. Crimson and vivid green fish darted in the depths. The sun cast shards of light through plankton. A shadow – a turtle, a shark? – plunged towards the reef's breaking waves.

Afterwards, we strolled back along the beach and the phrase that some ultra five-star hotels in the Maldives and other high-class sun, sand and flop destinations promise sprang to mind: "no shoes, no news" (though whether they really do with most people's smartphone twitchiness is not so certain). On Makunudhoo there really was no need for shoes – and the only news on its best beach was of scuttling crabs and shadows in the deep. Afrad took me to his small coral-stone house and introduced me to his wife. We sat in an immaculate courtyard by a fruit tree covered with a fishing net to fend off crows. His house was next to where an old fish-processing plant had once been. Afrad plucked a pale white fruit shaped like a bell pepper from the tree. It was juicy and tasted of apples and celery. His wife gave me a glass of squash.

'This is rainwater,' Afrad said. The water had been collected in a tank off the roof of the house. He sat close to his wife, and silence fell for a while.

'I am happy now,' he muttered, seeming to refer to his new job as a ferryman. He could see more of his wife, not sailing for days in pursuit of yellowfin tuna. 'I'm happy now,' he repeated, as though his thoughts were slipping out as words.

The Resort Workers

Makunudhoo was a perfect spot for a banishment: even those with tickets to leave found it difficult to escape. High winds had already caused delays and on the morning of my supposed departure, word came from the ferry's captain. 'Too strong, too strong!' summarised Mohamed Shakir, who went to investigate on my behalf. Moody lead-grey clouds rose like witches' hats on the horizon. Passengers began pleading: 'Cappi! Cappi!'

This seemed to be Dhivehi nickname for 'captain', who was sensibly hiding well away from view on the far side of the deck.

While we waited, Mohamed Shakir stood with me complaining about the lack of 3G coverage on Makunudhoo; the internet-whenever-you-want-it was apparently coming to Banishment Island soon, but there had been delays. He also moaned about the island's electricity supply: only one of the three generators was working and this last source of power was partly broken. There had been several blackouts. 'Every day we have to stop the generator. Here we do not have available two things: oil and ice. Once a week there is a delivery, diesel for the generator. And for ice, fishing boats have to go very far.'

The Cappi eventually relented, partly due to pressure to take yet another elderly man to hospital for urgent treatment. The ill man was hacking violently, drooling and being supported by family members. I wondered if he would last the journey.

Mohamed Shakir and I said goodbye and the ferry eased out of the harbour, with Afrad and a fellow crew member standing stock still on the bow. Their left arms were tucked behind their backs and their feet were splayed apart, a heron-like posture that appeared to be the best for reef spotting. The Cappi would follow their signals.

The passage to Kulhudhuffushi was rocky. By the time we arrived, via several stops, the ferry was packed to the rafters. The passenger next to me clung to a cage full of jittery budgerigars, their song drowned out by the engine. The elderly coughing man was, I was pleased to see, still alive. We filed away and I spent an afternoon at the Green Bite Café waiting for the overnight boat to Male, Mr B and his mafia associates nowhere to be seen.

The Male ferry was not exactly a beauty: a white hulk of a vessel with rusty streaks on the hull and simple sleeping quarters in cabins above a cargo hold. I had booked a 'bed', which consisted of a thin sponge mattress with a thick green plastic covering. My berth was squeezed into one end of a long row on A deck. The mattress was about two feet wide and six feet long – almost exactly coffin-shaped. Just about every space on the morgue-like deck was taken by sleeping berths, apart from two narrow walkways along which passengers negotiated the occasional protruding foot. Fans angled downwards from a pea-green ceiling.

I could hardly grumble. The journey to Male was 170 miles and I had paid 800 rufiyaa (£31) for bed and passage. I had been lucky enough to secure a last-minute place thanks to a charming Kulhudhuffushi taxi driver – they did exist – whom I had met at the Green Bite Café. Mohamed Ali was a balding former merchant seaman with a well-weathered face and a worldly air who had visited Gibraltar, Argentina, Rotterdam and London.

'Very cold, very big,' he commented of Britain's capital. His favourite place in the world was Montreal: 'Very, very,

very nice!' The boat people of the Maldives certainly got about.

Drifting south had a dream-like quality. Once on board the *Faalhu* (which means 'everyone knows' in Dhivehi, a fellow passenger told me) there was little to do but to sit on the sloping roof of A deck and watch the curling, caterpillar islands come and go. Some of those with the cheapest tickets were on this roof, where I found them lounging at sunset between extractor fans and air-conditioning units (B deck had a/c). The horizon seemed to have caught fire, turning into a yolk-coloured furnace. The sky beyond was peach, scarlet and shades of grey where rain clouds had formed. A pleasant wind from the motion of the ferry sliced through the heat.

The journey consisted of chatter (of people) and hum (of engine). I had decided to keep a low profile – I was the only Westerner among the 170 passengers – but the Maldivians are full of curiosity.

On the roof I met character after character. Hassan, a 19-year-old dive instructor, worked at a high-end resort that regularly attracted celebrity guests. 'I remember one Russian who came with his wife for a week,' he told me. 'He sent his wife back and brought his girlfriends: maybe three of them. He would smoke cigars and drink champagne. Actually he was a very chubby man. He never went to the dive centre.'

Hassan was as fit as a dolphin and seemed a little aggrieved at the Russian's womanising luck. His friend Ahmed, a watersports instructor, got onto the hot topic of tips. 'One Italian man, he gave me 400 dollars for a week,' he said, although there were some notoriously stingy guests: 'There was another Italian. He stayed with us for six months! He used to have four or five computers in his room. But he would allow no room-boy. Nobody could go in except the cleaner. My friend was the cleaner. He gave no tip to anyone for six months until right at the end. Then he gave my friend 10 dollars!'

The rooftop resort workers, either sitting cross-legged or lying out using bags as pillows, emitted a round of jokey sighs and gestures: Westerners! Ahmed sipped his Red Bull and Abdullah, a worker in a hotel kitchen, took over. A friend of his had had better luck: 'There was this Arabic guy. Very rich with two childs and wife. He would spend lots of time on private boat. For two hours it was costing him 4,000 dollars. He would give the three-person crew 1,000 dollars if they ever saw manta rays or whale sharks – 333 dollars for two hours' work!'

The vast gap in wealth between tourists and Maldivians seemed to be so engrained and normal it rarely appeared to be questioned, merely marvelled at when extremes were too obvious to ignore. I asked the group if they ever felt frustrated at the disparity.

'I don't feel anything,' said Hassan bluntly.

'Don't you mind when some guests are rude and flash their cash?' I asked, trying to prompt a response.

'Yeah, sometimes,' was all I could draw him to say. Abdullah's only comment was: 'It's too expensive: people spend lots of money.'

There seemed to be little danger of a Marxist Maldivian Front taking up the cudgels on behalf of workers' rights.

That said, there was occasional 'trouble' that suggested stirrings of discontent. The Tourism Employees Association of Maldives (TEAM) represented workers and was often outspoken in its condemnation of employers' treatment of staff. A recent case in which three workers had been dismissed from Sheraton's Full Moon Resort on Kaafu Atoll had provoked a mini-uprising, with four employees who had backed their colleagues being arrested. They too were sacked. TEAM argued that those who had initially lost their jobs had been targeted for dismissal, as they were trade union leaders on the island who were about to negotiate with management for higher wages. This incident came after unrest at the One&Only Reethi Rah on Baa Atoll. More than 90 per cent of staff had taken part in demonstrations that could have led to a full-blown strike over alleged ill-treatment and poor pay. Police had been dispatched to monitor the situation, which had subsequently calmed, although it was unclear whether workers' demands had been met. At both the Sheraton and the One&Only, management said that they were negotiating with staff and that guests' experiences had not been affected.

In reaction to the incidents, the secretary general of TEAM, Mauroof Zakhir, was quoted in a report on *Minivan News* saying that resorts should not call in police unless there had been a violation of the law. The arrival of armed officers was likely to intimidate workers who were simply sticking up for themselves, he believed. Fear of losing precious jobs might cause employees with legitimate requests to back down. However, pointing out that a quarter of the politicians in the People's Majlis, the Maldivian parliament, were resort owners (a figure I found difficult to verify), Zakhir was realistic: 'It is unlikely anything will come out of parliament that will give protection to the workers.'

On the roof of the *Faalhu*, about 30 Maldivians, and possibly Bangladeshis, lay soaking up the day's final rays. Most were probably resort staff. At least 26,000 people were employed in the country's tourist industry.

Minivan News was, I discovered, a great source of information on resort workers. Stories suggested that bargaining positions with bosses were weakening. A new law had been passed making it illegal to take any action that might incite fear among tourists or to call for a tourism boycott. The interpretation of what might constitute 'fear' was unclear, yet the fine for transgressions was as much as 150,000 rufiyaa (over £5,000). Zakhir feared that resort owners, in conjunction with the police, were also unfairly using clauses in a Freedom of Peaceful Assembly Act to clamp down on any sort of worker gathering whatsoever.

Behind the scenes at the five-star resorts, a lot was clearly going on. Up on the *Faalhu*, though, all of this seemed a long way from the reality of people's lives. Adam, who had switched off his iPod to listen to the others' stories, told me he had been earning US$12,000 a year, a decent wage. He had, however, set his sights on Egypt, where he believed he could make even more as a dive instructor in the Red Sea.

Adam also said he had been working at a resort where the owners had ignored local advice and built the main jetty on the windward side of the island. They had done this so that the shape of the resort would fit the European architect's designs. There had, however, been a problem. 'Waves smashed down the jetty,' he explained. 'It was bound to happen. We all knew. They had built a treehouse bar next to the jetty. This was ruined too: covered in sea water.' Many of the water villas at the resort had also been smashed by waves, as the architect had failed to take account of the force of the ocean.

Hassan, Ahmed, Abdullah and Adam had a bit of a chuckle about this. It was as close to rebelliousness as they would come in my presence.

Others, however, were more outspoken. One reservations manager, speaking of life under the regime of Gayoom, said: 'He really caused hell in the country. Even if anyone said anything about him: straight to jail. I remember once that there was the case of a person in a restaurant in Male.

He said to a waiter: "This rice is too hard!" Someone over-heard him. *Raees* means president in Dhivehi. Somebody misunderstood and reported him. He was taken straight to a police station.'

Another told me in confiding tones: 'Most Maldivian men in the tourist industry do drink, but we're not allowed to. Including me. Yes, I do drink, but my mother doesn't know!'

A companion of his said: 'There was this Russian in the presidential suite: 17,500 dollars a night. He had three girl-friends with him the whole time, but they were changed each week. For every girl he would buy the most expensive thing in the shop. I think he was mafia. I seriously think he was mafia. He would say to the cleaner: "Call me God!" He was very demanding. Everything had to be done perfectly. Oh my God! But he paid for it, so we did what we were told.' He made it clear he was less than impressed by such osten-tation and ambivalent ways. The Russians had really got a name for themselves among the Maldivian workforce.

When the sun dropped I descended the ladder to A deck and lay on my green foam mattress. Despite my coffin space I fell asleep instantly, managing to ignore a passenger to my right who was dozing with his eyes three-quarters open. I'd never seen anything like it before. All that was on view were the whites of his eyes, which looked like poached eggs. Beyond him a woman in a burqa lay next to her skull-capped husband. The sexes were, surprisingly, mixed.

I slept for some time before feeling a tap. It was Three-Quarter Eyes.

'Feeding,' he said, pointing to his mouth.

We went downstairs to a galley near a giant pile of flip-flops; mine were amid the jumble. Here we were served large portions of steaming chicken curry with fluffy white rice, a hot chilli and garlic sauce, and a carrot and cabbage salad. All was included in the price. I ate my curry sitting on a polystyrene box that probably contained iced fish. Then I returned to mattress A-20 and faced the wall to avoid seeing Three-Quarter Eyes. The lights went out ten minutes after dinner, and so did I.

After sleeping for seven hours, at 4.30am I sat up abruptly, blinkingly taking in A deck. There was a refugee boat quality to the scene with all the bodies scattered about. Dozens of us were lying there, snoring and occasionally coughing. Women had pulled headscarves over their faces as a form of curtain. Yet although the *Faalhu* was definitely 'roughing it' compared to most people's idea of a trip to the Maldives, I had had one of the deepest sleeps I could remember.

I carefully stepped over outstretched limbs. Outside was pitch black. I mistakenly entered a prayer room believing it was the bathroom, before coming to the bridge. The captain and his assistants sat on swivel stools. A man who turned out to be the chief cashier was in charge of a stall selling XL energy drinks and salt-and-vinegar crisps.

We were travelling at 11.8 knots. The chief cashier kindly made me a cup of black coffee. No one else was about, apart from the odd bearded man who entered the prayer room, from which I could hear a faint moan of worship. The cashier told me the *Faalhu* was 85 feet long, though it was too early for him to be very talkative.

Male appeared in the distance, a series of orange dots with red lights blinking on its tombstone-like tower blocks. Airport Island was to the west, a sodium glare with a pulsing radar tower. Ebony water fizzed past the hull. Gradually, the outline of the capital emerged against a thin blue sky. Motionless clouds hung above, as though waiting for daylight before waking and moving on. The closer we came to

Male the more ghost-like it became, a lost world coming into focus after the many tiny uninhabited islands the *Faalhu* had passed during the night.

Members of the crew emerged, smoking by the bow. The captain yelled orders. With dawn breaking, we turned into the crowded harbour. Deck hands splashed overboard and swam with ropes so they could be gathered on shore or on the decks of other ships, allowing our vessel to be pulled into place. It was chaos. A crew member on another ship tumbled backwards pulling a rope and fell into the sea, prompting much laughter. Various tugs of war ensued, the teams yanking with all their might.

'Is it always like this?' I asked a neighbour.

'Always,' he replied.

Mountains of cargo stood near the docks forming a patchwork of maroon, brown, jade and blue. We crept forth passing the *King Marine* and the *Vidhuvaru* ('lightning' in Dhivehi). The *Faalhu* was equal in size or bigger than almost all the others.

My companion told me he was a businessman involved in importing between Male and the north. He was on a trip to collect 'kitchen items: kettles, plates, mugs, knives – so many things'.

He looked like a sharp customer. I asked him how his company was doing.

'Not rich yet,' he said, laughing. 'Trying to get rich!'

Light rose pink and orange as the *Faalhu* slipped slowly into the docks. By some miracle of ropes and endeavour, the ferry edged backwards into a slot by the dock no wider than its girth. The night boat had returned to the capital, with its skyscrapers and hustlers, movers and shakers.

And I was about to meet some of the biggest shakers of them all.

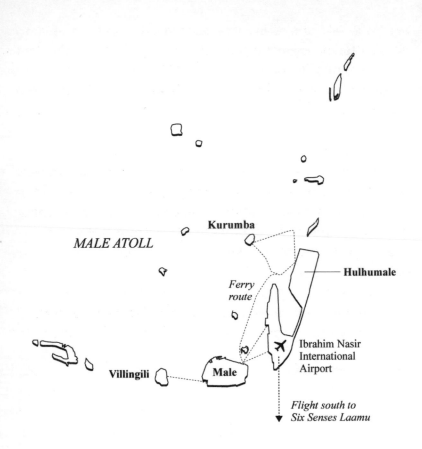

MALE ATOLL

Kurumba

Hulhumale

Ferry route

Ibrahim Nasir
International
Airport

Villingili

Male

*Flight south to
Six Senses Laamu*

PART FOUR
Talking Politics

An interview with an exiled man who says he was
tortured during the rule of former president Gayoom
and witnessed murders by prison guards, a meeting with
Gayoom himself on Male, an interview with
Mohamed Nasheed – and a posh hotel or two

*'Once a priest, always a priest; once a mason, always
a mason; but once a journalist, always and for ever
a journalist.'*
Rudyard Kipling

The Torture Victim

A month or so before leaving for the Maldives, I was standing by the bronze statue of Sherlock Holmes near Marylebone Tube in London. Vehicle horns blared. White van men switched lanes and tailgated, so close to the vehicles ahead they looked as though they were being towed. Double-decker buses shifted gear. Cyclists darted and weaved. A siren wailed. A pelican crossing bleeped. Exhaust fumes rose to a cindery sky. Tourists streamed in the direction of the watermelon-shaped dome of Madame Tussauds.

I had come to the statue to meet a man who had given up on the Maldives. His name was Naushad Waheed and he was the brother of the country's president at the time of my visit, Dr Mohammed Waheed Hassan. We had arranged to meet for coffee to talk about why Naushad had become disillusioned with the Indian Ocean idyll of so many honeymoon brochures.

Naushad arrived late, wearing a yellow short-sleeved checked shirt and faded jeans. He was short in stature and had a moustache, hooded eyelids and an avuncular manner. For some reason that was hard to pinpoint, perhaps because we were at a station, he made me think of a old-fashioned railway guard. He apologised for his train being delayed, just as a railway guard might, and we went in search of a post office. He had a letter to send with a document to a Maldivian friend living in Bristol who was travelling back soon. The paperwork related to the forthcoming presidential election: he was requesting permission to be an observer of the vote at the Maldivian High Commission in London, and the document needed to be delivered in person to the correct department in Male.

Mission accomplished, we found a Starbucks and sat in a downstairs room by a sign saying 'MAKING A CUP OF COFFEE IS AN ART'. Sipping on a latte, Naushad told me he was a professional painter and cartoonist. His occupation, after a period working as a civil servant and playing in the main football league on Male (as a defender for Club Valencia), had landed him in trouble. A political cartoon critical of the regime had been brought to the attention of the authorities during the rule of former president Gayoom. This and other such 'disloyalty' – the various charges included treason, theft and terrorism – had resulted in eight spells in prison, the longest stretch from 2002 to 2006, after which he, his wife and two children moved to Britain for safety.

During the Gayoom regime, both Naushad and his Stanford University-educated brother Dr Waheed had been involved in the opposition, to varying degrees. And when multi-party democracy arrived in 2008, with the Maldivian Democratic Party taking over, Dr Waheed was appointed Vice President, while Naushad was made Deputy High Commissioner in London.

For a while all went well during a golden period of 'people power'. However, this came to an abrupt halt in February 2012, when Dr Waheed took over from ousted president Nasheed; though many regarded him as a 'puppet' leader, a temporary figurehead put in place until the real players behind the upheaval took a stronger grip on power. There was a widespread belief that the Gayoom family would eventually, somehow, come out on top once more.

Never in my wildest dreams had I thought I would become so embroiled in Maldivian politics. Nevertheless, the almost Shakespearean relationship between Naushad and Dr Waheed had really caught my attention – perhaps not quite

Claudius and Hamlet, no stabbings or poison forced down anyone's throat, yet pointed and poignant in its own way.

When they were young, Naushad in his teens and Dr Waheed in his mid-20s, their mother had found herself in trouble with the regime and had been arrested. Naushad described what happened. 'I saw her dragged out of her house by the police,' he said calmly. 'While she was chatting with some of her friends at home, she had said that she believed that President Nasir was better than Gayoom. One of her friends reported this. That is why the police came. Officers took her through the streets to the police station. Some people were throwing stones and spitting on her as she was led there. People supporting the regime did this. Thugs. I saw this and so did my brother. He was by the front gate when they took her. They wanted to shame her. She was kept in the police station one night and brought back home. I think they took her to the police station three times: the same way each time. All of us in the family were anti-Gayoom. Many things happened to us. Once she was banished for treason to an island for six and a half years. All of my brothers were once in prison together. All of my brothers, that is, except Dr Waheed. He was working abroad at the United Nations. Myself and Mohamed Nasheed and our small group were supporting him then: we thought my brother might make change for the country according to our thoughts...'

Naushad's voice trailed off. Even after eight years of safety in the UK, he still seemed almost shell-shocked by his life.

'I might be one of the worst cases in the history of our movement,' he continued quietly. 'There was a time when they tortured me for one and a half years. Routinely. Every night. It's not just me that they tortured. It was all of us in prison. They do that, you know, for their own pleasure. They are sick men...'

'What has happened to them now?' I asked.

'Some of them have been kept free on the street. Some of them have jobs in the police and defence posts.'

He paused; the colour had drained from his face. 'I don't think I will be able to describe the torture. It is not easy to come up with words. It was physical: batons, boots. When I was in solitary confinement, I was kept in a hut with roofing sheets, metal galvanised sheets. It was six by six feet. The longest I was held there was four months.'

We were silent for several moments before Naushad, speaking in a whisper, added: 'I want the truth to be told. Several times I was stripped and had sticks into my back. Genitals. Abu Ghraib. This sort of thing.'

Naushad was in the prison on Maafushi island in 2003 when Hassan Evan Naseem, who had been jailed for drug offences, was beaten and killed by guards. Evan Naseem had been wrongly accused of causing trouble with another inmate and had resisted when prison guards came to take him from his cell for punishment. As an officer came for him, he struck out. Because of this, he was taken to an area of solitary confinement known as 'The Range', where he was severely beaten by a dozen guards. He lost consciousness in the early hours and was taken to a hospital on Male, where he was pronounced dead. When word got out of his death the next day there was a prison revolt. During this, officers shot and killed three further prisoners and injured seventeen.

'I saw them killing inmates with live bullets,' said Naushad, almost inaudibly. 'It was with an AK-47. One of the worst, terrifying days in prison.'

These deaths led to civil unrest, a state of emergency and, eventually, the introduction of multi-party democracy in the Maldives.

Naushad paused again and sipped his coffee. Then he turned to his brother's 'betrayal'. He looked almost at a loss at what had happened, both sickened and confused. 'I love my brother as anyone loves his brother, but I think that all along he was pretending that he was supporting democracy. But now, he wants power. That's all, I think. I don't know. Power. Not the money.'

He shifted to ex-president Gayoom, whose family he believed had benefited from the new status quo.

'A dictator will always be a dictator,' he said simply. 'I just don't understand how my brother has been party to him after seeing all he has done to our mother.'

Naushad's mother had died while he was in prison and he had been unable to attend her funeral.

Naushad and I talked for an hour. It had been a crash course in the 'other side' of the Maldives from an eyewitness to the country's darker secrets. From the Maldives to Marylebone ... via a cell by the sea. If I was going to be gate-crashing paradise, I did not want to paint over the cracks.

Postcards and Bumblebees

At the Sea House Café in Male, the waiter asked if I would like fresh *lunboa* juice; he had remembered my order from my last visit. I closed my eyes for a while, listening to a downpour rattle on the roof and the trickle of water in a drainpipe as Bono sang 'Where the Streets Have No Name' on the stereo. The café felt like home. A rumble came from the ferry port, commuters on the early boat from Emergency Island. I wrote some postcards, thinking of Graham Greene's observation in his Cuban novel *Our Man in Havana*: 'A picture postcard is a symptom of loneliness.'

He makes the comment as his protagonist Mr Wormold, a vacuum cleaner salesman and reluctant British spy (espionage helps pay the bills), is drinking wine and eating a 'dry flat omelette, stained and dog-eared like an old manuscript'. He's on a tour of provincial towns and writing to his daughter in Havana. He marks a cross by the window of his room on the postcard, showing the hotel at which he is staying. My card captured the palace at Ultheemu and 'a local woman sweeping clean the sand: a regular task to maintain the islands in Maldives'.

Pretty dog-eared myself after the night ferry, I ate breakfast and walked to Skai Lodge, where I showered and left my bag. The owlish receptionist hardly said a word and gave me a room that was slightly worse than the one before. My new abode had a grimy window overlooking a dim, narrow space. Foreign voices, possibly Dutch, and Indian soap operas filtered through thin walls. I didn't mind at all – I'd grown fond of Skai Lodge.

I escaped into the familiar mayhem of Male: the mopeds, the bikes, the pavement jostle. The pastel-coloured president's residence was quiet; no sign of Naushad's brother President Waheed. I inspected the intricate carvings at the Old Friday Mosque, the country's most ancient (dating from 1656, not so long after François Pyrard fled to France). A wide-based minaret by the mosque looked like the funnel on a cruise ship, towering above a graveyard lined with ghostly coral stones.

Round the corner, I entered the Grand Friday Mosque by the Islamic Centre, removing my flip-flops and ascending marble steps to a balcony overlooking a space with a burgundy carpet, its pattern resembling rows of enlarged hot-water bottles. An attendant with a pinched face and yellow teeth told me that precisely 1,372 people could fit on the carpet, each with a hot-water bottle slot of their own. The mosque could handle a maximum of 10,700 worshippers on a busy Friday. I left and strolled beneath the cool shade of banyan trees in Sultan's Park to the tomb of Mohammed Thakurufaanu.

Places in this distant island nation were taking on greater meaning to me. I had come to the resting place of the hero! Conqueror of the Portuguese! As I gazed across a concrete courtyard to a small white structure, a man wearing a T-shirt saying 'BORN FREE, NOW I AM EXPENSIVE' informed me: 'Outside good. Inside problem.'

In other words, but very politely: 'Keep out!'

Doing as I was told, I returned to Skai Lodge and promptly fell asleep, awaking disorientated at 10pm. I went to get some food and found myself near the tsunami monument at the tail end of a Maldivian Democratic Party rally. Yellow banners lay all around the dusty lot and activists sat by a yellow concrete wall; discussing democracy, I assumed.

By the wall and a tree with a yellow wooden *ungoli*, people wearing yellow were taking down yellow posters by a small yellow stage. It was as though a conference on custard had just drawn to a close.

'15,000 people,' said a man wearing a yellow bandana and a yellow sarong, referring to the evening's attendance.

A woman in a yellow polo shirt cut in. 'Actually we really don't know the count.'

I seemed to have dozed through a major event of some sort. I was invited to sit on the yellow wall and the yellow activists ran through the policies of the Maldivian Democratic Party, telling me how important the new guesthouses were to providing income on small islands. I learnt about mariculture (which involved the farming of shrimps and sea cucumbers), the need for a minimum wage, better hospitals, schools (apparently only 6 per cent of students went on to higher education) and 'regular ferries'.

They had my vote with the latter.

The woman in the yellow polo surprised me by saying she had been arrested twice and taken to Dhoonidhoo, the notorious Prison Island. Her longest spell had been six days, when she had been put in a cell with 20 others for 'obstructing police activity'. She looked nonplussed about what she had done wrong and her relatively quick release suggested the police were not sure either.

Another woman wearing yellow, in her 20s, said: 'I was arrested once at the airport, handcuffed and walked away by the police. They told me I was a "danger to society". It was scary but I found it quite funny. They went to all that trouble, just for me! I was held for two hours.'

'You are sitting next to a terrorist, by the way,' said the first woman in yellow. This had been another of the charges against her. It seemed hard to believe: she was friendly and down-to-earth, chilling out with her friends, discussing mariculture and improved education in the evening breeze. Hardly Carlos the Jackal.

She was making a joke of it. 'Yes, you have two very dangerous people here. One terrorist: that's me. And one assaulter of the police.' She pointed to her friend.

They both burst out laughing.

Then they talked about their fears for the up-and-coming election, questioning whether police, whom they believed (from the sounds of it correctly) were suspicious of the Maldivian Democratic Party, might turn a blind eye to vote rigging. They were also unsure about the country's courts, describing the Maldives as a 'judicial dictatorship' that was packed with figures from the old regime with a barnacle grip on underlying power.

They were eloquent, committed and welcoming. Around midnight they dispersed, bumblebees buzzing into the night.

The Former 'Dictator'

Two days later I was to meet the former 'dictator' himself. Ex-president Gayoom was the source of much mystery and, as I well knew by now, contention. He had ruled the country for 30 years from 1978, after rising to power at a time when many were disgruntled by a failing economy and the snooping of the secret police under President Nasir. By the end of his time in charge there was widespread concern about human rights, as Naushad's case had highlighted.

There was also the small matter of where much of the money belonging to the tourist resorts was going. In 2006, a pressure group named Friends of Maldives published a list of 23 resorts believed to have links to Gayoom's regime. Holidaymakers travelling to these islands were 'filling the coffers' of those involved, according to its British-based spokesman David Hardingham. The government at the time vehemently denied this, describing the list as 'misguided and ill-informed'. There was no avoiding it: tourism and politics in the Maldives were intricately linked, bound together tightly with knots that were difficult to unpick.

I had never met a ruler of a small set of islands before (if you don't count the once British prime minister John Major). In order to do so, I had to jump through a few hoops. These began with a phone call to a leading figure in Gayoom's Progressive Party of Maldives.

Ahmed Nihan was a member of parliament for the PPM. His constituency was the island of Villingili, a short hop to the west of Male. In 20 minutes I was on a pleasant little island with colourful houses, a gorgeous sand beach – where it was possible to swim in a gentle, swirling current and see the jagged skyline of the capital – and a new guesthouse named Chill Inn. The latter smelt of fresh fittings and was a short stroll from the ferry terminal. A walk around the entire island took half an hour, during which you were bound to see fruit bats swooping low around dusk, when kids played football energetically in sandy lots and the sun cast golden beams through palm groves.

Nihan, as he preferred to be known, was a slick, slender character wearing a pink shirt with a pen tucked in its top pocket and a stripy tie. He was in his early 40s, with brushed-back curly hair and a Samsung phone that was never far from his hands; shortly after arriving, he showed me he had more than 14,000 followers on Twitter. Nihan smoked Marlboro Light cigarettes one after the other. Before becoming an MP for the island, which had 15,000 inhabitants (perhaps many were Twitter fans), he had worked in human resources at a Club Med hotel. He had shiny cheeks and a fervent look in his eye.

We sat at a table in a Chinese restaurant overlooking the sea and ordered Red Bulls. I explained to Nihan that I was hoping to talk to Gayoom and he told me he could fix this for me the next day. That settled, we discussed the environment. Niham believed there was a possibility that coral might grow faster than expected, thus counteracting the rise in sea levels. This was 'an eco system balance created by almighty God ... many Maldivians say that we are living in the middle of the Indian Ocean with the blessing of Almighty Allah: the great blessing from the great Lord that we are remaining on these beautiful islands.'

He told me he had encouraged former President Gayoom to start a Twitter account. Tourism was doing well, he said, on the back of rich Russians. He also explained that nobody was exactly sure of the number of Bangladeshis working in the Maldives: 'Even the government doesn't know.'

Nihan had been to London twice and visited Stormont in Northern Ireland as part of an official Maldivian entourage. On his last trip to London he had stayed close to Heathrow airport on a stopover on the way back from Canada: 'I was in the Holiday Inn by the M4 junction. I was there alone and it was quite chilly in the night. I wanted to have a beef steak but I could not find anywhere close by.' He had been about to give up, but had eventually found what he was after. 'Not far away really. Quite close, on the left side, less than a mile. I got my beef steak! I was a happy Muslim!'

I had visions of a shivering Maldivian wandering down dual carriageways in search of a steak, puffing on Marlboro Lights as articulated lorries roared past. Despite the perfectly ironed short, smooth style and Red Bull-fuelled energy level, Nihan had the successful politician's common touch; I could see him going far.

So via the MP for Villingili and a telephone call with Ismail, Gayoom's private secretary, I arranged to meet the country's former ruler of 30 years. The set-up was as follows: between noon and 2pm the next day I would receive a phone call from Ismail giving me an address, which I would then have ten minutes to reach. Given that everywhere on Male was about ten minutes away by taxi, this was perfectly feasible.

That was how I found myself riding in a cab down a pot-holed road, arriving at a nondescript office block on a back street. I had been called at 12.50pm. I took a lift to the fifth floor and came to a landing with two doorways with peepholes. I knocked on one and waited, feeling nervous. I was sure I was being assessed through the doorways; I could sense eyes on me.

After a minute or so, a lock clicked and Ismail opened one of the doors, ushering me inside. He had an anxious air and was very softly spoken, with the hint of a lisp. He was middle aged and his hair was brushed forwards, Julius Caesar-style. His fluffy moustache twitched. A gold pen glistened in his shirt pocket.

I was led to a cramped waiting room with leather sofas, cheap plastic chairs and a couple of bodyguards. They stood square shouldered in crisp shirts and chinos, eyeballing me for a while before leaving for a side room.

'Where are you staying?' Ismail asked edgily. These were just about his first words to me.

'Skai Lodge,' I replied and he looked blank. I had a card for the guesthouse and I showed it to him. Most Western visitors to Male stayed at Traders Hotel by Shangri-La, near the president's residence.

'Ah yes,' he said, examining the card. 'I know.'

This seemed to be important: either an elaborate 'test' to see if I was telling the truth, or a way of understanding me better, or perhaps a means of discreetly saying: 'Now we know where you are.'

Maybe I was reading too much into it. Air-conditioning chilled the waiting room as I inspected various gold certificates honouring Gayoom that were kept in a glass cabinet and a model of a *dhoni*. From behind a door I heard the murmur of voices. This door opened and Ismail invited me into a room with a large tan-coloured wooden desk with a laptop and neatly placed books with Arabic written in gold on their covers. Pens, papers and an air-conditioning control were in an orderly line, everything just so. Islamic calligraphy in a gold frame was on one of the whitewashed walls, while on another was a picture of the Dome of the Rock on Temple Mount in Jerusalem; an inscription said it was a gift from President Mahmoud Abbas, head of the Palestine Liberation Organisation. A leather sofa and armchair were by an oval glass coffee table in front of the desk. Behind the desk, sitting on a black swivel chair, I found former president Maumoon Gayoom, who I knew was aged 75.

He had a squashed, round face with a Cheshire cat smile that pushed his cheeks up, making his visage seem even more circular. Wide almond, piercing eyes shot out from behind metal-framed glasses, above which his eyebrows were raised like question marks. The expression in the eyes did not seem to match the smile, which I found disconcerting. A thin covering of grey hair was swept to one side across his mainly bald head. He wore a striped short-sleeved shirt with a pen in the chest pocket; this appeared to be the Progressive Party of Maldives 'look'. Not much more than five feet tall, he had a small pot belly. He asked me to sit on the leather sofa, while he took the armchair beneath the picture of the Dome of the Rock and Ismail drew up a plastic chair close by, scribbling notes on a pad.

Earlier on the phone I had said to Ismail: 'I will not ask too many questions about politics.' I had not wanted to jeopardise the chances of the interview taking place.

Ismail had answered flatly and with a sense of hard-won spin-doctor irony: 'There's nothing other than politics.'

Nevertheless, I did not want to start with human rights, which might have brought an abrupt halt to proceedings, so I asked Gayoom about the environment. Like Nihan, he believed that growth in the reef could help protect the islands: 'We are facing a very grave risk. If, as scientists predict, sea levels are going to rise gradually by say 40 or 50 centimetres it's going to be very alarming for us … but when I was president I was told that by the end of the last century there would be such a rise and it did not happen.'

'Are you a climate change sceptic?' I asked.

'I can't say I am sceptical, but there's coral growth rate. It's growing, growing, but I don't think anyone knows accurately what the rate of growth is.'

'Does the world care enough about low-lying countries such as the Maldives?'

'I don't think so,' he replied sharply. 'If they did, something would have happened. If we allow emissions to rise as they are then one fine day we will find we are swimming.'

'What would happen then? Would the islands have to be evacuated?' I asked.

'There is always speculation about that, though I've never thought it practical that we would move. Where to? It's difficult to envisage India giving us a lot of land for nothing, or even Australia doing it. It's a bit far-fetched to me.'

After a bit more 'green talk' we turned to political prisoners during his time in office. Gayoom's fixed Cheshire cat smile narrowed almost imperceptibly. He shifted in his seat. I asked him how he defended himself against accusations of human rights abuses.

'Well I don't…' he began, his smooth delivery faltering for the first time. He paused, almost visibly putting his thoughts in order. He said there had been a 'gross misrepresentation' of his regime's human rights record, which he blamed on members of the opposition.

This was his response in full: 'They had the help of foreign organisations to project this as a country where there was no protection of human rights. That is all wrong. We did protect human rights and anybody who has been imprisoned has been based on a conviction in a court of law. Nobody is in prison without a trial. There has been no torture to speak of. Only a few cases. You must have heard of Evan Naseem. He was killed and that was a very bad situation. I feel very sorry about that. But that was one isolated case. Otherwise all these stories about torture and that sort of business is all exaggerated to achieve a political end. To an end [designed] to character assassinate me and to make it difficult for me to be re-elected. I was re-elected in 2003 after that particular incident. It was only in 2008 that I lost. Not because of that, it was because all the other parties got together. In the first round I got 40 per cent of the vote. Mr Nasheed got 25 per cent. But in the second round all the other parties got together so he got 54 per cent and I got 46 percent. I increased in the second vote. So if people had believed that I am a dictator, or I had violated human rights, they wouldn't have given me that many votes.'

There seemed to be a glaring slip in what he said – 'only a few cases' turning into 'one isolated case' – and the logic that imprisonment was just if based on a trial did of course depend slightly on who was making the judgement. I let it go and asked him about political parties: why hadn't he introduced them earlier in his rule?

'Because I didn't think the country was ready for that,' he replied swiftly, saying that education was poor when he came to power in 1978. He had, he said, improved this. 'First you have to know what democracy is, what parties mean.'

'Are you rich? Do you have interests in tourist resorts and stop others from investing in projects that are not connected to you or your family?'

He gave me a steady stare, his Cheshire cat grin narrowing a fraction more. 'Of course people might think that,' he replied. He paused. Again I could sense thoughts being shuffled into place behind his glasses. 'One thing I must tell you: I am a poor man. I don't have any money, neither me or my family. We are not in the high echelons of society. I have been president for 30 years and I don't own a single share in a tourist resort, in any commercial venture. I am living on what I get from my pension from the government. That's all. I have no business interests whatsoever. Right now, none of my family has. We are very ordinary people. A very ordinary family. What you say about money and all that, we don't get anything.'

Gayoom went on to say that former president Mohamed Nasheed had simply resigned. It had not been a coup. He did not go into any details.

We talked for a while about the calligraphy on the wall. It was his own work. I finished the glass of orange juice Ismail had given me and we stood up.

'What is your prediction for the forthcoming presidential election?' I asked.

'We are going to win … at least 55 per cent,' he beamed. The full Cheshire cat was back, and the look in his eyes for a moment matched his smile.

'Not 97 per cent like in the old days?' I asked, referring to his elections prior to multi-party democracy. 'Those days are over?'

His expression narrowed once again and he merely looked at me in a 'let's leave it there' manner. So I did. Ismail showed me nervously to the door past the bodyguards and into the lift. Out on the street, I stepped into the sunshine of another bright Maldivian day.

The Ousted Leader Responds

Trouble was brewing down by Male's docks. Lemon-yellow flags with a blue symbol depicting scales of justice swung above the heads of a large crowd by the water's edge. Streets had been cordoned off by riot police with batons and shields. An air of menace hung over the harbour.

A protest of some sort was in full swing. In one corner was a swarm of yellow demonstrators yelling slogans, in the other the security forces of this world-famous holiday destination.

'Money, money, yes sir!' cried an elderly man in a yellow cap, directing his message to the police. 'The military commanders, for them it's OK! Money in pocket! Open the gates! We're ready to go in!' They wanted to get to the President's Office.

Amid the melee, a local with a ponytail tapped me on the shoulder and explained that the crowd was waiting for Nasheed's return from abroad. Then he grabbed my arm and drew me closer.

'They are asking who you are: "Who is he?"'

I asked who 'they' were.

'Secret police.'

I had not expected this either. If 'they' were indeed secret police, I couldn't help thinking, they weren't doing the best job of maintaining their cover. To one side I could see a furtive man with his eyes locked on me. He couldn't be making a less obvious attempt at 'observation'.

Warm tropical rain swept across the docks as a diminutive figure in a suit arrived on a boat. This was Mohamed Nasheed. The crowd cheered and riot police clutched their batons more tightly. I caught a glimpse of the ousted leader as he was whisked through a tunnel of lemon-yellow supporters. He had wizened, gentle eyes.

'Open the gates!' shouted the elderly man in the direction of the President's Office, to no avail.

And then Nasheed was gone. The demonstrators began to disperse. The furtive secret police officer disappeared; or at least, I could no longer detect him.

After the demonstration, the man with the ponytail arranged to meet me at a café. He did not want us to be seen going there together, so he gave me the name of the place and told me to turn up in 20 minutes. I pottered by the docks like a regular tourist, though none was around, taking a few snaps of boats. Then I went to the café. There, I heard the whispered story of Mohamed Nasheed.

Proper voting, the man with the ponytail said (though I already knew), had been introduced in 2008 after 30 years of authoritarian rule by former president Gayoom, who had held 'elections' of the type that meant he always remained in power.

My new friend asked me not to use his name: 'It could cause problems.' He did not specify what. He said he had seen the 'bloodied corpse' of Hassan Evan Naseem at the cemetery along with '7,000 to 8,000 others' who had gone to witness the grim sight. This had fuelled his and many others' activism back in 2003.

We talked for about an hour in the shelter of the café as another shower pelted down. He was pleased I had come to the Maldives to stay at guesthouses on its lesser-known islands. He said that tourism cash was going to the country's elite and that more people should visit inhabited islands: 'It's the only way we're going to make money out of tourism.'

He also arranged for me to talk to Mohamed Nasheed. This involved sending a text to a mobile number and awaiting a reply with another 'safe' number. This procedure was required to avoid having our call bugged by the secret police. Eyes and ears, it seemed, were always watching and listening. I did as I was told and was soon speaking over a scratchy line to the former president.

It was a snatched conversation with poor reception. Nasheed expressed worries about the potential bans on alcohol and spa treatments at tourist resorts suggested by radical Islamists who were backing the country's new leaders. Such a move would have a 'drastic effect on tourism', he said. He told me he was concerned that greater pressure was being exerted on women to wear headscarves, that resorts should be properly taxed to pay for schools and hospitals, and that there should be an immediate presidential election – no dilly-dallying for months, as seemed likely. The country, he said, needed to return to a 'more moral trajectory'. And as he said this, the line went dead. I tried to call back but could get no reply.

It was difficult to get hold of Nasheed again. He had apparently become cautious about talking to the press. A friend of his who asked not to be named said: 'He feels increasingly let down that the West recognised the new government and that people did not take up his cause in the Western press.'

Eventually, after much toing and froing, I arranged to speak over the phone, using the same process as before: sending a text and a receiving a return text with a number for a 'safe' line. By chance, we were never in Male at the same time, so this was the only way. The interview was not long after speaking to Gayoom and I began by asking Nasheed about the day he lost power.

He started to run through the events of 7 February 2012. He had, he said, been rung by his opponents and told that 'if I didn't resign they would get hold of my wife and children. I thought they were in a safe house, but I was told that they knew where they were and could get them at any time.' They had also said that 'if I did not resign unconditionally they would force themselves within the Maldives National Defence Force building and they would endanger my life'. He had had little choice but to sign away his presidency.

Nasheed denied that he had abused the powers of office, a charge levied against him by some. He also said that, rather than being an act of altruism, Gayoom's decision to allow political parties and proper elections at the end of his 30 years of authoritarian rule had been forced on him: 'Basically he was not in control [of the country]. International pressure had so much to do with Gayoom having to do that. When [multi-party democracy] finally came in 2008, the Maldives was the only country in the world without political parties. Even China had one!'

I explained to him what Gayoom had said about the country not being ready for democracy. Nasheed's voice rose in disbelief.

'Not at all!' he answered. 'All countries are always ready for democracy. The dictator's idea that people don't understand, I don't believe that.'

I mentioned Gayoom's comments that he and his family had nothing to do with tourism; that he had never acted to protect his own financial interests. To this, Nasheed sighed and replied that many of Gayoom's family members seemed to be doing quite well for themselves: 'I just think it's too visible for him to deny that.' And he pointed out that the husband of Gayoom's daughter Dhunya had an involvement in six tourism resorts.

Nasheed believed that a minimum wage should be brought in to protect employees' rights at resorts, as well as those of abused overseas workers such as those I had met from Bangladesh. He said the police should not be brought into resorts – such 'heavy handedness' was unfair – and that vague laws to ban the 'incitement of fear among tourists' would inevitably 'affect freedom of expression and assembly and collective bargaining'.

I asked him about the state of human rights during the 30-year regime that had ended in 2008. Nasheed had been held in solitary confinement for 18 months. He paused and static danced on the line.

'Well, I was tortured twice. There is nothing more I can say.' Just like Naushad, he had become subdued and softly spoken as he mentioned this.

We switched to discussing guesthouse tourism, of which he said: 'Our one natural resource is our beauty and our location, the beaches and the sea. It's so strange that we are not willing to sustainably use that resource, but [we are] exhausting it on a few islands owned by a few people. I don't think that should be the situation. [Tourism] has a strong multiplier effect on the economy.'

I asked him if he believed that the country might have to be evacuated within 70 to 100 years due to rising waters, as some scientists suggested.

'Yes,' he replied.

I asked him if he still believed he would one day be president.

'Yes,' he replied.

And then we talked about Liverpool and Wiltshire. Nasheed had studied for his A-levels at Dauntsey's School, just outside the market town of Devizes, before reading maritime studies at Liverpool Polytechnic, graduating in

1989. He said he missed the Wiltshire countryside, roast beef and Yorkshire pudding, and Liverpool nightclubs.

'I liked jazz. Almost every week I'd go to the Casablanca, the Bierkeller and the Cavern Club,' he said, pausing as though imagining those simpler days. I asked him if he liked the Fab Four.

'Oh yes, I liked the Beatles, there's no doubt about that.'

The Cargo Ship Security Guards

I'd been having a curious few days on Male. There was more than a little bit of politics in the Maldives. Beyond the white sand ideal of the holiday resorts, a cauldron was bubbling. I had travelled in my great figure-of-eight around the country and found myself immersed in the ins and outs of a power struggle that could lead to any number of outcomes. I was coming to the end of my journey and I could sense the clock ticking … but then I got an offer I could not refuse.

In the breakfast room of Skai Lodge, fans whirred and mosquitoes clung to the walls, unwilling to take on the man-made breeze. Mimal had produced a tuna curry lunch with a mountain of white rice, his head swivelling from side to side as he enquired about the health of England cricket captain Alastair Cook as well as Kevin Pietersen's future in the team; there had been much discussion in the press about the latter.

I told him Pietersen was likely to be dropped for being too surly.

'Oh no. Very very good player. Bam! Bam!' he said, shifting his shoulders as though performing a couple of hook shots. And with that he had gone to serve a couple of guests on another table.

The other Skai Lodge dwellers had backpacks, cameras and laptops. They were unshaven, heavy set and looked like they spent a lot of time in the gym. They had crew cuts and were leaning back in their chairs, which creaked as though they might collapse, carefully examining the menu.

'Chips,' said one of them in a Mancunian accent. 'Two chips!'

Mimal scuttled into the kitchen.

'That'll be safe, mate,' the man confided to his companion, who was in the middle of a mini-crisis as he had just left his iPhone in a taxi. I'd heard them talking about it earlier and the hotel front desk was attempting to locate the driver.

They were a far cry from the Maldivian tourist board image of a honeymooning couple. After the Mancunian had had a brief chat with his wife via Skype about his likely arrival time home, I asked them if they had been on holiday.

'4,300 cattle,' was his offbeat reply. 'They were dropped in Lebanon. Then it came back.' 'It' was a cargo ship. 'Through the Suez Canal. That's where we got on. From Egypt to the Maldives, through the Internationally Recommended Transit Corridor, down the Gulf of Aden.'

They were security guards on a cargo ship that had transported cattle from Australia to Lebanon and was returning Down Under for another load. Russ and Andrew, who said nothing and seemed preoccupied by his iPhone, were called in to provide protection against pirates operating out of East Africa. They were ex-military and worked for a private security firm.

'Somalia, Yemen. There's a lot of piracy. Skiffs.'

Russ had a clipped, sergeant-major manner.

'Were you attacked on your recent trip?' I asked.

'No. But we have been before. Seven skiffs. Five pirates in each. They fired flares. Then they went away. Rules of engagement. International law. Paper trail is enormous: even if you fire one shot of a live round. You've got to be petrified to use real guns.'

Russ told me they wore body armour and helmets and were issued with 5.56mm rifles.

'Is it exciting work?' I asked.

'No, mostly pretty boring. Point A to B stuff. But then the adrenalin kicks in. You see boats. You think they're fishermen not pirates. Then they come at you. At speed. AK-47s.'

Their journey from Suez to the Maldives had taken ten days. They hadn't enjoyed it.

'As soon as we got on: the stink of bullshit,' Russ said. He pulled a face. 'They were cleaning it out. Decks were 140 metres long. Seven floors.'

It didn't sound like a pleasant job. And there had been fatalities on the journey over.

'Mainly bigger cattle bullying the weak ones,' Russ explained. 'Then there were the feeding problems. They were very fussy eaters. If they got even a little bit of bullshit in their trough, they wouldn't eat. Dangerous to go down there. One of the members of the crew was gored in the side. By a horn. Another was kicked...'

My phone rang. It was a public relations contact back in Britain who had heard I was in the Maldives; I had texted my Maldivian number to a few contacts in case of an opportunity like this. Would I like to go and see a nearby tourist resort named Kurumba? It was, she said, the first to have opened in the Maldives, in 1972, and was a short boat ride from Male in one of the superfast speedboats I'd so often seen buzzing by Petrol Island. She could send for a boat and I could be there well before sunset. She could also arrange a complimentary room for the night.

I had been planning to catch a few ferries to see the north of Kaafu Atoll during my last few days. This was the atoll directly above Male and was jam-packed with resorts, of which Kurumba happened to be one. Was I crazy? Of course I wanted to go.

I said farewell to Russ and Andrew, who were finishing their chips and ordering more, looking like international mercenaries at a loose end. They had a couple of hours until their flight and I hope Andrew got his phone back.

Coconuts and Beach Slippers

Before I knew it I was on a plush tan leather seat in an air-conditioned chamber with matching tan carpet, surging towards an island quite unlike any I had so far seen. Slim attendants in lime-green polo shirts and shades delivered iced water and cool towels with which to dab my face and hands. The nose of the boat rode high through the waves as we skipped past Emergency Island. Within a matter of minutes we were pulling into a wooden jetty with a Chinese-style pagoda, where I was soon being greeted by Myat Su.

From Burma, she wore a crisp white shirt with a lime-green collar and tan chinos. Her job was 'front of office supervisor'. She gave me another cool towel, then handed me a tub of coconut ice cream. 'It is our signature welcome,' she said; *kurumba* is 'coconut' in Dhivehi.

I was to eat this as we drove by golf buggy to my beach-side villa. This was living! Captain Mosa Rasheed back on Isdhoo never came up with chilled towels or coconut ice cream. Not so long ago I'd been sleeping on the morgue deck of the *Faalhu* next to Three-Quarter Eyes. Now I was on a golf buggy with a signature welcome ice cream heading for the lap of luxury.

Myat Su drove me past a circular infinity pool and a deck with sunshades, a jewellery shop (selling US$7,000 diamond necklaces) and a series of fine-dining restaurants. As we hummed along, I learnt that there were eight eateries serving Indian, Lebanese, Italian, Chinese and Japanese food. Tennis and snorkelling were included free, she said, giving me the introductory spiel. There were 180 villas on the island, which was about 40 acres in size.

We took a tight corner and moved into the interior. The gardens were lush and perfectly kept, with bright flowers amid verdant shrubs and palm trees with sloping trunks. Labyrinthine pathways twisted in all directions. Glimpses of magnolia-coloured villas flashed between fronds; the gardens were clearly designed to ensure as much privacy as possible.

My villa was a palace. Beyond a bed wide enough to sleep five on the *Faalhu* ferry, Myat Su and I stepped into a minimalist lounge with a driftwood lamp and sawgrass matting on a dark-wood floor. A wi-fi transmitter flickered next to a massive Sony television and an iPod docking station. Out on my terrace I found a 'day bed' with apple-green cushions and wicker armchairs. On the other side of the villa, beyond the dressing room behind the bed ('extra hangers can be requested if you need more'), I found a private courtyard with a hot tub, shower and his-and-her basins with coconut-scented soaps.

The price of a week at the resort was about £1,400 with flights from Europe. This was the amount it would cost for each person staying in a room with breakfasts included, but no other meals. So £2,800 was the basic cost for a couple, to which you might realistically add about £600 for lunches and dinners – and that's a pretty conservative estimate. With a spa treatment or two, you were probably looking at a weekly bill of about £4,000 to £5,000. This was based on one of the cheaper rooms, but it was quite possible to blow a whole lot more.

David and Victoria Beckham and kids had recently visited another resort, the One&Only Reethi Rah in the North Male Atoll, where they booked four of the best suites and were estimated to have spent £250,000 over 11 nights. This came to £6 a minute, as calculated by *The Sun* newspaper. At the time of the visit, its reporter pointed out that Victoria, 'Posh Spice', had been able to be very posh indeed, enjoying the hotel's 'swirling vitality pools, crystal steam rooms, saunas and stimulating ice fountains'.

The Beckhams' break in the sun was equivalent to the annual wages of 64 Maldivians. It was crazy when you thought about it.

I tried not to. Yes, I was breaking my self-set rules of travelling around the edge of paradise – at Kurumba I was getting the full-on paradise package – but I was ready for a taste of how the other half lived, with fresh eyes after sleeping next to sacks of onions on cargo ships and on mattresses on the floors of spare rooms.

After pointing out my complimentary cocktail – a 'mixed berries mule' with Finlandia vodka and ginger beer – a Lavazza espresso machine and my 'beach slippers', Myat Su and I had a chat about Burma. I think she found it unusual that a guest should be interested in her homeland. She had come to the Maldives in 2008 after a tip-off about a job from her late uncle, who had been an in-house resort doctor. She had applied for a front desk job and got it. She stayed in staff accommodation hidden behind thick foliage in the centre of the island, and had been able to save money from her wages to maybe one day return to Southeast Asia and buy her own home.

When Myat Su was a child, she told me, she had met Burma's pro-democracy figurehead Aung San Suu Kyi during one of the Nobel Peace Prize winner's spells not under house arrest.

'I see her and she shook my hand,' said Myat Su. 'Actually that was quite dangerous. My parents never saw her. My friends said: "Maybe someone take a picture of you with her. Tomorrow the police will come round." I was a little bit worried, but I was very happy to have met her. She told me to try hard in school so people were more educated in the country.'

That was the thing about paradise, you never knew who you were going to meet next. One minute it was cargo ship security men with tales of pirates on skiffs, and then someone who had shaken hands with Aung San Suu Kyi.

Myat Su left and I went for a swim. The shallow water was warm in the artificial lagoon, created by a curve of concrete breakwaters (they were not the world's most beautiful breakwaters). Beneath the surface of the sea, purple and yellow fish darted between crops of coral and for a while I lost myself in life down below. Then I lay on my apple-green day bed flicking through a glossy coffee-table book entitled *The Kurumba Story* by Royston Ellis. The back-page biography of the British writer, who was also the author of a Maldives guidebook and a strangely gushing biography of President Gayoom, explained that Ellis was a beat poet who lived in Sri Lanka and had once performed on stage with Cliff Richard's pop group The Shadows, Jimmy Page of Led Zeppelin and The Beatles. The spelling of the world's most famous all-time pop group was down to Ellis, according to the biographical notes. He had, apparently and intriguingly, suggested Beatles instead of Beetles to John, Paul, George and Stuart during a visit to give a poetry reading at Liverpool University in 1960.

I took a sip of my mixed berries mule. After many days of teetotal living since the Heineken-fest with the *Minivan News* reporters, the vodka hit the spot. While I read, I looked up now and then as a fruit bat flapped by in the mild early-evening air.

Tourism, officially at least, had begun in the Maldives on 3 October 1972, said Ellis, when the first paying guests arrived at Kurumba. The resort had been the brainchild of an ambitious Italian travel agent and a group of Maldivians who spotted the potential of tourism. One of them was Mohamed Umar Maniku, who still had an interest in Kurumba. His description of the early days, just 40-odd years ago, is of a different world: 'We scavenged door frames from old boats. Coconut thatching was very cheap. And we used gunny bags, jute, in places like the restaurant as the ceiling. The rooms had a tarpaulin on the sandy ground to start with. We bought cheap mattresses from Sri Lanka. We based our idea for rooms on what some of us had seen at the Ceylon Intercontinental Hotel in Colombo, each room with an attached bathroom and wardrobe. At first there were no fans, just open doors.'

Grainy black-and-white pictures showed tourists with spear-fishing harpoons (since banned) on a rudimentary jetty and wobbly looking frond-thatched roofs. A reprint of a brochure from the 1970s revealed that full-board rooms were US$14 per person per night, with a US$1 airport transfer fee.

By 1987 more than 130,000 tourists were visiting the Maldives each year – a number to which you could add a zero at the time of my trip, 40 years after the start of recognised tourism.

I went to the bar where I had an appointment with someone who could shed some light on holidaymaking today. Mr C was one of the resort's employees, although again I'm giving him a false name.

Russians were popping champagne corks in scoop-shaped chairs close by as Mr C hailed a waiter. We were on an open-sided candle-lit deck with a pleasant breeze lifting off the water. Jazz music played. Mr C ordered a soft drink for himself and a blueberry mule for me. 'Mules' appeared to be all the rage on Kurumba.

We talked about how tourism had changed over the years since the 1980s, when Mr C remembered that showers and baths were supplied with water 'from the ground, it was smelly and salty, but we never had any complaints'. He had worked at Kurumba for many years.

Then we discussed religion. Reminding me of the Moroccan traveller Ibn Battuta's ancient efforts, Mr C said that since the 1990s 'Islamist extremists had encouraged women to wear headscarves, some of them must wear black and cover their faces'. Maldivian women working at the resort, however, were requested to don uniforms such as Myat Su's outfit. Islamists were, he said, putting pressure on the government to ban alcohol, pork and spas. This, he said firmly, would not be a good idea. Tourists, in particular the Russians, would not stand for it: 'They want an even bigger selection of alcohols! They want them available in rooms! They want them in rows by the poolside! Strange drinking hours! Champagne during breakfast! They start drinking from breakfast, then they keep going!'

He sounded disbelieving whenever he mentioned the Russians. The most expensive bottle of champagne was US$800, he told me, while a bottle of fine wine could be as much as US$1,500. Four and a half bottles of the priciest plonk equalled the country's average annual wage.

We dined on sushi and sashimi, crab cakes, grilled tiger prawns and lemongrass crème brûlée, washed down with a French 2008 sauvignon blanc (for me, not Mr C). My meal, excluding the wine, came to about £55, though as a guest of the resort I did not have to pay a penny. And I won't pretend otherwise, although you probably imagine that I'm biased: it was a first-rate gourmet treat, exquisitely prepared and very tasty.

In the morning, Mr C showed me the island's power plant, desalination works, staff quarters, recycling station and mosque. Kurumba was like a small country. As I looked in the shop, waiting for my boat back to Male (the assistant telling me that the highest monthly takings had been US$120,000: 'most of the Russians come with young ladies and they like diamonds'), I got another phone call. It was an editor back in Britain. A press trip was leaving to go to the Six Senses Laamu resort, not far from Isdhoo and its Buddhist *stupa*. Would I like to go?

The Press Trip

A press trip is usually made up of a group of journalists taken somewhere by an organisation that is trying to promote a product. Destinations can vary tremendously. You might be led off to Salford docks to see the latest regeneration scheme, the product being the 'new city' and its brash development of apartments and entertainment venues on once-derelict land. You could find yourself in the Swiss Alps sampling fondue halfway up a ski slope, the product being the local delights of St Moritz or Laax or wherever it may be. Or the tourist board of Taiwan might arrange an exploration of its hidden gems by bullet train, the focus or official 'line' being why Taiwan is so wonderful and should not therefore be overlooked in favour of big bad China.

Something is always being sold, be it an attraction, a position, or a business opportunity. Alliteration is important. You may be led around the marvels of Mexico, the secrets of Sicily or the splendours of South Africa (almost always avoiding the harder realities of life such as townships and slums), and you are encouraged to see the places through the eyes of those who have paid your airfare and provided you with room and board.

In this instance the product was the tourist island of Six Senses Laamu, which wanted the world to know about its surfing holidays. This was how I found myself on a journalists' junket a few days later, landing with a sense of eerie déjà vu at the airport at Kadhdhoo.

Another superfast speedboat whisked us to another jetty lined with smartly dressed staff with ice-cool towels and welcome drinks. The 'us' consisted of a bearded writer for a travel magazine (who took notes on his mobile phone), a tall woman with blonde hair working for an in-flight glossy (whose note-taking came in fits and starts using a pad that occasionally made an appearance) and an impeccably dressed public relations representative from a firm based in London that had been hired to provide an escort (who patiently and politely dealt with the various quirks of her journalists). Our ages ranged from 20s to 40s, the PR being the youngest and with the most on her plate: three potentially troublesome hacks.

The island was amazing. The beaches were perfect; if you ignored the one that was lined with sandbags to provide protection from wave erosion. Our accommodation was simply superb (the PR should be happy with that).

While the villas at Kurumba had been elegant and sophisticated, Six Senses Laamu's versions were outrageously OTT. On arrival, I was given an old-fashioned bicycle with 'TC' carved on a slice of wood and attached to the frame. Each guest was allocated one to get about, the personalised tag provided so bikes did not get mixed up at the racks outside the restaurants or the spa. On this bike I pedalled along a long, thin wooden causeway that split into two branches that curved outwards and rejoined one another at the far end, completing a circle. From above, the shape must have resembled a cooking spoon.

I wobbled forwards, wondering how many guests tumbled with their bikes into the crystal-clear turquoise sea; a member of staff later informed me that this did 'not occur every day but it has happened'. Then I arrived at my water villa, which had a wooden exterior with a palm-frond roof. I entered a spotless chamber of chilled air with a massive double bed at its centre facing out to sea beyond a terrace – known as the 'Private Water Garden' – where there was a series of levels with padded day beds and mesh 'hammocks'.

The latter were pinned to the wooden deck on all sides so it was impossible to slip out. On the hammock you could idly regard the waves lapping at the telegraph pole-style supports of the villa as fish flitted by and crabs clambered up to dry off in the sun.

Cleverly crafted his-and-her sinks were carved into old-fashioned travellers' chests on a raised section behind the bed. This area led to an enclosed outdoor shower – the whole villa was designed so that no matter where you were no passers-by could peer in – and a reinforced glass-bottomed bathtub. This provided an alternative opportunity to relax with a view of the fish. Up a twisty staircase I came to a crow's nest space that was ideal for watching the sunset. The whole effect was of being in an incredibly comfortable treehouse, with free wi-fi, a 37-inch flatscreen television and a Bose entertainment system.

How much for this version of paradise plus? Well, at the time of my visit the cost of a week's full-board stay was from £2,469 per person with flights from the UK and transfers included. Suffice to say that you'd have to put in a few shifts on the night boat as a tuna fisherman to cover that.

As you might expect, the bearded travel magazine writer, the in-flight glossy scribe and myself had the most marvellous time. We were taken to the surf shack, where we were introduced to a man named Steve from Nottingham. He was the resort's surf instructor. He was also extremely mellow and soon confiding in me: 'I had 25 years of partying, but I'm OK now. I gave up drink. Last year I climbed Kilimanjaro. Then I turned 40.'

Steve had learnt to surf in Jacksonville, Florida when he was in his 20s and he had been in the Maldives for two and a half years. His former jobs included being a personal trainer in Brighton, a surf instructor in Woolacombe in Devon and a watersports supervisor in Mexico and Sri Lanka. He had sandy-brown hair and piercing eyes, and described himself as a 'soul surfer' rather than a competitive surfer: 'Competition takes away the joy of riding a wave.'

Surfing in the Maldives, I learnt from Steve, has a cult following. There are certain points in the archipelago where the reefs are perfectly positioned to push up the swell of the sea and create enormous waves. One of those spots was right by Six Senses Laamu, next to an uninhabited island we could see from the surf shack. It was known as the 'Ying Yang'. Each set of waves across the country had its own name and there was also 'Pasta Point' (in the North Male Atoll, breaking within view of an island that had once been home to an Italian-owned resort) and 'Chickens' (also in North Male, near a former poultry farm island).

Many of them had been discovered, and named, by an Australian. Tony Hussein Hinde had helped develop surfing tourism in the Maldives after coming to the country on a yacht that was almost shipwrecked when he arrived in 1973, before the ban on hippies in the 1980s. He loved the waves so much, he stayed and ended up converting to Islam and marrying a local woman, with whom he had two children. He also set up a surfing holiday company, Atoll Adventures, which took visitors on chartered 'safari boats' to visit the waves; some of the world's best surfers went to the Maldives to go to these remote sites. Sadly, Hinde died in 2008 while out at sea. He was found floating face down in the water by fellow surfers.

After explaining in some detail why the waves of the Maldives are so good – because the reefs make the size of the waves consistent, whereas waves breaking on sandy beaches can vary as the seabed sands can shift – I was given a surf board. This was bright orange and emblazoned with the slogan 'LIQUID SHREDDER'. Having only just heard of Hinde's tragic end, and having little idea what I was letting myself in for, I listened carefully to Steve's safety tips and advice on how to stand up on the board.

His principal rule of surfing was simple: 'Go like Usain Bolt!'

He eyed me keenly to see if I was taking this in, as he sprang up from the sand and pointed to the heavens: 'Like Usain Bolt!'

By this he meant I should leap up on the board, adopting a position similar to the celebratory pose of the great Jamaican sprinter. I did this a few times in the shade of the surf shack and then we went out to the waves on 'The Corner'. These were tiddlers, but high enough for me. After a few attempts and many yells of 'Usain Bolt! Remember Usain Bolt!' from Steve, I stood up a couple of times, relishing the feeling of movement, of swooping along (briefly) before the inevitable tumble into the spume. The board was attached to my leg by a cord or else I would certainly have lost the 'LIQUID SHREDDER'. Several times I was carried close to the reef, but the hardest part was swimming back through the waves to have another go. It was exhausting and I soon realised that the fitness required to be a surfer is on a different level to any other sport I'd tried.

Finished off, I went on a speedboat with the bearded travel writer and the PR to 'Ying Yang'.

The bearded travel writer had brought his own boogie board (a shorter version of a surf board that you don't stand on) and was a proficient surfer, but even he was amazed by the size of the waves, which were over six feet high. Beneath his beard, he turned quite pale as he saw the *Hawaii Five-0*-sized swell. Then he muttered something that sounded like:

'It's going to rip.' He jumped overboard and paddled to the waves.

The PR and I, unsure we would ever see him again, watched on as he sailed along the top of a giant ridge of water towards the reef, disappearing in an almighty crash. Yet somehow or other he survived, returning to inform us that the waves had been 'awesome' and were also 'epic'.

We stayed four nights and dined at a different high-class restaurant each evening. On one occasion we were taken to the 'Wine Tower'. This was round the corner from the main cocktail bar where a DJ span tracks in a sound system built into a grand piano made of pieces of driftwood (swiftly established as the preferred post-meal haunt of the press trip).

The Wine Tower was literally that: a tower of wine within a thatched building above a jetty. The bottles were stacked in shelves within the tower, at the centre of which a staircase led to a table on a reinforced glass floor. There we were served a series of cheeses and matching vintages. It was chilly in the Wine Tower, so we were given fleeces and hot-water bottles were placed beneath our feet. Each wine was carefully selected to enhance the taste of the particular cheese. These combinations were overseen by a flamboyant head sommelier named Melroy, who wore a purple pyjama-style outfit with a Nelson Mandela collar. He told us that the tower contained more than 400 labels and then he gave us a list of them, which began with a quote by the Irish poet Thomas Moore: 'So life's year begins and closes; Days though shortening still can shine; What though youth gave love and roses, Age still leaves us friends and wine.'

And so we sampled New Zealand sauvignon blancs with 'hints of asparagus' and Sardinian grenaches that were 'peppery with an aftertaste of cherries and liquorice' along with various cheddars and bries, our toes being warmed by hot-water bottles in a tower on a jetty in the middle of the Equatorial sea.

This was, I must say, wonderfully relaxing. On another evening we enjoyed a beach feast of lobster and steaks, illuminated by flames flickering in pits dug into the sand – a really splendid meal that would have cost us US$250 each 'plus plus' (this meant plus tax and a service charge). Our journalist group was carefully positioned to one side of the honeymooners and made an animated point of interest for the romantic couples, whose eyes darted our way, clearly not quite sure what to make of us. Who were these marauding Brits, some of them clutching note-books? Afterwards, we strolled down the beach to meet the 'Resident Astronomer'. A high-powered telescope was angled towards Saturn, and we could – amazingly – make out the rings of the distant planet. The sky was so cloud-less and clear that the heavens had seemingly opened up for a private show. A few sauvignon blancs to the good, we marvelled at the yellow planet and the dusty, undulating craters of the moon.

Activities with 'plus plus' prices for regular guests were listed on a board by reception. As well as star-gazing and surf-ing, 'Robinson Crusoe Picnic Island Experiences' (US$350), 'Tai Chi with Benson' (US$25) and 'Full Moon Meditation with Emily' (US$25) were offered. There was also an oppor-tunity to learn to cook Maldivian cuisine – we tried this, watching a chef prepare a curry before eating the tasty result (US$130). We also sampled dinner at a 'Deck-A-Dence', yet another seafood blowout with accompanying wines, on a wooden deck over the water close to the cocktail bar with the driftwood piano. Then we relaxed on hammocks with throw cushions, watching the milky moonlight catching the tips of the waves.

And that was how you do a press trip in the Maldives.

In the interests of full disclosure, here I should explain that Kurumba was owned by a Maldivian-run consortium named Universal Enterprises, which at the time of writing oversaw six 'secluded pristine island resorts on the deep blue oceans of the Maldives: powder white beaches, swaying coconut palms, exotic frangipani and hibiscus'. Six Senses Laamu was run by 'Singapore-based HPL through its subsidiary Leisure Frontiers Pvt Ltd', which promised to use its 'unique insight to target markets and to operating in the destination'. Neither was on the list of 23 resorts believed to have links to the former regime that had been published by the Friends of Maldives in 2006.

But who really knew who owned what?

PART FIVE
Rubbish Island and Broken Buddhas

Seeing where the tourist island resort waste goes and the museum where Buddhist relics were smashed to pieces by Islamist extremists, plus thoughts on Airport Island

'The sea is calm tonight.
The tide is full, the moon lies fair.'
Matthew Arnold

1. National Museum
2. Sultan's Park
3. Grand Friday Mosque
4. Fish market
5. Official Residence of President
6. Skai Lodge
7. Sea House Cafe
8. Tetrapod monument

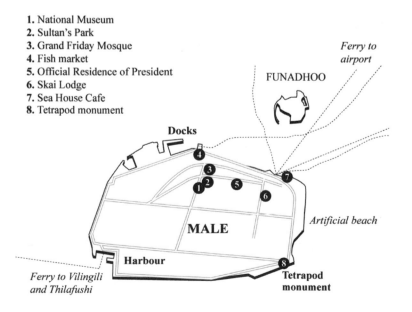

Being Human in the Dump

On my penultimate day in paradise I went to Rubbish Island. Its real name is Thilafushi and it is an artificial island, large parts of which are literally made of rubbish. You might wonder what happens to the waste created by 1.3 million annual visitors to a nation with 400,000 or so inhabitants in the middle of the Indian Ocean. Well, Thilafushi is the answer.

I caught a ferry there, a journey of about 40 minutes to the west of Male. My friends from *Minivan News* had suggested I might need permission to go; a BBC report had described the place as 'apocalyptic', while a writer for the *Guardian* said it was a 'dirty secret' growing at the rate of a square metre a day as ships transported garbage from the resorts. The authorities had become wary of outside visitors to this day-trip 'story', but I hopped off the workers' ferry and walked unchallenged along a filthy track into the heart of the island, soon arriving at a field of plastic bottles.

The bottles spread out like dunes, rolling into the distance on one side of the track. On the other, food wrappers, old tyres and rusting cans were heaped. Thick, brown smoke billowed from patches of this wasteland, which was tended by Bangladeshis with bandanas covering their mouths. There were about 150 such people handling the tourist waste on Rubbish Island.

I asked one of them what it was like to work there. I don't think he understood what I said, though he got the gist of my enquiry. 'Arrrgh,' was all he would say.

This was a truly grim place, bringing me back to earth with a jolt after the luxury of Kurumba and Six Senses Laamu. There was little point in hanging around. I retraced my steps, passing a metal recycling plant, expecting to be picked up by officials at any moment. I wasn't.

I went to the Café on Spot for a drink. This was a dilapidated building with a cracked sign on a corner near a yard in which men were hammering metal. Inside, though, it was cool and peaceful. A cheerful man by the counter wore an orange T-shirt bearing the words 'BEING HUMAN', which seemed a difficult notion to imagine on Thilafushi. His body was an unusual shape; perhaps it had evolved from his work poking about in the trash. His torso was skeletal, yet his arms bulged with muscles looking like a crab's claws.

'English?' he asked me, grinned and popped a samosa short eat in his mouth with one of his claws. Conversations on Rubbish Island appeared to consist of one word or sound.

I made my way to the dock where the ferry had dropped me. It was beyond a mosque and a municipal building. There was a little public garden with a gazebo surrounded by palm trees. At the far end of the garden was the dock. I had an hour to kill before the return ferry, so I lay down on a wooden bench in the gazebo and had a rest, using my camera case as a pillow. I enjoyed the quiet.

After a while, though, I heard voices, laughter and the sound of splashing. People were indeed being human: kids were leaping off the edge of the dock into the water, performing dives and crazy, leg-wiggling jumps. Where they had come from I have no idea – there must have been families living on Thilafushi. It seemed unlikely, and desperately sad, but to some people Rubbish Island was home.

Fundamentalists and the Whale Sub

Back on Male I visited the National Museum, entering between two ornate crimson pillars; the building was paid for by the Chinese, who opted for this oriental design. I was the only tourist and, as I examined former sultans' costumes near a teak desk that once belonged to an English governor of Sri Lanka, I was approached by an assistant curator named Ashraf Ismail. He was scholarly looking with spectacles, a red short-sleeved shirt and matching tie. Beneath a high forehead, olive-brown eyes regarded me curiously. He was interested in any outside visitor; it did not seem as though many folk passed by from the Four Seasons or Six Senses. Before long he was leading me to a space where there had once been display cabinets. He pointed to a dent on the tiled floor.

This was where one of the heavier pre-Islamic relics had struck the ground during the assault on the museum by fundamentalists in February 2012. Ashraf Ismail described what had happened: 'There was a mob attack. They targeted anything with a face or a figure: Hindu and Buddhist relics. I think there were 11 or 12 people. They barged in. We were closed. It was 8am. They just smashed everything that was pre-twelfth century. The exhibits were very brittle. There are a few we can repair, but it will take a long time. Some things were turned to dust. These are not articles that can be bought in the shops. They are destroyed. Gone.'

Ashraf Ismail let that sink in. His delivery style suggested: 'This is what goes on while politicians worry about keeping office and tourists go to fancy hotels.' Emotion flickered behind his glasses. Then he adjusted his tie, as though pulling himself together. 'This is actually a huge loss to our country's history,' he said. 'The exhibits showed evidence of the ancestors of the Maldives. They are part of our identity. Even if the artefacts have been destroyed, the history remains. It's our job to tell the next generation.'

Ashraf described how the vandals had returned to the museum at 11am on the day of the attack. As there had been great uncertainty in the country at the time – it was the period of the ousting of former president Nasheed and there was a breakdown in law and order – they had been bold enough to come back. They wanted to destroy the CCTV tapes of their earlier actions, but the control room office was locked. Disgruntled, they pulverised a few more statues that they had earlier missed. To those behind the assault on the museum the relics were not mere historical displays, they were promoting an illegal religion. They believed they were rightfully ridding the country of an evil influence, though they were, of course, breaking the law: the displays were of historical import, protected by statute as they were not in a place of worship.

Ashraf introduced me to his colleague Hamdha, who said: 'I heard glass smashing. I was scared. I could see them from the second-floor balcony. They went out of the front entrance, running. They had scarves covering their faces.'

They were not, however, so lucky on their second visit. 'When they returned, the police came and arrested some of them,' Hamdha told me.

Around six men are said to have been taken into custody, although it is uncertain what became of them, she said.

This attack had happened at a time when there was widespread concern that extreme Islamists were being courted by certain politicians, who hoped to use their numbers as a power base to win election. During my visit, it felt as though there was a shift towards a more stringent Muslim code, as hinted at by the temporary ban on spas at hotels, the suggestion of making booze illegal at hotels (which would, by all accounts, appear to be highly unlikely to occur), and the increase in the number of women wearing headscarves.

Ashraf and Hamdha's story had reminded me of 'wedding vow-gate'. In 2010, international headlines were made when a man presiding over the renewed wedding vows of a couple at the five-star Vilu Reef resort on Dhaalu Atoll branded them 'pigs' and 'infidels' in Dhivehi. The ceremony had been caught on camera, posted on YouTube and gone viral. The couple had been completely unaware of what was happening.

After reading out from a page of staff regulations as though conveying Dhivehi expressions of devotion, the man in charge of the intimate occasion had intoned: 'You are swine. The children that you bear from this marriage will be bastard swine. Your marriage is not a valid one. You are not the kind of people who can have a valid marriage. One of you is an infidel. The other, too, is an infidel, and, we have reason to believe, an atheist, who does not even believe in an infidel religion.'

As he had said this, the couple had smiled warmly and another local man had said in Dhivehi: 'Can see her breasts!'

Further commentary had ensued. And as they kissed at the end of the ceremony, a voice was heard saying that they must 'suck mouths, suck mouths', a derogatory term used by Maldivians for the act of kissing.

In response to the global coverage, the resort later expressed its 'deep concern and regret' about the incident. It had not been the best PR.

I spent my last afternoon at the National Museum before catching the 'Whale Submarine'. This was a ride that left from near the President's Jetty and involved plunging in a surprisingly large canary-yellow submarine to the edge of a reef. The organisers promised that this was 'the most outstanding attraction of the Maldives today' and that it was 'your chance to visit the underwater world without getting wet'. How could I miss out?

Inside the sub, I sat on a purple suede seat alongside mainly Asian tourists. We watched through portholes, cameras aloft, as turtles slid into the shadowy depths and mad-eyed moray eels grinned like conmen from beneath shards of coral. The eels looked harmless, yet they would shoot forth in a flicker to devour their prey, said one of the guides.

Pop songs played over the submarine's stereo – 'You Are Not Alone' by Michael Jackson echoed through our narrow chamber as we reached the seabed, 23 metres beneath the surface. Large mauve fish peered in with goggling eyes. Schools of yellow and blue damselfish sprinkled down from above. They seemed to find the submarine mildly interesting.

'Faith' by George Michael began to twang. A couple of divers from the submarine company bubbled and waved, sent down as though to make up for a shortage of marine life. The music switched to 'La Macarena' and a few Chinese honeymooners jiggled to the jaunty beat.

Quite an experience: I can recommend the whale sub.

Full Circle

My trip around the country had come full circle. A series of snapshots of this Indian Ocean archipelago had formed an album in my mind's eye, and I shuffled through them as I made my way to Skai Lodge, slowing to a walk near a football pitch where elderly men were, as ever, playing checkers by a wall.

Not all of the pictures were so wonderful: the haze and squalor of Rubbish Island and the eerily empty museum cabinets where the destroyed Buddhas had once been, for a start. Yet on balance, I had overwhelmingly positive images on which to draw: the sheer joy of the fish-eating party in Makunudhoo (never have I seen so many fish consumed so happily or rapidly); the serenity and dignity of Ultheemu's palace of the hero, the deep-down pride with which locals held Thakurufaanu so abundantly clear; the quiet dedication and good humour of the dried-fish workers on tsunami-struck Vilufushi; the drama and skilled work of the tuna fishermen of Addu hurling skipjacks onto the deck.

I found it extraordinary that I could potter about this paradise on *dhoni* ferries, cargo ships and the odd propeller plane and have it more or less to myself. Some places I visited had never seen a tourist at all, according to those I met. I was in one of the most established places of beauty on Earth (why else would all the five-star resorts have been built?) and yet no one was about.

I could stay at charming little guesthouses, or rent rooms from locals, who sometimes simply invited me as a guest. From the ground up, I could get a feel for the rich culture of an ancient maritime nation as well as the strong sense of community of a people living in the middle of a mighty ocean. Beyond the hurly-burly of Male, and even in the busy capital, most Maldivians were only too ready to pass the time of day. Other than Bangladeshi workers, few foreigners managed to gatecrash paradise.

It was incredibly odd when I stopped to think about it: out beyond the Makunudhoos and Isdhoos were 100 'tourist' islands packed with people from every corner of the globe. These islands and the people on them, the occasional day-trip aside, were almost entirely sealed off to the locals. And those who worked on them were, generally speaking, paid to keep a low profile (other than dive instructors and concierges, perhaps).

It did indeed feel as though a whole new country had opened its doors. Four years before my visit, my journey would have been against the law. And as far as I knew, nobody before had gone Maldivian island-hopping quite the way I had.

Yes, there were troubles with ferry timetables and last-minute changes of plan, but that was always how I intended it to be. I did not have all the answers before I went. Boats came, or they didn't. Religious festivals intervened. I got used to sitting by an empty dock, wondering if the *Naza Express* or some such ship was on its way.

As a journalist, I asked questions. I wanted to know as much as I could about the country: the good and the bad. Sure, I relaxed by the beach and enjoyed the sun, but I also wanted to find out about the social set-up, the bubbling politics, the 'reality' of the Maldives. I might have simply splashed about in the waves and waxed lyrical about spectacular sunset after spectacular sunset, but I could not help myself: I had a notebook and I was curious to find out more.

There was, as I had soon discovered, so much going on: the deposed president, human rights abuses, fears of rigged elections, human trafficking, corruption, hard drug use, fundamentalism, the question of women's rights in an Islamic state, a high divorce rate, freedom of the press, overactive secret police, the social division between tourist and locals, the maltreatment of resort workers. A heady mix. Go to just about any country and there are 'issues', but the Maldives was almost flamboyantly (and unexpectedly) alive with controversy of one sort or another.

I was lucky to be visiting in the run-up to an important presidential election. People had opinions and would happily take a load off their chests, sometimes understandably asking for anonymity. The flags billowed, yellow and pink. Powerful interests shuffled for position, while the democratic party held rallies down by Male's artificial beach. There was tension in the air, a tug-of-war over the future.

In the event, Abdulla Yameen Abdul Gayoom, the half-brother of former President Gayoom, representing the Progressive Party of Maldives, was elected president of the Maldives in September 2013. This election took place in controversial circumstances following several delayed ballots that were believed to have given the Progressive Party of Maldives time to 'organise'. Many observers believed that a better description would have been 'buy votes', although there is no clear evidence of this. An independent observer told me that ballot boxes had not been rigged – official reports said as much – but money had passed hands to sway voters' minds. This observer, whose opinion I trusted but whose anonymity I promised, said that such questionable tactics had involved both the PPM and the Maldivian Democratic Party. He gave me no proof. 'Powerful figures would arrive with money and it was distributed among the islands. It's a kind of feudal system,' he told me. The PPM scraped through after being beaten by the MDP in the first round of voting, the latter initially receiving 45 per cent of the vote to the PPM's 25 per cent. As more than 50 per cent was needed to take power, a second round of voting was held during which other parties joined the PPM to tip the balance to 51 per cent against the MDP's 49 per cent. Dr Waheed, Naushad's brother, had stood as an independent candidate in the first round, attracting just 5 per cent support.

What happens next in the Maldives is, of course, about more than yellow and pink flags. Put all the politics to one side and there is the looming matter of the rising sea. I had never before visited a country that faced oblivion. That is the stark reality if the scientists are right. I tried to put myself in the shoes of an islander on a remote atoll, but it was impossible to do so. You can only truly appreciate a crisis when it stares you in the face. However, by visiting tsunami-struck Vilufushi and seeing some of the most isolated islands, I had picked up on a sense of genuine bewilderment: was it really possible that the islands could 'go under'?

When I talked to Dr Bubhavant at the observatory on Hanimaadhoo, the reality struck home when he said: 'This is the future of the planet. Antarctica is melting!' I realise that some people find it tedious and 'worthy' to go on about such things, and I appreciate the inherent paradox of flying somewhere emitting plane fumes and then discussing 'green' issues, but his passion spoke volumes.

After François Pyrard was shipwrecked in the sixteenth century, he found himself at sea with locals in rough waters travelling through narrow channels between jagged reefs: 'I was never so afraid as on one occasion when I was with some of them in a little boat of not more than four armlengths, in a sea towering above me two pikes high, more stormy and swollen than ever was. Every moment it seemed that a wave would carry me off the boat, wherein I had much trouble to hold myself, while they recked nothing of it, and only laughed; for they fear the sea not a whit, and are exceedingly adroit in managing their barques and boats, being brought up to it from their youth, as well as the great lords as the poorest will have a boat of his own, and a rich man will have many.'

That relationship with the sea is changing, as I found with children who were too afraid to learn to swim on Vilufushi, and with adults who were rightly concerned about the possibility of a national evacuation. Pyrard went on to describe the Maldivians thus: 'In truth they are half fish, so accustomed are they to the sea, in which they pass their days, either swimming or wading or in boats. I have seen them many a time within the reefs where the sea is calm – I have seen them, I say, swim after fish, which they have suddenly caught sight of while bathing, and catch them in their course.'

The Maldivian connection with the sea is closer than anything an outsider can comprehend. Life on the flattest country on the planet requires mental adjustment, as the foreign teachers I met described. Standing on a beach facing inland to one of the long, straight roads on a little island was like looking along the surface of a spirit level. There are no bulges, no hills. If the sea rises, as it did on Boxing Day 2004, the best advice is to climb the nearest tree (and do it quick).

All in all, on my journey this nation had quietly opened its doors to me and had proved to be by turns blissful, troubled, joyous, delicious, fraught, and always very, very watery. With the blazing sunsets on the South Equatorial Channel, gyrating currents in deserted lagoons, kaleidoscopes of coral, cascades of fish, crescents of perfect white sand, peaceful coral-stone villages, colourful birds, emerald jungle ... there is no doubt about it, the Maldives has to be one of the most beautiful, colourful – and sometimes complicated – places on the planet.

Epilogue

As a travel writer for *The Times* for 17 years I have been to many picturesque spots: sun-soaked Caribbean islands with cricket greens and rum shacks, verdant rainforests in the depths of Southeast Asia, vast open land-scapes populated by kangaroos and venomous snakes in the Australian Outback, African deserts, hidden coves with little tavernas by the Mediterranean Sea. I have also experienced many an adventure: mad tornado chases across America's Mid West with 'twister-spotters', train rides through deso-late stretches of North Korea, encounters with unfriendly brigade men at checkpoints in Libya.

Famous sights? You name them, I've probably been: the mystical mountaintop remains of Machu Picchu, the rose-red ruins of Petra in Jordan, the marvellous and curious Grand Palace in Bangkok. Tick, tick, tick. I've lived a charmed existence, notebook in hand, searching for stories in corners of the globe that I'd never imagined I would visit when I was younger and training to be a reporter, starting with shifts on the *Coventry Evening Telegraph* covering stories about pubs with ghosts near the infamous ring road and locals 'furious' about travellers' camps.

It has been an incredible experience and during this time spent globetrotting I have witnessed at first hand the many major upheavals in the world of travel of recent years.

The pace of change has been staggering. Not only are faraway places just a click away on low-cost airlines, there is also now an almost infinite supply of facts and figures, images and blogs on just about everywhere on the planet. Live cameras are angled at Californian beaches and moun-tain tops in the Alps. Bloggers inform us of the latest news and gossip in the Faroe Islands and Angkor Wat. Tweets fill us in on live events from Shanghai to San Diego. Google Earth watches from above, taking pictures from the heavens that we can call up on smartphones tucked in our pockets that have more powerful hard drives than were used to launch the Space Shuttle.

When I began at *The Times* in 1997, if I wanted up-to-date news on events in, for example, Cairo, there were computers on which you could perform rudimentary searches using an internet dial-up service. This was often very slow and limited, so instead I would go to a gloomy basement in an old rum warehouse in Wapping in London's East End. I would sign a docket and take neatly folded, yellowing newspaper cuttings to my desk, remove a rubber band and sort through the articles, each hand-pasted on a piece of paper stamped with the relevant newspaper's name and publication date. One internet terminal existed for the entire features floor and it was not used for web searches, just for writers filing stories.

In my first year at the paper, I wrote an article under the headline 'TAKE A TRIP AROUND THE NET', which came with a standfirst reading: 'CYBERSPACE CAN BE HELPFUL FOR TRAVELLERS. TOM CHESSHYRE DESCRIBES THE QUICKEST ROUTE TO USEFUL INFORMATION'. Among my insightful tips was: 'The most common way to begin any research is to key the destination you are thinking of visiting into the internet "search engine" that usually appears on the opening page of the internet site.' People in those days were only just getting used to newfangled devices such as 'search engines'. I recommended trying Alta Vista, Excite and Yahoo! The piece was published on 13 September 1997, which, I now see, happened to be two days before Larry Page and Sergey Brin registered the Google domain name in the

United States. Hard to imagine, I know, but Google did not even exist.

Travel journalism has also changed in the years since I began. Publications' budgets have fallen on the back of reduced advertising (the internet playing its part yet again). Meanwhile, the PR machine has grown ever stronger. These days PRs far outnumber travel journalists, many of whom have had to give up this area of reporting as there are not enough commissions to go round. The ball would appear to be firmly in the PR industry's court, whereas once there was a finer balance between journalists and the 'other side'.

As travel journalists cannot afford to finance flights and accommodation, they approach the PRs of tourist boards or travel companies in the hope of support. Trips are offered in return for editorial, and this is all perfectly run-of-the-mill. The PR scratches the journalist's back, and the journalist returns the compliment by pitching a story to a publication in the hope of securing a commission. The journalist travels overseas to find a story and tells it – one hopes with impartiality and a fair eye – in a paper, magazine or, increasingly, online.

But the story is unlikely to include politics or 'difficult issues', which, by and large, are not considered the domain of travel journalism. They tend to be regarded as matters for the foreign pages, as though an invisible line has been drawn between the two. Most 'holiday destinations', not only the Maldives, have stories beyond the sun lounger, be it the United Arab Emirates, China or the Dominican Republic. Yet when reading most travel writing, it sometimes feels as though there is little interest in the world beyond 'holiday sights', hotels, restaurants and 'attractions'. The constraints under which the narrator, journalist or author, is often writing make for an unnecessarily limiting position and everyone is left worse off.

Should any hard realities outside the holiday 'bubble' make their way into print – and quite rightly they do from time to time when they are relevant to the story – the PR involved will tend to get rather upset. It is quite likely that the PR will blacklist the journalist from further trips, especially if the writer is a freelance. A further probability is that the PR will mention the experience to colleagues at networking events. In one fell swoop, the journalist will be marked out.

To a certain extent this PR–journalist set-up is unavoidable. The truth is that we increasingly live in a leisure world. Tourism keeps the wheels of the economies of many nations spinning. The PR machine, even if many journalists do not always like it that much, is integral to this. That is why the idea of the Maldives as 'honeymoon heaven' lives on.

Travel journalism has mainly become consumer travel journalism. There is nothing whatsoever wrong with this. Done well, it is incredibly useful: we save up diligently for our holidays and we want the very best tips on how to spend our hard-earned cash. In the Maldives, however, I wanted to take a different approach. I paid my own way, other than where I briefly joined the 'press trip', and the aim of that was to show as many sides of the country as I could. What is more, I deliberately left the Google world behind; although it had a habit of creeping up on me.

As Paul Theroux says so memorably in *The Last Train to Zona Verde*, I wanted to see things with my own eyes, not with the help of the World Wide Web. What I found was an almost forgotten country deep in the Indian Ocean, one that was brim full of life yet at the same time teetering on the edge of so many troubled possibilities.

Acknowledgements

It is difficult to know where to start when it comes to thanking those who helped with this book, many of whom are mentioned in the text. Back in the UK, David Hardingham of the Friends of the Maldives provided useful contacts. I would like also to thank Jane Knight, travel editor of *The Times*, my brother Edward for his proof reading, Kate Quill and Lysbeth Fox for their words of encouragement, and my mother Christine Doyle and father Robert Chesshyre for putting up with me talking about Maldivian politics so much. Thanks also to Lucy Highton of Trailfinders, Natalia Dowling-Kennedy of Sadler & Co, and to Matthew Swift for the book's (swiftly delivered) maps. Special thanks go to Sally Lansdell for her sharp-eyed editing, Nadia Manuelli for her promotional ideas, and Nicholas Brealey of Nicholas Brealey Publishing, without whom this book would not have got off the ground. I conducted the travels at my own expense (apart from the press trip I describe), in my own time and without a publishing deal, so I was more than pleased in his interest, and subsequent editing.

Bibliography

Steven Amsterdam, *Things We Didn't See Coming* (Harvill Secker, 2010)

J.G. Ballard, *The Drowned World* (Fourth Estate, 2012; first published 1962)

Ibn Battuta, *The Adventures of Ibn Battuta* (University of California Press, 2005)

H.C.P. Bell, *The Maldive Islands* (first published 1883)

H.C.P. Bell, *Excerpta Maldiviana* (Asian Educational Services, 1998; first published 1922)

T.C. Boyle, *Water Music* (Granta, 1993)

Danny Danziger & John Gillingham, *1215: The Year of the Magna Carta* (Hodder & Stoughton, 2003)

Imogen Edwards-Jones & Anonymous, *Beach Babylon* (Bantam Press, 2007)

Royston Ellis, *A Man for All Islands* (Times Editions, 1998)

Royston Ellis, *Maldives* (Bradt, 4th edition, 2008)

Royston Ellis, *The Kurumba Story* (Universal Enterprises, 2012)

William Golding, *The Spire* (Faber and Faber, 1964)

Arthur Grimble, *A Pattern of Islands* (John Murray, 1952)

Hammond Innes, *The Strode Venturer* (William Collins, 1965)

Patrick Leigh Fermor, *A Time of Gifts* (John Murray, 1977)

Norman Lewis, *Voices of the Old Sea* (Hamish Hamilton, 1984)

John Masefield, *Spunyarn* (Penguin Classics, 2011)

Tom Masters, *Maldives* (Lonely Planet, 2012)

George Monbiot, *Heat* (Allen Lane, 2006)

George Orwell, *Down and Out in Paris and London* (Victor Gollancz, 1933)

François Pyrard, *The Voyage of François Pyrard of Laval to the East Indies, the Maldives, the Moluccas and Brazil* (The Hakluyt Society, 1887)

Xavier Romero-Frias, *The Maldive Islanders: A Study of the Popular Culture of an Ancient Ocean Kingdom* (Nova Ethnographia Indica, 1999)

Paul Theroux, *To the Ends of the Earth* (Ballantine Books, 1990)

Paul Theroux, *The Last Train to Zona Verde* (Hamish Hamilton, 2013)